A DICTIONARY OF INTELLECTUAL PROPERTY LAW

A Dictionary of Intellectual Property Law

Peter Groves

Solicitor, Consultant to CJ Jones Solicitors LLP, London and author of the IPso Jure blog (www.ipsojure.co.uk)

Edward Elgar
Cheltenham, UK • Northampton, MA, USA

Published by
Edward Elgar Publishing Limited
The Lypiatts
15 Lansdown Road
Cheltenham
Glos GL50 2JA
UK

Edward Elgar Publishing, Inc.
William Pratt House
9 Dewey Court
Northampton
Massachusetts 01060
USA

A catalogue record for this book
is available from the British Library

Library of Congress Control Number: 2010930126

ISBN 978 1 84980 777 7 (cased)

Typeset by Servis Filmsetting Ltd, Stockport, Cheshire
Printed and bound by MPG Books Group, UK

CONTENTS

PREFACE

Lord Macnaughton asked and answered a pertinent question in *IRC v Muller and Co's Margarine* [1901] AC 217 at 223: 'What is goodwill? It is a thing very easy to describe, very difficult to define.'

The intellectual property universe is full of expressions that are very difficult to define, but we need to understand them because intellectual property is inescapable. We encounter it in our daily lives, more extensively each day and in new ways. It underpins the value of whole industries. Its owners demand stronger and stronger protection, and use their rights with growing enthusiasm. It sometimes seems to have become invested with magical properties.

At the same time there is widespread ignorance about it. It is time to stop talking about it as if it were a single, seamless, continuous, integrated area of law, because if we approach it that way we place excessive expectations on it. It is time, in short, to drop the idea of intellectual property.

Intellectual property has its own vernacular, and – especially among lawyers, for whom precision in the use of language is crucial – knowing the vocabulary is essential if we are to understand and discuss the subject, so a dictionary is a contribution to ensuring accuracy and comprehension. Happily, I have been able to refer to what every lawyer needs: a precedent, in the form of *The Economist Pocket Lawyer* (Oxford: Blackwell, 1986), by Stanley Berwin, with whom I once had the pleasure of taking lunch when his new firm – the one without Leighton – was still young. As, now I think of it, was I.

Is it a paradox to compile a guide to an anachronism? No, because although as a catch-all expression 'intellectual property' has – I believe – stopped being helpful, even become positively damaging, it still serves the useful purpose of bringing together a number of important topics. The required change in mindset is to recognise intellectual property rights as islands rather than as a complete world in themselves, and this guide will, I hope, enable people more readily to do that.

This modest attempt to assist and educate the reader is mainly concerned with English law. Intellectual property is, however, an international subject, and practitioners and students will encounter words and expressions from other English-speaking jurisdictions (US patent law, for example, has its own extensive vocabulary) and in other languages too, so it includes some foreign terms. Readers will identify some arbitrary choices of what to include and what to leave out, and will no doubt find some inaccuracies (for which I take full responsibility). My aim has been to include everything that a person encountering intellectual property might wish to know about, and suggestions of additional or revised definitions will be greatly appreciated, in anticipation of further editions.

Please visit the Dictionary of Intellectual Property Law blog (www. dictionaryofiplaw.com) for new definitions and to post suggestions and comments.

ACKNOWLEDGEMENTS

Thanks to Bob Cumbow, Dave Musker (for the speed as well as the number of his suggestions), Barbara Cookson, Stephen Kinsey, Patrick Wheeler, Susannah Rolston, Wing Yan, Laura Winston, Lara Broschat, Adi Barkan-Lev, Hannes Iserentant, Tony McStea (I am particularly obliged for so much material), Scott Alprin, Nic Garnett, Chris Hemingway, Sarah Driver, Bart van Wezenbeek, Ron Klagsbald, Mikk Putk, Nils Victor Montan, Rodrigo Borges Carneiro, James Olcott, Rebecca Kaye (the *Archers* listener) and Paul Sumpter for suggestions; Rachael Elliott for finding the earliest uses of the expression 'intellectual property'; Julia Cresswell for alerting me to Oxfordshire County Council's generosity; Andrew Keogh for the Land of Lost Content; Marta Safin for research help; the IPKat for reaching out to his or her readers; and Nick Gillies for guidance, Berwin and the outboard motor story, for which, sadly, I could find no place in this work.

I dedicate this book to all of them, and to other friends who did not, for one reason or another, respond to my requests for suggestions.

1-click

See **One-Click**.

71(3)

From Article 71(3) of the European Patent Convention. The notification that the EPC is prepared to grant a patent, on the basis of a particular description and claims, known as the ***Druckexemplar***. The applicant has four months in which to approve the text and pay the fees.

A

A priori

Denotes deductive reasoning or arguing, proceeding from causes or abstractions to effects or conditions. The opposite of empirical or inductive reasoning, reasoning from experience, the term for which is a posteriori.

'A' Publication

The publication of the patent application, which takes place in most systems 18 months after the application is filed unless it is following an accelerated procedure such as that in the UK. Signified by the suffix 'A' in the serial number. See **early publication, publication codes.**

Abandonment

The state of an application (or of an invention) when the applicant has failed to react to an **official action (office action)** within the stipulated time. In the case of a US trade mark application, abandonment may take place if no statement of use is filed at the appropriate time. See also **withdrawal**.

Abandonment and refiling is a technique used in the patent world, when the applicant still wants to secure protection for the invention but has not made sufficient progress towards making a commercial product or does not wish to file foreign applications within the priority period. If the application is completely and irrevocably withdrawn, with no rights remaining (which must be stated clearly in the request to withdraw), the application is treated as never having been made and a new application can be made for a patent for the same invention. The application has not been published in this time so the subject-matter remains confidential and does not form part of the **state of the art**. Priority is lost, so the applicant runs the risk that someone else has filed an application or otherwise taken his place in the queue in the meantime.

Absolute Grounds

Registration of a trade mark may be refused, or declared invalid, on absolute or relative grounds: they are called by these names in the **Community**

trade mark system, and in the national trade mark laws of the EU Member States. The absolute grounds are matters inherent in the sign registration of which is applied for. It might be outside the statutory definition of a trade mark; it might lack **distinctiveness**, be **descriptive**, or be **generic**, in which cases it can be saved by evidence of **acquired distinctiveness**; in the case of a **shape trade mark**, it might fall within the statutory exclusions; it might be contrary to **public policy** or accepted principles of **morality**, or deceptive (**deceptiveness**); its use might be prohibited by law; it might be a **specially protected emblem**; or the application might have been made in **bad faith**. See also **relative grounds**.

Absolute Novelty

The level of novelty required in the European patent system, and in the laws of the **European Patent Convention (EPC)** contracting states. Novelty is destroyed by the publication of anything, anywhere in the world, in any language, by any means including written or oral publication or use, before the application date or the priority date. See **state of the art**.

Abstract

One of the elements of a patent application, a short summary of the invention which is used as a classification and indexing tool by the patent office. It is not examined, confers no legal rights and may benefit from some assistance in its drafting from the patent office concerned.

Abstraction test

A test devised by Judge Learned Hand to work out whether non-literal copying had taken place. Expression and idea are treated as ends of a continuum, and infringement is found if the allegedly infringing work crosses the line between the two.

> Upon any work . . . a great number of patterns of increasing generality will fit equally well, as more and more of the incident is left out. The last may perhaps be no more than the most general statement of what the work is about, and at times might consist only of its title; but there is a point in this series of abstractions where they are no longer protected, since otherwise the author could prevent the use of his 'ideas', to which, apart from their expression, his property is never extended. . . . Nobody has ever been able to fix that boundary, and

nobody ever can. *Nichols v. Universal Pictures*, 45 F.2d 119, 121, 7 USPQ 84, 86 (2d Cir. 1930)

There have also been other tests used to deal with the problem: the 'pattern' test, where infringement is found if the pattern of the work is taken (in a play, for instance, the sequence of events, and the development of the interplay of characters), the subtractive test and the totality test. The **abstraction–filtration–comparison test** is in the ascendant. See **substantial similarity**.

Abstraction–Filtration–Comparison (AFC) Test

An approach to detecting whether copyright has been infringed, formulated in *Computer Associates v Altai* [1992] 20 USPQ 2d 1641, 982 F.2d693 (1992). Commonly used in computer software copyright cases, but also applicable to non-literal infringements of other types of copyright works. Overcomes the drawback of Whelan v Jaslow, where the court identified one underlying idea and deemed everything else to be protectable expression.

The first stage is to determine the appropriate levels of abstraction at which to consider the elements in which copyright is claimed, on a scale running from the most fundamental statement of the idea of the copyright work at one extreme to the precise expression of that idea by the author at the other. The second stage requires that any non-copyright elements (for example ideas) be filtered out, so that there remains only material that is truly the stuff of copyright protection. The third stage asks the judge to compare that residue, or golden nugget, against the defendant's programme to ascertain whether there has been an infringement.

This approach was adopted, and slightly adapted, in the English case, *John Richardson Computers v Flanders and Chemtec* [1993] FSR 497, by Rimer J (who, sadly, delivered his judgment in prose). The lack in British copyright law of an express exclusion of copyright protection for ideas, which in US copyright law is of fundamental importance for the successful application of the three-stage test, made this approach inappropriate in English law, as **Jacob J** observed later in *Ibcos Computers Ltd v Barclays Mercantile Finance Ltd* [1994] F.S.R. 275.

Also referred to as the successive filtering test.

Accelerated Procedure, Accelerated Processing, Accelerated Examination

A common feature of patent and trade mark procedures allowing the applicant, on payment of an additional fee, to have the application dealt with more speedily than would otherwise be the case. The **Patent Examination in Highway** is a mechanism for making accelerated examination readily available in certain international situations.

Accelerating the application process often has the undesirable effect of bringing forward the time when further fees are payable, but there are many reasons why an applicant might be prepared to accept this if the rights can be granted sooner.

See also **petition to make special**.

Acceptance

The stage in the application process, particularly for a trade mark, when the office to which the application has been made considers that the mark is ready for registration. It is then advertised or published in an official journal (nowadays, frequently on-line only) and depending on the applicable laws is then open to opposition for a set period of time. Some patent systems also have pre-grant opposition (Australia being one).

Access Control Technology

A synonym for technological protection means used in the Digital Millennium Copyright Act in the US. The Act provides that the Library of Congress may issue exemptions from the prohibition on circumventing access control technology where that technology prevents lawful use of material. Similar provisions exist in the laws of other countries, thanks to the **WIPO Treaties**.

Account of Profits

In English law, the equitable remedy of an account of profits is an alternative to an award of damages in an infringement action. The theory is that the profits made by the defendant should properly have been made by the claimant, and the defendant should therefore be required to account for the profits wrongly made. It remedies the defendant's unjust enrichment.

Consequently, the top limit of an award will be what the defendant has made from the infringement. This will frequently be less than the amount of damages that would be awarded. In the right case, however, it might yield a great deal more. If the claimant is unable to prove any damage to their own business, an account of profits would be preferable. This will happen where the defendant is making bigger profits than the claimant. It is not open to the claimant to argue that the defendant should have made more: the claimant must take the defendant as they find them.

The profits must have been earned from the infringement, and difficulties can arise where only a proportion of the defendant's profit can be attributed to the infringing activities. It would be unfair to the defendant if the claimant were awarded all the profits where it is possible to allocate them between infringing and non-infringing activities. A manufacturing process that uses an invention as a small part of the overall process is an example.

The court will make allowances to the defendant for the proper expenses associated with making sales, including advertising and marketing. Account will also be taken of any increase in the value of goods or services once they have been sold or provided, and any additional features of the products or services that are outside the scope of the invention. The assistance of forensic accountants with knowledge of the relevant industry is often required to calculate the amount of the profits.

Acquiescence

Consenting to something by remaining silent. Where the proprietor of an earlier trade mark or other earlier right has acquiesced for a continuous period of five years in the use of a registered trade mark in the UK, being aware of that use, it ceases to be entitled to apply for a declaration that the registration of the later trade mark is invalid or to oppose the use of the later trade mark (Trade Marks Act 1994, section 48(1)). Equity and common law will also deny remedies to a claimant or plaintiff who has acquiesced in the act about which complaint is made.

See also **laches**, which is different (though not unrelated).

Acquired Distinctiveness

An applicant who seeks to register a trade mark may be able to overcome objections based on absolute grounds of refusal if it has acquired distinctiveness. Another way of putting this is to say that it has a **secondary**

meaning. The words or other symbols making up the trade mark may have an ordinary meaning, but when they have become distinctive of a particular trader's goods or services, then other things being equal the sign should be registered as a trade mark.

ACTA

The Anti-Counterfeiting Trade Agreement, a proposed plurilateral trade agreement dealing (as the name suggests) with counterfeit goods. A plurilateral agreement, in contradistinction to a multilateral one, is made between two or more countries but not a great number of them: Deardorff's Glossary of International Economics (http://www.personal. umich.edu/~alandear/glossary; *Terms of Trade: Glossary of International Economics*, Singapore: World Scientific Publishing Company, 2006). Signatories have a particular interest in the subject-matter of the treaty, and reservations are less freely available than under an ordinary multilateral treaty. In the World Trade Organization (WTO), the expression denotes an agreement which gives member countries the choice of whether to agree voluntarily to new rules, whereas the main WTO agreement binds all members.

The intention to create ACTA, which has been negotiated in secret outside the structure of international organisations, was first announced in October 2007 by the US, the EU, Switzerland and Japan. Other countries have since joined. It seeks to establish international standards for enforcement of intellectual property rights – not being limited to **counterfeit goods (counterfeiting)**, but also covering **piracy**, including Internet piracy. Its focus is developing countries where enforcement could be improved – Brazil, Russia and China are specifically mentioned in the imaginatively named 'Fact Sheet: Anti-Counterfeiting Trade Agreement' published by the European Commission (http://trade.ec.europa.eu/doclib/html/142039. htm). The draft agreement, which has been the subject of several leaks, also seeks to impose obligations on Internet Service Providers. It has been heavily criticised, both for its substantive content, including the effect it will have on the free software movement, and for the secrecy in which it is being negotiated.

ActionAid Chip

An invention claimed in a UK patent application filed by the development charity, ActionAid, to draw attention to the harm it claims is done to development by patents, particularly plant patents (see **enola bean**). Equivalent to a French fry in some parts of the world. The patent claimed a ready-salted chip, but was refused.

Added Matter

If it were possible to add matter to a patent application by amendment, that added matter would enjoy a priority date earlier than it should. The new matter ought to be the subject of a new application with its own priority date. Similarly, if a later application claims the priority date of an earlier one, new matter must not be added. Article 123 of the European Patent Convention prohibits added matter in divisional applications or new applications for the subject matter of earlier applications, and deals with added matter introduced in amendments. Section 76 of the UK Patents Act is in similar terms, though as an implementation of the EPC provision it has been described as 'cack-handed' by **Lord Justice Jacob**.

Addition, Patent of

A patent which covers an improvement in or modification of another patent, and is directly associated with that other patent. It must be restricted to matter that is an improvement or modification of the invention in the parent patent. It does not have to be renewed as the parent patent does.

Where such patents are provided for (India and Australia, for example, and formerly under the Patents Act 1949, section 26, in the UK) the law does not require that the addition is inventive over the parent patent, so the patent of addition is subject to a relatively relaxed examination process. However, a patent of addition will give no longer protection for the additional subject matter than that given by the parent patent – they will expire at the same time.

Additional Damages

Damages in, for example, an infringement action are intended to put the parties back into the position they would have been in had the infringement not occurred, by redistributing the proceeds of the infringement. They are not intended to penalise the infringer, on the principle *nulla poene sine lege.*

The Copyright, Designs and Patents Act 1988 (which abolished **conversion damages** in copyright infringement cases) provided (in section 97(2)) for the court to award 'additional damages' where, having regard to all the circumstances and in particular to the flagrancy of the infringement and any benefit accruing to the defendant by reason of the infringement, the justice of the case may so require. Section 191J(2) provides in identical terms for performer's property rights, and section 229(3) does so for design right. Section 14 of the Trade Marks Act 1994 provides that in an action for infringement the same relief is available as in respect of the infringement of 'any other property right', which must logically mean that any remedy available for infringement of copyright is available there too, and that must include additional damages.

In *Cala Homes (South) Ltd v McAlpine Homes East Ltd (No2)* [1996] FSR 36 the court said that additional damages are akin to exemplary damages and awarded them in addition to an account of profits (stretching the literal meaning of 'additional damages'). The House of Lords overruled this approach in *Redrow v Bett* [1998] 1 All ER 385, [1999] AC 197.

Addressee

A patent specification is addressed to those likely to have a practical interest in the subject matter of the invention, and such persons are those with practical knowledge and experience of the kind of work in which the invention is intended to be used. The addressee comes to a reading of the specification with the common general knowledge of persons skilled in the relevant art, and he (or, once and for all, she) reads it knowing that its purpose is to describe and demarcate an invention. He is unimaginative and has no inventive capacity.

Administrative Council

The Administrative Council of the European Patent Organisation is one of the two organs of the **European Patent Organisation**. The other is the **European Patent Office**.

Administrative Patent Judge (US)

A judge of the **Board of Patent Appeals and Interferences**.

ADR

Alternative dispute resolution; includes a variety of techniques which offer an alternative to conventional legal proceedings, such as arbitration and mediation. Presumably centuries ago legal proceedings were offered as an alternative to more physical means of resolving disputes. WIPO, and national intellectual property offices, offer ADR services.

Advocaat

According to the English humorist Alan Coren, a drink made from lawyers (*The Sanity Inspector*, London: Hodder & Stoughton, 1974). In fact a drink made from eggs, sugar and brandy, one of the leading manu-facturers of which is the Dutch company Ervin Warnink BV. In *Ervin Warnink BV v J Townend & Sons (Hull) Ltd* [1979] AC 731, [1980] R.P.C. 31 the Dutch company sued the maker of an inferior product marketed under the name Keeling's Old English Advocaat. In the House of Lords, the case gave rise to Lord Diplock's five-part test for **passing off** (a mis-representation by a trader in the course of trade to prospective customers of his or ultimate consumers of goods or services supplied by him, which is calculated to injure the business or goodwill of another trader, and which causes actual damage to the business or goodwill of the trader bringing the action). His Lordship warned against the logical fallacy of the **undis-tributed middle**. The case established the extended concept of passing-off, including any situation where goodwill is likely to be damaged as a result of the misrepresentation.

AdWords

The name for a 'pay-per-click' advertising programme offered by Google, the Internet search engine company. Advertisers specify the words which, entered by a user into the Google search engine, will trigger the display of the advertiser's material in the form of 'sponsored links'. The system was alleged to infringe patents owned by a business called Overture, later taken over by Yahoo!, with which Google negotiated a perpetual licence, but more significantly it raises novel and far-reaching trade mark issues. Apart from the fact that AdWords are often incapable of performing an origin-identifying function – they can be utterly non-distinctive – businesses are allowed to bid for AdWords that correspond to registered trade marks, and not only registered trade marks belonging to the bidder. On 23 March

2010 the Court of Justice of the European Union held that no infringement is committed by Google in allowing trade marks to be used in this way, though its customers for AdWords might infringe.

Agreement on Trade-Related Aspects of Intellectual Property Rights

See **TRIPS**.

AIPPI

Association Internationale pour la Protection de la Propriété Intellectuelle (or International Association for the Protection of Intellectual Property).

Air Pirates

In the words of US trade mark lawyer and **blawger** Marty Schwimmer: 'Any excuse to recall the Air Pirates case'. *Walt Disney Productions, Inc., v. The Air Pirates et al.*, 199 U.S.P.Q. 769; 581 F.2d 751, was a case in the United States Court of Appeals for the Ninth Circuit in 1978 (but filed in 1971) which examined the scope of the **parody** defence in US copyright law. The defendants produced a magazine, in the underground or countercultural tradition, in which Walt Disney's creation engaged in activities not previously associated with him, like dope-smuggling, or sexual congress with Minnie. The Court of Appeals upheld the granting of summary judgment to Disney on copyright infringement, but remanded the (less notorious) trade mark infringement and unfair competition claims where the court felt that summary judgment had been inappropriate.

Dan O'Neill, one of the founders of Air Pirates and the artist of the Mickey Mouse parodies (other members of the group drew other strips), continued to draw the character notwithstanding court orders until, faced with the impossibility of collecting the $190000 damages they had been awarded and with $2 million spent on legal costs, the Disney Corporation dropped contempt charges and settled the case on the basis that no more infringements would be committed.

Alappat, In re

In re Alappat 33 F.3d 1526, 1545 (Fed. Cir. 1994) is a key US judgment on patentability of computer programs. The court said: 'We have held . . . that programming creates a new machine, because a general purpose computer in effect becomes a special purpose computer once it is programmed to perform particular functions pursuant to instructions from program software.' See **machine-or-transformation test** and **Old Piano Roll Blues**.

Aldous, Lord Justice (Sir William Aldous) (1936–)

The judge assigned to the Patents Court from 1988 (when he succeeded Whitford J) to 1995, when he was appointed to the Court of Appeal and succeeded in the Patents Court by Jacob J. Retired from the Court of Appeal in 2003. Justice of Appeal for Gibraltar since 2006.

Allegation of Use

A US trade mark application may be based on actual use in commerce, an intent to use (ITU) or a foreign application. In the case of an ITU application, the trade mark must be used in commerce and an allegation of use filed before the registration can issue.

There are two types of allegations of use: (1) an amendment to allege use, which is submitted prior to a mark being approved for publication; and (2) a **statement of use**, which is submitted within three years of the date of the issuance of the notice of allowance. From the time that the mark is approved for publication until the issuance of the notice of allowance, an allegation of use cannot be filed. This is known as the 'blackout period'. The requirements for an amendment to allege use and a statement of use are the same, and the differing terminology used to describe the documents is based only on whether the submission was made prior to the blackout period or after it. However, the remedies for curing a defective allegation of use are different depending on whether the document in question is an amendment to allege use or a statement of use.

The allegation of use must attest to use in commerce in connection with all of the goods or services listed in the application, unless the applicant deletes the goods or services that are not in use or files a request to divide in conjunction with the allegation of use. An applicant is required to file a sample of its mark in use in commerce, called a **specimen of use**, for each class of goods or services.

If an amendment to allege use (filed prior to publication) is found to be unacceptable, an applicant can usually return the application to 'intent-to-use' status by filing a simple document. On the other hand, if a statement of use is found to be unacceptable, the applicant may be constrained in terms of returning the status of its application to 'intent-to-use'. Therefore, if the applicant is not positive that its specimen of use will be deemed acceptable when filing its statement of use, the applicant may wish to file an 'insurance extension', which will provide the applicant with an additional period of six months to submit an acceptable specimen of use.

Allowance

In US procedure, the **acceptance** of the application.

Analogous Use

In US trade mark law, use of a sign that falls short of being trademark use (for example, use in a catalogue) but which may nevertheless be sufficient to create a basis for priority or even to confer prior rights sufficient to cancel a later trademark registration.

ANDA

In the US, Abbreviated New Drug Application: see **Hatch–Waxman Act**.

Andean Community of Nations

An international community comprising Bolivia, Colombia, Ecuador, Peru and (originally but no longer) Venezuela which has a common industrial property system (the present TRIPS-compliant system being introduced, with encouragement from the United States, in 2000, replacing one that was considered restrictive and patentee-unfriendly). The patent system bears a close resemblance to the EPC. There is also a common regime on copyright and related rights and a Regime for Protection of the Rights of Obtentors [sic] of new Plant Varieties.

Annuities

See **renewal**.

Anticipation

1. A novelty-destroying reference; a problem for a patent, because a patent claim will be anticipated if someone following the instructions given by a piece of prior art would inevitably infringe the patent. The reference must contain explicitly all the essential features of the alleged invention.

    Lord Hoffmann summarised the position in English law thus in *Synthon BV v Smith Kline Beecham plc* [2006] R.P.C. 10 (§§ 22, 23):

    > . . . the matter relied upon as prior art must disclose subject-matter which, if performed, would necessarily result in an infringement of the patent. That may be because the prior art discloses the same invention. In that case there will be no question that performance of the earlier invention would infringe and usually it will be apparent to someone who is aware of both the prior art and the patent that it will do so. But patent infringement does not require that one should be aware that one is infringing: 'whether or not a person is working [an] . . . invention is an objective fact independent of what he knows or thinks about what he is doing': *Merrell Dow Pharmaceuticals Inc v H N Norton & Co Ltd* [1996] R.P.C. 76, 90. It follows that, whether or not it would be apparent to anyone at the time, whenever subject-matter described in the prior disclosure is capable of being performed and is such that, if performed, it must result in the patent being infringed, the disclosure condition is satisfied. The flag has been planted, even though the author or maker of the prior art was not aware that he was doing so. . . .

    > But the infringement must be not merely a possible or even likely consequence of performing the invention disclosed by the prior disclosure. It must be necessarily entailed. If there is more than one possible consequence, one cannot say that performing the disclosed invention will infringe. The flag has not been planted on the patented invention, although a person performing the invention disclosed by the prior art may carry it there by accident or (if he is aware of the patented invention) by design. Indeed, it may be obvious to do so. But the prior disclosure must be construed as it would have been understood by the skilled person at the date of the disclosure and not in the light of the subsequent patent.

2. 1971 album (and title track therefrom) by Carly Simon.

Anticommons

The mirror-image of commons property. A neologism coined by Michael Heller in 'The Tragedy of the Anticommons: Property in the Transition from Marx to Markets' (*Harvard Law Review*, 111, pp. 621–88, 1998), which describes a coordination breakdown where the existence of numerous rights holders frustrates the achievement of a socially desirable outcome. It mirrors the older term 'tragedy of the commons', which describes coordination breakdowns arising from an insufficiency of rights holders. Heller observed empty shops in Moscow alongside street kiosks full of goods, but the theory (which, naturally, has its opponents) is relevant to other coordination failures such as patent **thickets**, **submarine patents** and nail houses (the latter being outside the scope of this work).

Antitrust

The body of law in the United States of America designed to control **monopolies** and restrictive practices and to preserve competition. Known as **competition law** in other parts of the world, although the expression 'antitrust' is used extensively in the European Union to describe parts of the body of competition law there.

Anton Piller

A form of order, made on an *ex parte* application, known to the English courts that enables a claimant in an intellectual property infringement action to collect evidence of the infringer's activities. It can be seen as a sort of civilian search warrant. It takes its name from *Anton Piller KG v Manufacturing Processes Limited* [1976] Ch 55 though the first such order was made by Templeman J (as he then was) in *EMI Limited v Pandit* [1975] 1 All ER 418. This novel form of order was in fact devised by Hugh **Laddie** who was then at a relatively early stage in his career at the Bar.

An order would only be granted if the three-step test set out by Ormrod LJ in the *Anton Piller* case were satisfied:

1. there is an extremely strong prima facie case against the respondent;
2. the damage, potential or actual, must be very serious for the applicant; and
3. there must be clear evidence that the respondents have in their possession incriminating documents or things and that there is a real

possibility that they may destroy such material before an *inter partes* application can be made.

The order has now been replaced by the statutory search order under the **Civil Procedure Act 1997** (although the nickname is still often used, and in some common law jurisdictions the case remains the basis of orders that the courts might grant).

ANZAC

The Australian and New Zealand Army Corps, whose legendary reputation is intimately linked with the Gallipoli landings (1915) and whose participation in that disastrous campaign was a crucial event in the development of those countries' national consciousness. It might seem something of an anachronism, but the Anzac (Restriction on Trade Use of Word) Act 1916 makes it an offence in the UK to use the word without permission from the government of Australia or New Zealand. It cannot therefore be used as, or form part of, a trade mark, and objections will be raised under section 3(4) or (5) of the Trade Marks Act should such an application be filed. Legislation of the same vintage and to like effect applies in Australia and New Zealand, where Anzac Day (25 April) remains more significant as a commemoration than Armistice Day or Remembrance Day elsewhere. The potency of the word as a trade sign, were this to be allowed, far from diminishing with the passage of time appears to be growing.

Apostille

A form of legalisation of documents provided for under the Hague Convention of 1961. Many countries formerly required patent documents to be notarised and then legalised by their consulate or embassy. Signatories to the Hague Convention dispense with the requirement for legalisation as far as other Convention countries are concerned: instead, local authorities apply the apostille to the notarised document.

Apparatus Claim

A patent claim to a piece of equipment.

Appellation

The common element (though an etymologically different word might be used) in the name for systems throughout the world, such as the Appellation d'origine contrôlée (AOC) used in France, the Denominazione di origine controllata (DOC) used in Italy, the Denominação de Origem Controlada (DOC) used in Portugal, and the Denominación de Origen (DO) system used in Spain, to denote and protect local and regional names for produce.

Appellations of origin are the subject of the **Lisbon Agreement**, Article 2 of which contains this definition:

> geographical name of a country, region, or locality, which serves to designate a product originating therein, the quality and characteristics of which are due exclusively or essentially to the geographic environment, including natural and human factors.

The European Union **Protected Geographical Status** system works in parallel with the national systems, and in some cases is subordinated to the pre-existing appellation system, particularly with wine.

Apple

The distinctive part of the corporate name of, first, the company set up in 1968 as a corporate vehicle for The Beatles' business activities (Apple Corps Ltd); and secondly, a US computer manufacturer incorporated in 1977 as Apple Computer, Inc. (now just Apple, Inc., reflecting its expansion into other areas of consumer electronics) by Steve Wozniak and Steve Jobs. The suggestion that Jobs chose the name because he was a Beatles fan appears to be a myth: the official version is that Apple wanted to appear before Atari in the telephone directory. An account of the ensuing litigation could easily fill a book this size. See *Sosumi*.

Applicant

In the case of a patent, the applicant may be a natural or legal person but not in the USA, where the application must be filed in the name or names of the inventor or inventors (who must necessarily be natural persons). The application is then commonly assigned to someone who is the actual owner of the patent, which in the case of employed inventors is their employer.

Application

An ambiguous expression. An application must be filed in order to secure those intellectual property rights that rely on grant or registration, but the expression could be used to designate the documents presented to the office or it could mean the legal state of affairs arising from the filing of the papers. The first might be withdrawn or granted and cease to exist: the second is a matter of fact and will endure, as Peter Prescott QC (sitting as a deputy High Court judge) observed in *Oxonica Energy Ltd v Neuftec Ltd* [2008] EWHC 2127 (Pat).

Application Number

The number assigned to an application for a trade mark, patent etc. The same number will in some systems become the registered number, while in others a new number will be assigned to the right concerned on grant.

Applied Art

Design and aesthetics applied to everyday objects, as opposed to fine arts which are intended purely to stimulate the intellect. Industrial design, graphic design, fashion design, interior design, decorative art and functional art are applied arts, and photography and architecture might also be considered to fall into the category. The expression is used in the Berne Convention which requires works of applied art to be protected, but only mandates protection for 25 years.

Arbitrary, Arbitrariness

A desirable characteristic in a trade mark, which cannot (in theory) be descriptive or generic.

Architecture, Work of

One of the forms of artistic work according to the Copyright, Designs and Patents Act, section 4(1), being a building or a model for a building. A drawing of a building would be a graphic work and protected as such (if it qualified) irrespective of artistic quality, whereas such a quality would have to be present in a work of architecture for it to be protected.

ARIPO

The African Regional Industrial Property Office. Established in 1976, ARIPO deals with the protection of all types of IP, including trade marks, patents, industrial designs and utility models. Members are Ghana, Gambia, Kenya, Lesotho, Malawi, Mozambique, Sudan, Sierra Leone, Swaziland, Tanzania, Uganda and Zimbabwe, where it has its headquarters – most of non-Francophone Africa (which has **OAPI**) but not South Africa or Nigeria. A **PCT** application may designate ARIPO, and individual members may also be designated. Trade mark registrations are governed by the Banjul Protocol, to which only eight of the members are party: it allows a 12-month examination period, which is criticised as not long enough for some of the members. The Harare Protocol on patents, industrial designs and utility models, on the other hand, is very successful, partly at least because it has 15 signatories.

Article

The entity the design of any aspect of the shape or configuration of which may be protected in the UK under Part III of the Copyright, Designs and Patents Act 1988 (**unregistered design right**). Cf. **'product'** in the **registered designs** legislation.

Article 61 Application (EPC)

An application pursued by a person, other than the original applicant, who has been adjudged to be entitled to the grant of a European patent.

Artist's Resale Right

The right for the creator of an **artistic work** to participate in the proceeds of subsequent dealings in the work itself (as opposed to the copyright or any other rights in it). Based on the reasonable assumption, supported by history, that artists might sometimes be obliged to part with their work for the price of a meal (or perhaps for the meal itself), some countries enacted legislation giving the artist a continuing interest in the artwork. The Artist's Resale Right Regulations 2006 implement EC Directive 2001/84/EC of the European Parliament and of the Council of 27 September 2001 on the resale right for the benefit of the author of an original work of art (OJ No L 272, 13.10.2001, p.32) and the option given by Article 14*ter* of the Berne Convention.

The right applies where the resale price is at least €1000 (the Directive permitted a threshold between zero and €3000) and the rate of royalty is up to 4 per cent. Only living artists will benefit from the UK law, at least until 2010 as the government has secured a delay in the full implementation of the Directive. It wishes to extend this to 2012, and if possible to make it permanent. The London auction industry perceives the right as a major threat, especially because there is no such right in New York.

Artistic Craftsmanship, Work of

The third category of artistic work according to the **Copyright, Designs and Patents Act 1988**, section 4(1). The statute does not elaborate: this category of artistic works has been recognised since 1911, but deliberately left open. A work must be artistic – protection is not irrespective of artistic quality – and craftsmanship must have been exercised in its making. In *George Hensher Ltd v Restawile Upholstery (Lancs) Ltd* [1976] AC 64 the House of Lords confirmed that artistic quality was necessary, so everyday works of craftsmanship will not qualify, and in the course of presenting their opinions five law lords canvassed about nine possible definitions of the expression – eventually being persuaded by the fact that witnesses had described the armchair in suit as 'flashy' and 'vulgar'. The discussion in that case of the Arts and Crafts Movement is instructive. In *Lucasfilm v Ainsworth* [2008] EWHC 1878 (Ch) it was held that various props made for the Star Wars films were not works of artistic craftsmanship, though in the earlier case *Shelley Films v Rex Features* [1994] EMLR 134 various artefacts associated with the film *Mary Shelley's Frankenstein* were held to fall within the category.

In *Merlet v Mothercare* [1986] RPC 15 the creator of a waterproof cape had designed it without any artistic considerations in mind, so it was not a work of artistic craftsmanship. In *Burke v Spicers Dress Designs* [1936] Ch 400 at 408 (referred to in *Merlet*) it was suggested that even 'a beautiful frock' might not be a work of artistic craftsmanship. Following *Burke*, some cases suggest that the same person must bring the artistry and the craftsmanship to the project, though later cases cast doubt on this (see in particular *Vermaat v Boncrest* [2001] FSR 43, where there was held to be no copyright because the work concerned was so simple).

Artistic Work

A category of copyright work, defined in section 4(1) of the **Copyright, Designs and Patents Act 1988**. It means a **graphic work, photograph, sculpture** or **collage**, a **work of architecture** or a **work of artistic craftsmanship**. The list is exhaustive – there is no possibility of squeezing in anything that is not included in the definition, though the expressions used are wide and open-ended. The first group of works receive protection irrespective of artistic quality – in other words, an artistic work does not have to be artistic, or looking at it another and more defensible way, judges are not required to act as art critics.

Assignation

In Scotland, an **assignment**; in England, a tryst.

Assignment

A transfer of legal or equitable title to property, or both, and the document that achieves this (which is often, though not always, in common law jurisdictions a deed). One of the defining features of a **chose in action** is that it can be assigned, and most types of intellectual property are choses (or things) in action – but patents, expressly, are not. However, the Patents Act 1977, section 30 (in Scotland section 31) specifically states that patents may be assigned, so their exclusion from the scope of choses in action is of limited (perhaps even no) importance. So too may applications for patents be assigned.

In UK law, an assignment (in Scotland, assignation) of a registered trade mark must be in writing and signed by the assignor (Trade Marks Act 1994, section 24(3)), as must an assignment of copyright (Copyright, Designs and Patents Act 1988, section 90(3)) or unregistered design right (section 222(3)), or a registered design or an application for one (Registered Designs Act 1949, section 15B).

'Many rights,' Berwin observes, 'including the rights of a book publisher and of a software user, are "personal" rights which may not be freely assigned unless the contract otherwise provides. This may cause difficulties on the sale of a business.'

Associated

Under section 30 of the (UK) Trade Marks Act 1938 trade marks that shared important features and differed only in details would have to be associated with each other. The consequence of this was that they could not be assigned separately.

Where for any purposes under the 1938 Act the use of a trade mark had to be proved, the use of an associated trade mark (or of a trade mark with additions or alterations not substantially affecting its identity) would be regarded as equivalent. See **analogous use**.

Associated Design

In the UK, section 4 of the Registered Designs Act 1949 permitted, until 9 December 2001 when the changes required by Directive 98/71/EC came into operation, the registration of an existing registered design for other articles, or with minor modifications or variations ('not sufficient to alter the character or substantially to affect the identity thereof'). The prior registered design would not count against the novelty of the later application, but the later application would not secure a longer period of protection than the first registered design had. It worked just like a **patent of addition**, in fact.

Section 4 was repealed in 2001. It was not compatible with the Directive, nor was it necessary given that designs would no longer be registered for specific articles (products, in the terminology of the revised law) and registration would give rights that would extend over designs that do not create a different overall impression on the informed user.

The concept of an associated design is also found in other countries. In Taiwan, for example, Article 110 of the Patent Act permits the proprietor of an earlier design patent to file an application for a design patent for a similar design without the earlier one compromising the novelty of the later application (though if someone else has filed a similar application in the meantime, the opportunity to file for an associated design will have been lost).

Association, Likelihood of

The Trade Marks Act 1994 suggests that association is a type of confusion, so that a likelihood of confusion includes a likelihood of association. This form of words appears in sections 5(2) and 10(2) of the Act. In

Wagamama Ltd v City Centre Restaurants plc [1995] F.S.R. 713 **Laddie J** declined to consider Benelux law (alleged to be the source of this concept); observed that the narrower concept appeared, illogically, to be said to include the broader; and decided that there was no requirement that words in a statute should always bear a meaning. However, the CJEC has subsequently given a meaning to those words in *Sabel BV v Puma AG* [1997] ECR I-6191 and later cases.

Attorney–Client Privilege

See, in general, **legal professional privilege**. There are particular issues for intellectual property practitioners, though: *In re EchoStar Communications Corp.*, 448 F.3d 1294 (Fed. Cir. 1 May 2006) decided that when an accused infringer chooses to rely on an opinion of counsel in defending an allegation of wilful infringement, it waives the attorney–client privilege with regard to any attorney–client communications relating to the same subject matter. *In re Seagate Technology, LLC*, 2007 WL 2358677, Misc. No. 830 (Fed. Cir. Aug. 20, 2007), removed significant ambiguities created by that case.

The work product doctrine in the US also provides protection, on a similar basis, for documents and so on created in anticipation of litigation from discovery by the other side.

Audio–Visual Work

In US copyright law: 'works that consist of a series of related images which are intrinsically intended to be shown by the use of machines or devices such as projectors, viewers, or electronic equipment, together with accompanying sounds, if any, regardless of the nature of the material objects, such as films or tapes, in which the works are embodied'.

The definition, which is apt to cover video games and similar matter unimaginable when it was coined, corresponds to the definition of 'film' in UK copyright law, the UK legislature having opted to use the established expression for a range of technologies while the US has adopted a novel, technologically neutral term. The laws of both countries will cover video games under this rubric.

Auslegeschrift

German, formerly an examined and published patent application. See *Offenlegungsschrift* and *Patentschrift.*

Author

The creator of a **work** for the purposes of copyright law and usually the first owner of **copyright** in it. The Copyright, Designs and Patents Act 1988 employs a broad definition of author, including the creators of material such as sound recordings, broadcasts and cable programmes, which are regarded in the *droit d'auteur* countries as a different type of intellectual property: see **related rights**, **neighbouring rights**, and see **hire**, **work made for**.

Authors' Rights

The equivalent of (but far from identical to) what common lawyers call copyright, throughout the civil law world. French *droit d'auteur*, German *Urherrberrecht*, Italian *diretto d'autore*, Spanish *derecho de autore*, Polish *prawa autorskie*, Russian авторское право, Swedish *upphovsrat*, and so on.

AXMEDIS

Automating Production of Cross Media Content for Multi-channel Distribution. A research project partly supported by the European Commission Information Society Technologies (IST DG-INFSO) programme of the Sixth Framework Programme.

Ayyangar Report

Shri Justice Rajagopala Ayyangar was appointed in April 1957 by the Indian government to report on the revision of the patent and designs laws. His report, including notes on the clauses of the lapsed 1953 Bill, is a far-ranging assessment not only of Indian patent law but also of the principles of patent law in general, with many lessons from the UK and other Dominions. Available from http://www.spicyip.com/ip-resources.

B

'B' Publication

The publication of a granted patent.

Background Intellectual Property

Pre-existing **intellectual property** (which must be carefully defined) available to a party to, for example, a cooperation agreement which will benefit the joint venture. The expression is commonly used in agreements relating to such arrangements, where it is likely that both sides will contribute background IP to the project and will wish to be able to take it with them at the end of the arrangement. The agreement will also make clear that neither party has the right to use the other's background IP, certainly after the joint venture has finished but also (depending on the precise nature of the arrangement) possibly while it is extant.

Bad Faith

An absolute ground for refusal of registration of a trade mark – or grounds for it to be declared invalid. Trade Marks Act 1994, section 3(6), and Article 51(1)(b) of the CTM regulation (which makes bad faith grounds for invalidity but not for refusal).

Bait and Switch

A form of trade mark infringement in which prospective customers are lured to the defendant's goods or services by use of the trade mark, then converted to customers of the person making unauthorised use of the trade mark with no further use of the trade mark (for example on the defendant's goods). For an example, see *Whirlpool Corporation & Ors v Kenwood Ltd* [2009] EWCA Civ 753 (23 July 2009). Equivalent to **initial interest confusion** in US trademark law.

Banderole

A small flag or pennant, typically long and thin, flown from the mast-heads of ships, carried in battle, hanging from trumpets; but more commonly these days stamps used in some countries to show that dues, such as taxes, have been paid. In Turkey, for example, a requirement for any material (printed, audio, visual) that was used in a public place.

Bangui Accord

See **OAPI**.

Banjul Protocol

See **ARIPO**.

Banks Report

The British Patent System, Report of the Committee to Examine the Patent System and Patent Law, Cmnd 4407 (1970). The Committee was established in 1967 with a remit to consider 'the desirability of harmonising national patent laws and the degree of protection obtained by the same invention in different countries.' The Sainsbury Report, *Relationship of the Pharmaceutical Industry with the National Health Services, 1965–1967*, (Cmnd 3410) had made recommendations about patent law which, if implemented, would have led to a clash with Europe, including retaining or even reducing the 16-year term, a short monopoly period followed by licensing of right, and simplification of the existing compulsory licensing regime to make life easier for generics manufacturers. In the interim the Wilson government had decided to seek membership of the European Economic Community. Although joining the EPC was not mandatory, the UK government wanted to be seen as a team player.

Bare Licence

A personal right or permission to use another's property which is revocable at will and perhaps not a contractual licence at all. There might be no consideration such as would support the grant of a contractual licence. It is a defence to an infringement claim, and if the bare licensee exceeds the terms of grant he will be an infringer. Scrutton LJ summed this up nicely, though in a non-IP case: 'When you invite a person into your house to use the staircase, you do not invite him to slide down the bannisters' (The Carlgarth (1927) P 93 at 110). In the trade marks field, a bare licence is a problem because it contains none of the quality control provisions that are essential to safeguard the proprietor's interests. The agreement could be unenforceable, the trade mark could be abandoned, or rights could be forfeit by the licensor to the licensee. Before the Trade Marks Act 1994, permission to use a trade mark had to be given in a registered user agreement which, once registered at the Trade Marks Registry, ensured that the use of the mark accrued to the benefit of the owner and kept the mark safe from a non-use challenge. See also **naked licence**.

Basmati

A variety of long-grained rice, noted for its fragrance and delicate flavour, grown in India and Pakistan. RiceTec, a Texas corporation, obtained US Patent No. 5 663 484 on 'basmati rice lines and grains' in 1997, causing international outrage, allegations of biopiracy and a diplomatic crisis between India and the US. India threatened to take the matter to the WTO as a violation of TRIPS, which would have been embarrassing for the USA. Eventually RiceTec withdrew some claims, the USPTO refused others and a more limited varietal patent, covering three strains of rice developed by the company and not using the name 'basmati', was granted in 2001.

Bayh–Dole Act (US)

Otherwise known as the University and Small Business Patent Procedures Act of 1980. It deals with ownership of intellectual property arising from federal government-funded research. US universities, small businesses and non-profits have control of their inventions and other intellectual property resulting from such funding, reversing the presumptions about title that had pertained before then. The Act was sponsored by Senators Birch Bayh of Indiana and Bob Dole of Kansas.

Beauregard Claim

A claim to a computer-readable storage device containing a set of instructions that will cause a computer to perform a process. Formerly unpatentable as being merely printed matter – a set of instructions – in *In re Beauregard* 53 F.3d 1583 (Fed. Cir. 1995) the Federal Circuit held that a computer program was patentable subject matter because it was claimed as an article of manufacture held on a disk. The importance of such claims is reduced by the use of non-physical means of distribution, over the Internet. In the UK, *Re Gale* explored similar territory.

Belgian Torpedo

A popular defensive strategy in patent infringement cases. The alleged infringer files a pre-emptive action seeking a pan-European declaration that it does not infringe the patent or any corresponding patent in another European country. Article 21 of the Brussels Convention provides that while the courts of one Member State are seised of the matter the courts of other Member States must stay subsequent infringement proceedings. Of course, it is based on courts in the Member State where the action is brought taking their time over trying patent cases. See also **Italian torpedo**.

Benelux

A union between Belgium, The Netherlands and Luxembourg. A customs union was created by the signature of the London Customs Convention in 1944, which was ratified in 1947 and operated from 1948 until it was supplanted by the Benelux Economic Union in 1958. A Benelux Trade Marks Convention was signed in 1962 and a Benelux Designs Convention in 1966. Offices to handle these systems were set up in The Hague, and in 2005 merged into the Benelux Intellectual Property Office.

Berlin, Sir Isaiah (1909–97)

Philosopher and historian of ideas. He is mentioned here because his essay *The Hedgehog and the Fox: An Essay on Tolstoy's View of History* (London: Weidenfeld & Nicolson, 1953) was referred to in Lord Hoffmann's opinion in *Designers Guild Limited v Russell Williams Textiles Limited* [2002] 1 WLR 2416. See **Fox** and **Hedgehog**.

Berne Convention

In full, the Berne Convention for the Protection of Literary and Artistic Works. An international convention dating originally from 1886, instigated by Victor Hugo. It was revised in Paris in 1896 and in Berlin in 1908, completed in Berne in 1914 by a Protocol (insisted upon by the United Kingdom in the interests of its Dominions, of which only Canada took advantage of it), revised in Rome in 1928, in Brussels in 1948, in Stockholm in 1967 and in Paris in 1971, and amended in 1979. The UK signed in 1887. The US did not join until 1988 (the legislation coming into force in 1989), because of concerns about registration and the mandatory copyright notice. It had 164 members in May 2010 (unchanged, in fact, since 2006), although through the **TRIPS** agreement (with its near-universal membership) its basic requirements apply even more widely than that.

The Convention establishes the principle of national treatment as the key one in international copyright relations, subject to the **comparison of terms rule**. It prescribes minimum periods of protection and prohibits any formalities such as registration or deposit.

See also **WIPO Treaties**.

Best Method, Best Mode

The (UK) Patents Act 1949 required an applicant to set out the best method of performing an invention. The Patents Act 1977 imposes no such obligation, which explains (in part, anyway) why licences of patents are commonly accompanied by licences of **know-how**. US patent law requires a disclosure of the best mode contemplated by the inventor of carrying out the invention (and, in a continuation-in-part application, if the best mode has changed it must also be updated). This helps to ensure that an **enabling disclosure** is given. Such a requirement is optional under **TRIPS**. See also **preferred embodiment**.

Bilski

Bilski v Kappos (Supreme Court 2010)(08-964) is the latest statement from the Supreme Court of the United States on patentability of business methods. The claimed invention was for a method of hedging risks in commodities trading. An *en banc* decision of the US Court of Appeals for the Federal Circuit had cast serious doubt on such patents and made the **machine-or-transformation test** the only test to be applied in determining the patentability of such subject-matter: **State Street**'s 'useful, concrete, and tangible result' test could no longer be relied upon. The Supreme Court, in a majority opinion delivered by Justice Kennedy, rejected the idea that the machine-or-transformation test should be the exclusive test for patentability in the field, preferring to apply the basic principles of the Patent Act under which the claimed invention was unpatentable subject matter. Justice Stevens's concurring opinion is a magisterial review of the patent system, concluding that the framers of the Constitution did not have patents like Mr Bilski's in mind.

The Supreme Court opinion is considered by the anti-software patents lobby as a missed opportunity.

Biogen Approach to Appeals

Important principles governing the conduct of appeals in the English courts, containing some universal observations about the roles of the different levels of court. Set out by Lord Hoffmann in *Biogen Inc v Medeva Plc* [1997] RPC 1 (House of Lords) at p. 45:

> The need for appellate caution in reversing the judge's evaluation of the facts is based upon much more solid grounds than professional courtesy. It is because specific findings of fact, even by the most meticulous judge, are inherently an incomplete statement of the impression which was made upon him by the primary evidence. His expressed findings are always surrounded by a penumbra of imprecision as to emphasis, relative weight, minor qualification and nuance (as Renan said, *la vérité est dans une nuance*), of which time and language do not permit exact expression, but which may play an important part in the judge's overall evaluation. It would in my view be wrong to treat *Benmax v Austin Motor Co. Ltd* [1955] A.C. 370 as authorising or requiring an appellate court to undertake a *de novo* evaluation of the facts in all cases in which no question of the credibility of witnesses is involved. Where the application of a legal standard such negligence or obviousness involves no question of principle but is simply a matter of degree, an appellate court should be very cautious in differing from the judge's evaluation.

Biogen Insufficiency

The principle, set out in *Biogen Inc v Medeva Plc* [1997] RPC 1 (House of Lords) that unless claims in the patent specification correspond to the teachings of the patent, the patent will be invalid.

Biotechnology Directive, Directive on the Protection of Biotechnological Inventions

Directive 98/44/EC of the European Parliament and of the Council of 6 July 1998, which deals with the patentability of certain biotechnological inventions and stipulates that certain matters are not patentable and that certain inventions the exploitation of which would be contrary to public policy or morality may not be patented. It defines the extent of protection, makes provision for compulsory cross-licensing and deals with the deposit of biotechnological inventions.

BIRPI

The Bureaux Internationaux Réunis pour la Protection de la Propriété Industrielle or Intellectuelle, the precursor to the World Intellectual Property Organization (which was created in 1967). Both names are mentioned in the treaty establishing **WIPO**. The plural is appropriate because BIRPI was formed (in 1893) by the amalgamation of the bodies set up to administer the Berne and Paris Conventions.

Bis

Latin ordinal number, second: encountered particularly in international conventions, for example Article 5 bis of the Paris Convention.

Bismag

Bismag Ltd v Amblins Chemists Ltd [1940] Ch 667 is a case famous not so much for what it decided but for Mackinnon LJ's comments about the drafting of the Trade Marks Act 1938:

> In the course of three days hearing of this case I have, I suppose, heard section 4 of the Act of 1938 read, or have read it for myself, dozens if not hundreds of times. Despite this iteration I must confess that, reading it through once again, I have very little notion of what the section is intended to convey, and particularly the sentence of two hundred and fifty-three words, as I make them, which constitutes sub-section 1. I doubt if the entire statute book could be successfully searched for a sentence of equal length which is of more **fuliginous obscurity**.

Black Box Filing

A notional container for patent applications for chemical compounds filed in India in the interval between that country acceding to the TRIPS agreement and enacting a new patent law that would finally permit such inventions to be patented. The interval was ten years, and expired on 1 January 2005. At that time the notional box was notionally opened and the applications within were finally examined.

Third parties who marketed the compounds before the end of the black box period may continue to market them, and patentees will have to be satisfied with a royalty (which will probably be small).

Blawg, Blawger

A **blog (weblog)** devoted to legal topics, and the person or persons who write it. Intellectual property lawyers are perhaps the most enthusiastic blawgers. Influential intellectual property blawgs include **IPKat**, **Likelihood of Confusion**, Patently-O, Seattle Trademark Lawyer, At last – the 1709 Copyright Blog (NB: not 1710), IP Finance, PatLit, Spicy IP, IP Tango, Afro IP, Class 46, Class 99, IP Watch, IP Wars, The Trademark Blog, and the **TTAB Blog**. Please note: other IP blawgs may be available. Modesty prevents the inclusion of the IPso Jure blawg in the foregoing list. A number of IP blawgs are collected on a Netvibes page: http://www. netvibes.com/ipso_jure#IP_blogs.

Blog

See **weblog**.

Blurring

Besides tarnishment, the other type of damage that can cause a famous mark to become diluted (**dilution**): damage to the distinctiveness of a trade mark caused by the unauthorised use of identical or similar signs on dissimilar goods or for dissimilar services. Very difficult to prove.

Board of Appeal

An internal appellate body that deals with appeals from decisions of examiners in many intellectual property offices, including the **EPO** and **OHIM**. In the UK, an appeal from an examiner's decision goes to a hearing officer and thence to an Appointed Person, an experienced legal practitioner discharging a judicial function.

Board of Patent Appeals and Interferences (BPAI) (US)

An administrative law board within the **USPTO**.

Bogsch Theory

The theory, named after former WIPO Director-General Dr Arpad Bogsch, which held that a satellite broadcast is a restricted act in all countries within its **footprint** and therefore requires licences from all right holders in that geographical area. Effectively consigned to history in Europe by the European Community's legislation in the field.

Bolar Exception

Roche Products Inc. v Bolar Pharmaceutical Co., 733 F.2d 858 (Fed. Cir. 04/23/1984) is a court case in the United States related to the manufacturing of generic pharmaceuticals, and to the conduct of clinical trials before the drug patent has expired using the patented drug itself. The **CAFC** decided in that case that such trials infringed, so Congress passed the **Hatch–Waxman Act** to change it. See **research exemption**.

In patent law, the research exemption or **safe harbor exemption** is an exemption to the rights conferred by patents, which is especially relevant to drugs. According to this exemption, despite the patent rights, performing research and tests for preparing regulatory approval, for instance by the Food and Drug Administration (FDA) in the United States, does not constitute infringement for a limited term before the end of patent term. This exemption allows generic manufacturers to prepare generic drugs in advance of the patent expiration.

In the United States, this exemption is also technically called § 271(e)(1) exemption or Hatch–Waxman exemption. The US Supreme Court recently considered the scope of the Hatch–Waxman exemption in

Merck v Integra. The Supreme Court held that the statute exempts from infringement all uses of compounds that are reasonably related to sub-mission of information to the government under any law regulating the manufacture, use or distribution of drugs.

In Canada, the equivalent exemption is also known as the Bolar provi-sion or Roche–Bolar provision.

In the European Union, equivalent exemptions are allowed under the terms of EC Directives 2001/82/EC (as amended by Directive 2004/28/EC) and 2001/83/EC (as amended by Directives 2002/98/EC, 2003/63/EC, 2004/24/EC and 2004/27/EC). In order to market a medicinal product a manufacturer must first obtain regulatory approval by conducting clinical tests and trials to prove that the product is safe and effective. Producers of generic medicines are able to use the original manufacturer's approval if they can demonstrate that the generic version is bioequivalent to the approved medicine. However, the generic producer runs the risk of patent infringement if they conduct clinical trials on a patented product before the patent has expired. The Bolar exemption means that these neces-sary studies, tests and trials will not amount to patent infringement. This removes significant differences in national laws (there was a broad experi-mental use exception in Germany, a narrow one in the UK).

The Bolar exemption was a small part of a comprehensive reform of the current European Union pharmaceutical legislation proposed by the European Commission in July 2001. This consists of three proposals: a regulation on marketing authorisations and the functioning of European Medicines Evaluation Agency (EMEA); a Directive on medicinal prod-ucts for human use; and a Directive on veterinary medicinal products.

Within the two Directives on medicinal products are proposals to allow the Bolar exemption. These can be found in Article 10, paragraph 5 of the Directive on medicinal products for human use and Article 13, paragraph 6 of the Directive on veterinary medicinal products. These paragraphs say:

> Conducting the necessary studies and trials with a view to the application of paragraphs 1, 2, 3 and 4 (paragraphs 1–5 on the Veterinary Medicinal Products Directive) and the consequential practical requirements shall not be regarded as contrary to patent rights or to supplementary protection certificates for medicinal products.

Agreement on the Regulation and the Directives was reached between the European Council, Commission and Parliament on 18 December 2003, and the Council adopted them in March 2004.

Bonn Guidelines

Bonn guidelines on access to genetic resources and the fair and equitable sharing of the benefits arising from their utilization. Made under the **Convention on Biological Diversity**.

Bono, Sonny (1935–98)

An American record producer, singer, songwriter, actor and politician. As a member of the US House of Representatives (for the 44th District of California) he was one of 12 sponsors of a bill to extend the term of copyright protection. Although that bill was not voted on in the Senate, a similar Senate bill did become law (the Copyright Term Extension Act) and was named after Rep Bono, who died in a skiing accident while the legislation was being considered. It is also known as the **Mickey Mouse Protection Act**.

Bowie Bonds

Asset-backed securities representing current and future revenues from 25 albums, 287 songs, recorded by David Bowie before 1990. The bonds were bought by Prudential Insurance, Inc., for $55 million and yielded an interest rate of 7.9 per cent. Weakness in sales of recorded music caused them to be downgraded to near-junk bond status in March 2004, though the growth of legal online music retailing (especially iTunes) has led to renewed interest in the area since then. See also **Pullman Bonds**.

Boyle, James

William Neale Reynolds Professor of Law, Duke University. Author of *Shamans, Software and Spleens* (Cambridge, MA: Harvard University Press, 1997) and *The Public Domain* (New Haven, MD, USA and London, UK: Yale University Press, 2008).

BPAI

Board of Patent Appeals and Interferences (US).

Brand, Branding

'[A] collection of intangible values as perceived by a consumer which are attributed to a name, symbol or design used to identify a product or group of products or services', according to the claimants' expert (Thayne Forbes of Intangible Business Limited) in the English case, *L'Oréal SA v Bellure NV* [2006] EWHC 2355 (Ch), at para 79. The judge, Lewison J, went on in the following paragraph of his judgment to say:

> A brand is designed to convey differentiation to a customer; and this requires more than merely a difference in the logo. A number of elements go in to the construction of a brand in order to achieve differentiation. These can be summarised (in the jargon) as the seven P's: Product, Place, Physical Evidence, People, Price, Promotion and Process.

Often, not quite correctly, used as a synonym for trade mark.

Breach of Confidence

A cause of action of considerable importance to intellectual property owners, largely because of the need to preserve secrecy in the pre-patenting phase of working with inventions. It can also be a very useful addition to the armoury of intellectual property rights, for example to protect the contents of copyright documents. Based in large measure on equitable principles, and dating back many decades, the modern action for breach of confidence is invariably based on the **Coco criteria**.

A breach of confidence may give rise to an action for damages and an injunction. Remedies will not be granted when it would be contrary to public policy to do so, or where the obligation is an unreasonable **restraint of trade**.

In the absence of a law on privacy in the UK, the law on breach of confidence has in recent years been invoked to try to prevent intrusions by the media into the lives of people whose exploits might assist with selling newspapers.

Breeders' Exemption

An exemption to plant breeders' rights or plant variety rights that allows breeders to use protected varieties as sources of initial variation to create new varieties of plants or for other experimental purposes.

Breeders' Rights

See **plant breeders' rights**.

Brevet

1. (English) An official or authoritative message in writing (including, for example, a Papal Indulgence, according to the *Oxford English Dictionary*); an official document granting privileges, from a sovereign or government, especially a document conferring a nominal rank (but no extra pay) on an army officer.
2. (French) *Brevet d'invention*, a patent. *Brevet* may also bear a more general meaning similar to that in English – so, a diploma, certificate, royal warrant, ticket, guarantee, or licence. Cf. *Octrooi*.

Bristol-Myers Squibb ('BMS') Conditions

A set of conditions elaborated by the Court of Justice of the European Communities in Case C-427/93, *Bristol-Myers Squibb v Paranova A/S*, Case C-429/93 *C. H. Boehringer Sohn, Boehringer Ingelheim KG and Boehringer Ingelheim A/S v Paranova A/S* and Case C-436/93, *Bayer Aktiengesellschaft and Bayer Danmark A/S v Paranova A/S*, governing when it will be permissible for a trade mark owner to prevent parallel importation of their products:

> Article 7(2) of Directive 89/104 must be interpreted as meaning that the trade mark owner may legitimately oppose the further marketing of a pharmaceutical product where the importer has repackaged the product and reaffixed the trade mark unless:
> *   it is established that reliance on trade mark rights by the owner in order to oppose the marketing of repackaged products under that trade mark would contribute to the artificial partitioning of the markets between Member States; such is the case, in particular, where the owner has put an identical pharmaceutical product on the market in several Member States in various forms of packaging, and the repackaging carried out by the importer is necessary in order to market the product in the Member State of importation, and is carried out in such conditions that the original condition of the product cannot be affected by it; that condition does not, however, imply that it must be established that the trade mark owner deliberately sought to partition the markets between Member States;
> *   it is shown that the repackaging cannot affect the original condition of the product inside the packaging; such is the case, in particular, where the importer has merely carried out operations involving no risk of the product

being affected, such as, for example, the removal of blister packs, flasks, phials, ampoules or inhalers from their original external packaging and their replacement in new external packaging, the fixing of self-stick labels on the inner packaging of the product, the addition to the packaging of new user instructions or information, or the insertion of an extra article; it is for the national court to verify that the original condition of the product inside the packaging is not indirectly affected, for example, by the fact that the external or inner packaging of the repackaged product or new user instructions or information omits certain important information or gives inaccurate information, or the fact that an extra article inserted in the packaging by the importer and designed for the ingestion and dosage of the product does not comply with the method of use and the doses envisaged by the manufacturer;

- the new packaging clearly states who repackaged the product and the name of the manufacturer in print such that a person with normal eyesight, exercising a normal degree of attentiveness, would be in a position to understand; similarly, the origin of an extra article from a source other than the trade mark owner must be indicated in such a way as to dispel any impression that the trade mark owner is responsible for it; however, it is not necessary to indicate that the repackaging was carried out without the authorization of the trade mark owner;
- the presentation of the repackaged product is not such as to be liable to damage the reputation of the trade mark and of its owner; thus, the packaging must not be defective, of poor quality, or untidy; and
- the importer gives notice to the trade mark owner before the repackaged product is put on sale, and, on demand, supplies him with a specimen of the repackaged product.

Also known as the Paranova conditions.

Broadcast

For the purposes of the **Copyright, Designs and Patents Act 1988**, a broadcast is an electronic transmission of visual images sounds or other information, which is transmitted for simultaneous reception by members of the public and is capable of being lawfully received by them, or is transmitted at a time determined solely by the person making the transmission for presentation to members of the public. Internet transmissions are not included, unless they take place simultaneously on the Internet and by other means, or are a concurrent transmission of a live event, or are a transmission of recorded images or sounds forming part of a programme service offered by a person responsible for making the transmission, being a service in which programmes are transmitted at scheduled times determined by that person. A broadcast may be encrypted, though it will only fall within this definition if decoding equipment has been made available to the public by or with the authority of the person making or providing the content of the transmission.

Brought to Mind

Not an expression actually used in trade marks legislation, but an important concept in determining whether an infringement has taken place. It is used particularly in dilution cases. In *Daimler AG v Sany* [2009] EWHC 2581 (Ch) the deputy judge held that the defendant's three-pointed symbol would not 'bring to mind' the claimant's well-known three-pointed star. The concept was also important in Case C-252/07, *Intel Corporation v CPM United Kingdom Ltd*, where the Court of Justice explained that the stronger the claimant's mark the more it would be brought to mind by the defendant's sign – which some people considered to be the exact opposite of what would actually happen.

Brussels Convention Relating to the Distribution of Programme-Carrying Signals Transmitted by Satellite

The Convention was concluded in 1974 and obliges contracting states (of which there are 33) to take adequate measures to prevent the unauthorized distribution on or from their territory of any programme-carrying signal transmitted by satellite.

Brussels Regulation 44/2001

The Brussels Convention on Civil Jurisdiction and Judgments (1968) contains detailed rules to determine which country's courts should have jurisdiction in civil cases, and also deals with the enforcement of judgments across national boundaries. As between EU Member States, it has largely been supplanted now by the Brussels Regulation (Council Regulation (EC) No 44/2001 of 22 December 2000 on jurisdiction and the recognition and enforcement of judgments in civil and commercial matters) which came into operation on 1 March 2002.

The general rule is that a legal or natural person domiciled in a Member State must be sued in that Member State. However, in matters relating to torts, an action may be brought in the courts of Member State where the harmful event occurred or might occur. Article 27 provides, in the interests of comity, that the court first seised of a matter has priority over other courts in which the matter might be litigated, an approach which works satisfactorily when the same cause of action arises in a number of different jurisdictions but which does not apply so neatly to intellectual property disputes, where there are similar parallel disputes rather than identical ones. This is what has led to the creation of the **Italian torpedo** and its Belgian relative: if they have been disarmed in recent years, it is because legal proceedings in those two jurisdictions have become speedier than used to be the case. The only fully effective anti-torpedo device is a pan-European patent litigation system, such as was proposed in the **European Patent Litigation Agreement** and later in the **Unified Patent Litigation System**.

Budapest Treaty

An international patent treaty that provides for the deposit of micro-organisms with an International Depositary Authority (of which there are 38), which overcomes problems with patent publication. When a patent application relating to the micro-organism is published, third parties may obtain samples of the micro-organism which can be used for experimental purposes. 72 contracting parties.

Budweiser

A native of Budweis, or České Budějovice, a city in Bohemia; by extension, a product of that town, and famously a beer brewed there since the thirteenth century. Since 1911 the brewery has been engaged in trade mark litigation in many jurisdictions with Anheuser-Busch, the US brewer which has enjoyed immense commercial success with its Budweiser brand beer, leading **Jacob LJ** to allude to a Hundred Years War (*Budejovicky Budvar Narodni Podnik v Anheuser-Busch Inc* [2009] EWCA Civ 1022 (20 October 2009)). The Czechs are now turning to protected geographical status regimes for additional protection.

Bundespatentgericht

The German Federal Patent Court. It hears appeals from decisions of the Patent Office (Bundespatentamt). *Patentanwälte* (German patent attorneys) are entitled to appear before it. An appeal lies from the court to the Bundesgerichthof, the Federal supreme court, but this happens very rarely.

Business Method

Subject matter that is not patentable as such under European (including UK) patent law, but which is more often patented in the United States since the **State Street** decision. See **One-click (or 1-click)**, and *Bilski*.

Business Name

The name under which a business is carried on, which is not necessarily the name of the company running the business, and is even less likely to be the names of all the members of a partnership. In the UK, the use of business names is regulated by the Business Names Act 1985, perhaps the most widely broken law on the statute book. Companies, partnerships and sole traders must not hide behind spurious business names: the Act requires disclosure of their identity, but is frequently ignored or flouted and rarely enforced.

The former Register of Business Names was abolished, by the Companies (No 2) Act 1981, in a frenzy of deregulatory reform in the early days of the first Thatcher government, for which I voted.

See also **DBA**.

C

Cable Programme

The (UK) *Copyright, Designs and Patents Act 1988* originally treated broadcasts (which involved the use of wireless telegraphy) and cable programmes as different things. In 2003, with the changes brought about by the EC Directive on copyright in the Information Society (and therefore, indirectly, by the WIPO Treaties) the two techniques for getting content onto the screens and loudspeakers of users were assimilated under the title 'broadcasts'.

Cable Programme Service

The service in which a cable programme was included, until the 2003 amendments to the UK copyright legislation described in the previous entry.

CAFC

Court of Appeals for the Federal Circuit, the US Court that hears appeals on patent cases.

Cancellation

A term used in the European Community trade mark system, covering both invalidation of a registered trade mark and revocation: there is a Cancellation Division of **OHIM**. Also used in the US patent system: a patent that is found to have been wrongly granted in re-examination proceedings is cancelled.

Carbon Copy Divisional

A divisional patent application which contains material identical to that in the parent from which it is divided.

Caricature

A 'grotesque or ludicrous representation or exaggeration of parts, as in a portrait, etc. . . . An exaggerated or debased likeness, or copy, naturally or unintentionally ludicrous'. The associated verb carries the related meaning, although the *Shorter OED* adds the figurative definition 'to burlesque'. Recommended by the Gowers Review as a matter for an exception to copyright, along with *parody* and *pastiche*.

CARICOM

The Caribbean Community, an organisation of 15 countries and territories in the Caribbean, dedicated to promoting integration and cooperation, ensuring that the benefits are fairly shared, and coordinating foreign policy. The Caribbean Single Market and Economy (CSME) is an integrated development set out in the Grand Anse Declaration of the 10th Meeting of the Conference of Heads of Government of the Caribbean Community which took place in July 1989 in Grand Anse, Grenada. Phase 2 of CSME (2010–2015) envisages, among many other things, a regional intellectual property regime.

Catnic

1. *Catnic v Hill & Smith* [1982] RPC 183 was the leading UK case on interpreting patent claims for some years, despite being one of the last cases decided under the Patents Act 1949. Catnic are manufacturers of building supplies, including in this case a steel lintel. They owned a patent for it, in which one face of the device was said, in typical patent language, to be 'vertically disposed'. The defendant made a lintel, on professional advice, in which the equivalent face was angled at 6 degrees. This allegedly made it easier to apply plaster to the lintel in situ.
2. The same case also gave birth to a defence – known, unoriginally, as the Catnic defence – to a copyright infringement claim. It states that copyright in patent documentation cannot be enforced against someone who copies it. In effect, the applicant for the patent has waived copyright as part of the price of obtaining the patent.

Caused to Wonder

A useful form of words in trade mark infringement and relative grounds cases, where confusion is an issue. As long ago as 1946, in the English case *Re Jellinek's Application* [1946] RPC 59, Romer J used it:

> It is sufficient if the result of the user of the mark will be that a number of persons will be caused to wonder whether it might not be the case that the two products come from the same source.

Cautionary Notice

In a surprisingly large number of countries, protection of a trade mark – and often other forms of intellectual property, too – is still something that can only be achieved by publishing a cautionary notice advising the world that ownership of the trade mark in question is claimed by the person giving the notice. The legal effect of such notices is generally untried and uncertain.

In some countries, although there is no trade mark registration as such, it is possible to register as the owner of an asset (for example at the Office of the Registration of Deeds in Myanmar) and to supplement this with a cautionary notice in a local newspaper. In the Republic of Maldives, where at the time of writing (May 2010) there is no trade mark law, protection is a matter of publishing a cautionary notice and protecting the mark by a passing action (the country having a legal system in which Islamic law and common law coexist).

A cautionary notice might also play a part in the registration process, where there is no official trade marks journal, as in (for example) Ethiopia.

Caveat

1. A warning or notification that some action has taken place on an application. A caveat is entered in the relevant office, which then informs the person registering it when one of the events specified in the caveat takes place.
2. Formerly, in US patent law, a legal document, an official notice of intention to file a patent application at a later date, filed with the United States Patent Office: discontinued in 1909. Similar to a patent application, with a description of an invention and drawings, but no claims.

CBD

See **Convention on Biological Diversity**.

CCC

See **Copyright Clearance Center**.

Cease and Desist Letter

Originally an American expression but one now often encountered elsewhere in the common law world, meaning a letter sent by the owner of intellectual property rights to someone who is believed to be infringing those rights, or indeed by any prospective plaintiff or claimant to a prospective defendant – it is not limited to the IP world. In English practice, such letters are conventionally called 'letters before action' and have the status of a formal step in the legal process under various protocols governing the conduct of litigation (see **Civil Procedure Act 1997**).

If the recipient of a cease and desist (or simply 'C&D') letter in the US is placed in reasonable apprehension of litigation, they may apply for declaratory judgment in their own jurisdiction.

A demand letter (LOD, or letter of demand) is a similar communication used in the US to intimate a claim for money.

Central Attack

The principle, enshrined in the Madrid Agreement, that cancellation of the basic national registration on the basis of which the proprietor had obtained international trade marks under the Agreement would also result in the loss of all those international trade marks. This was a consequence that UK trade mark owners in particular were not prepared to countenance, so central attack was one of the main considerations that prevented the UK from adhering to the Agreement. Instead it worked to secure a system for international registrations without the objectionable elements of the Madrid Agreement, which eventually emerged as the Madrid Protocol. Central attack is still an important concept, but the loss of the basic national trade mark (or application) results in the applicant being able to elect to have the international applications transformed into ordinary national applications (subject to payment of some hefty filing fees).

Certificate of Correction (US)

A certificate, affixed to the front of a US patent, showing an error made by the applicant in the patent and how it has been corrected.

Certification Trade Mark

A special type of trade mark, used not to represent the reputation of the user but to demonstrate that the user's goods or services have certain qualities. The best-known example is probably the Woolmark of the International Wool Secretariat, which may be used (according to the regulations which are filed at the Trade Marks Registry) on wool or cloth or garments made entirely from it. Use except in accordance with the regulations is an infringement.

UK trade mark law has allowed registration of certification trade marks for many years, though they remain a specialised area of trade mark law. Not all trade mark systems have similar provisions: some (including the European Community system) offer collective trade marks, which are in some ways similar, and which are also available in the UK.

Chakrabarty

See *Diamond v Chakrabarty*.

Chancery Division

One of the three divisions of the High Court of Justice of England and Wales, and the one to which intellectual property cases are assigned. They are then usually assigned to the Patents Court, part of the Chancery Division. The head of the division is the Chancellor of the High Court (until 2005, known as the Vice-Chancellor). In addition to its IP jurisdiction, the Chancery Division deals with property, trusts, equity, company law and taxation.

Chapter I and Chapter II

1. Parts of the Patent Co-operation Treaty procedure. Chapter I is compulsory, Chapter II is optional. The compulsory part involves

an international application, international search, international pre-liminary report on patentability, international publication and entry into the national or regional phase. The optional part comprises international preliminary examination, which must be 'elected' (sic) before 22 months after application of priority or within three months of the issue of the international preliminary report on patentability (whichever is the later).

2. Parts of the UK Competition Act 1998. Chapter I contains the prohibition on restrictive agreements and so on, and Chapter II the prohibition of the abuse of a dominant position. Both may be relevant to intellectual property owners.

Characterising Claim

A patent claim in the form '[prior art] characterised in that [whatever is considered to be inventive]'. Simple, and can be useful.

Chartered Patent Attorney

In the UK, a Fellow of the Chartered Institute of Patent Attorneys, which received its Royal Charter in 1891 (having been founded in 1882). To become a Fellow, it is necessary to have passed the UK Advanced examinations and to have accrued sufficient experience. Two nominations from existing Fellows are also needed.

Check Digit

Did you ever wonder how the application numbers of patents are made up? The check digit is the number that appears after the decimal point in some application numbers – not actually part of the application number (which is why you do not have to include it when doing an esp@ce search). It is there to confirm that the office has recorded the number correctly: it is generated by performing a calculation using the digits in the patent number, and if this operation gives a different number it is incorrect.

Chilling Effects

A collaborative archive, named after the perceived effect of an overenthusiastic application of the law of copyright. Created by several US law school clinics and the **Electronic Frontier Foundation** to protect lawful online activity from threats of legal action. It operates a website, Chilling Effects Clearinghouse (http://chillingeffects.org/), which publicises **cease and desist letters** issued by rights owners and enables recipients of such notices to receive advice about their legal rights and responsibilities.

Chivalry, High Court of

The English Court, the sole judge of which is the Earl Marshall (the Duke of Norfolk), which hears disputes about arms (as in **heraldry**). Having last sat in 1732, it was convened in 1954 to hear the **Manchester Palace of Varieties** case and has not sat again.

Chose in Action

In the common law world, an intangible personal property right which has no existence apart from its recognition at law. In particular, being intangible, it is not something that can be possessed. The owner can only enforce it by legal action. Choses in action include debts, shares, rights under contracts and shares in trust funds.

Intellectual property rights are deemed to be choses in action, except for a UK patent which is specifically said not to be 'thing in action' (Patents Act 1977, section 30). A UK patent does, however, possess the usual characteristics of a chose in action.

It used to be the case that no chose in action could be assigned except by or through the Crown, or with the debtor's consent. Now they can be assigned, the manner of assignment often being set out specifically in statute – which is the case with intellectual property. See **assignment**.

CII

Computer-implemented invention: essentially a software invention, though it also refers to business methods patents implemented by means of computers (for example online).

Cinematographic Work

An expression used in Articles 4, 14 and 14 bis of the Berne Convention but not defined there. Generally synonymous with a film.

CIP

Continuation in Part (of a patent application); or the Competitiveness and Innovation Framework Programme (of the European Union).

Circumvention

A word used in various provisions in UK copyright law, which seeks to control activities and contrivances designed to get round the various technical means employed by copyright owners and licensees to prevent or control copying and other acts restricted by copyright (and sometimes acts that are not restricted by copyright).

Citation

Prior art discovered by an intellectual property office in a search and mentioned in a search report or during the prosecution of the application is said to be cited against the application.

Civil Procedure Act 1997

The UK legislation that laid the foundation for the root-and-branch reforms of civil litigation contained in the Civil Procedure Rules of 1998. Part of the reform process involved the formulation of protocols dealing with different types of litigation, but no protocol for intellectual property cases was ever issued (a Code of Practice for pre-action conduct in intellectual property was however drawn up by the interested professions). The intractable problem in intellectual property cases was the conflict between the standard requirement in the issued protocols that a claim should be intimated in detail to the defendant before proceedings be commenced, and statutory provisions on **groundless threats** in several intellectual property statutes.

CJEC

The Court of Justice of the European Communities, commonly and inaccurately known as the European Court of Justice or **ECJ**. Since December 2009, it has been the Court of Justice of the European Union (CJEU) though the common name remains in use.

CJEU

Court of Justice of the European Union.

Claeryn

A brand of Dutch *jonge genever*, a spirituous drink. It was involved in an important trade mark case, *Claeryn/Klarein*, Case A 74/1, judgment of 1 March 1975, Jurisprudence of the Benelux Court of Justice 1975, p. 472. The defendant's product was a domestic cleaning solution and the case was an early example of a dilution claim: the drink trade mark won.

Claim

The claims are that part of a patent specification that define the scope of the monopoly protected by the patent. Building on the description of the invention (because it is a requirement that the claims be supported by the description, and no additional matter be introduced in them), they deconstruct the invention in a specific legal style, using language that often reflects the wording of the description. They are also likely to include some novel words or unusual formations, such as 'slideably', elements of a device are often 'disposed' in relation to each other, and there is never several or many things, always a plurality. The claims are often narrowed during the prosecution of the patent application (and, in certain circumstances, may be extended).

Typically, there will be one or more sets of hierarchical claims. Each set will have a main independent claim stating the invention in the broadest terms that the description can support, followed by dependent claims that are progressively narrower by virtue of introducing more specific features to the description. Grammatically, each claim takes the form of a noun phrase.

An independent claim may be to a product or to a process, and it is not uncommon in certain fields (pharmaceuticals, for example) to find product and process claims in a single patent application. Different countries have different approaches to claim drafting: in the UK, the United States and Japan, the claims tend to define the periphery of the monopoly (known as the peripheral claiming system), while in continental Europe the claims tend to focus on the core of the invention (the central claiming system). Neither system is used to the exclusion of the other, however.

Claims can be amended after grant, and often are during the course of litigation when the validity of a patent is in issue, but may not be broadened beyond the initial disclosure. In the US, the claims may not be broadened more than two years after the patent is issued.

Claim Broadening

See **added matter**.

Claim Construction

See **construction**.

Class Headings

The broad statements of goods or services set out for the 45 classes of the **Nice Agreement**. Whether an application that simply recites the class heading covers all goods in the class is a controversial matter.

Classical Trinity

The three elements for a **passing off** action in UK law, identified by Lord Oliver in *Reckitt & Colman Products Ltd v Borden Inc* [1990] 1 WLR 491, [1990] 1 All ER 873, [1990] UKHL 12, [1990] RPC 341:

> The law of passing off can be summarised in one short general proposition – no man may pass off his goods as those of another. More specifically, it may be expressed in terms of the elements which the plaintiff in such an action has to prove in order to succeed. These are three in number. First, he must establish a goodwill or reputation attached to the goods or services which he supplies in the mind of the purchasing public by association with the identifying 'get-up' (whether it consists simply of a brand name or a trade description, or the

individual features of labelling or packaging) under which his particular goods or services are offered to the public, such that the get-up is recognised by the public as distinctive specifically of the plaintiff's goods or services. Secondly, he must demonstrate a misrepresentation by the defendant to the public (whether or not intentional) leading or likely to lead the public to believe that goods or services offered by him are the goods or services of the plaintiff. Whether the public is aware of the plaintiff's identity as the manufacturer or supplier of the goods or services is immaterial, as long as they are identified with a particular source which is in fact the plaintiff. For example, if the public is accustomed to rely upon a particular brand name in purchasing goods of a particular description, it matters not at all that there is little or no public awareness of the identity of the proprietor of the brand name. Thirdly, he must demonstrate that he suffers or, in a **quia timet** action, that he is likely to suffer damage by reason of the erroneous belief engendered by the defendant's misrepresentation that the source of the defendant's goods or services is the same as the source of those offered by the plaintiff.

Although it is now becoming an old case, and there have been dramatic changes in trade mark law in the UK since the case was decided, this remains the definitive statement of the law of passing off – usually preferred to Lord Diplock's in **Advocaat**. It retains misrepresentation as the central concept, despite suggestions that the tort might be widened into a sort of unfair competition law.

Classification

1. For trade mark purposes, all goods and services in the world are divided into a plurality of classes. In the classification set out in the **Nice Agreement** there are 45 classes. Some countries operate national classification systems and many operate detailed classification systems within the broad framework of the Nice Classification. In the Community trade mark system, OHIM uses a variation referred to as EuroNice. Canada manages perfectly well with no classification system (leading me once to tell a client that there was no class system in Canada, an interesting sociological statement), which tends to reinforce the impression that classification is little more than a device for extracting additional fees from applicants.

2. For patent purposes, subject-matter is organised into fixed categories of technology so that it can be found more easily in a subject matter search. On receipt of an application, the receiving office will classify the invention so that it can be assigned to the correct examining group and can be added to the stock of prior art for examinations of future applications. WIPO's **International Patent Classification** (IPC) is the

most important such system, but there are several highly developed national systems in use – for example, in the USA.

Clean Room

The notion of a clean room (which is conceptually similar to a Chinese Wall) is encountered in the development of new products and software. A clean room design is one that is created from information obtained by **reverse engineering** but without direct reference to the product itself. It is designed to protect the developer of the second product from allegations of copying or breach of confidence or trade secrets. It is no help if infringement of a patent is alleged, of course, because a patent is a monopoly right which is infringed without the need for anything analogous to copying. The room is said to be clean because it is uncontaminated by any connection with the product that is being reproduced, or not being reproduced, as the case may be.

For a recent example from the British courts of the use of the clean room technique to prevent cross-pollination of ideas about a product, see *Virgin Atlantic v Premium Aircraft* [2009] EWCA Civ 1513.

A clean-room rewrite of a computer program featured in *Computer Associates v Altai* [1992] 20 USPQ 2d 1641, 982 F.2d693 (1992), when the defendants realised that their program infringed the plaintiffs' copyright (it had been written by an employee who had joined them from the plaintiffs and who had brought with him rather more than his common skill and knowledge) and withdrew it from the market. A team of programmers created a new program to do the same job in clean room conditions so the risk of copyright infringement was as far as possible excluded. It worked: at first instance and on appeal, the first version was held to infringe but the second did not.

Clearance Search

A search for earlier rights designed to determine whether a new trade mark is available for use without the risk of an infringement action being brought. See also **freedom to operate**.

Clinical Trials

Pharmaceutical products must undergo trials before being unleashed onto the public. This can raise problems in the case of generic products, because trials of these might be considered to infringe the patents protecting the proprietary products. Such trials often benefit from an exception, even though they might be considered a form of **springboarding**. See **Bolar exception, Hatch–Waxman Act**.

Co-branding

The practice of placing the trade marks of the repackager alongside those of the manufacturer on the packages of parallel-imported pharmaceuticals which have been repackaged.

Coco Criteria

The three essential elements of a claim for breach of confidence, laid down in *Coco v A N Clark (Engineers) Ltd.* [1969] RPC 41 by the judge, Megarry J – the future Vice-Chancellor:

- the information must have the necessary quality of confidence about it;
- it must have been imparted in circumstances importing an obligation of confidence (a requirement that has been somewhat modified as a result of the *Spycatcher* litigation); and
- there must be an unauthorised use of that information to the detriment of the party who communicated it.

It might now also be said that it must be reasonable to impose the obligation, and the information must be clearly identifiable, but the 'trinity' remain the starting point for every important breach of confidence case even now – an impressive record for a first-instance judgment on an interlocutory application which was settled by the defendant giving an undertaking.

Cognating, Cognate Applications

The process of combining two or more patent applications into one, which may be necessary at foreign filing time (when a plurality of priority applications, later ones covering improvements to earlier ones, may be combined into a single application) or in any circumstances when an early application – perhaps a provisional – is filed but the applicant later realises that there are further elements to the invention which ought to be included too. Applications for those further elements can be filed, and the multiple applications cognated, in some jurisdictions, including New Zealand, Australia and the USA.

Collage

A type of artistic work for the purposes of the Copyright, Designs and Patents Act 1988, protected irrespective of artistic quality.

Collecting Society

An organisation that exists to collect royalties on behalf of its members for the use of their copyright works, and to distribute the proceeds among those members. The expression has no definition in the Copyright, Designs and Patents Act in the UK (though there is legislation that deals with certain aspects of collecting societies' activities): for the Act's purposes, they are 'licensing bodies', and so are other organisations that issue licences to use the works of multiple authors.

Collecting societies gain the authority to grant licences and collect royalties either by the agreement of their members or by law. Because of the problems inherent in individual management of copyright, the idea of collective management of copyright is widespread – indeed, virtually universal among developed countries. Their regulation and the scope of their activities does however vary considerably: in Europe the usual model involves the author transferring the administration of all their rights in the relevant category, whereas in North America members retain their rights in parallel with the collecting societies.

Collecting societies grant blanket licences authorising the licensee to use material in the repertoire for the duration of the licence. Laws might contain provisions requiring that licensees who use material that turns out not to be in the collecting society's repertoire will have an indemnity. Societies enter into reciprocal arrangements with societies in other jurisdictions, so I expect to see payments for photocopying of this book from a range of different countries in due course. Collecting societies also grant individual licences in appropriate cases.

Also referred to as copyright collectives, collecting agencies.

Collective Licensing

The main activity engaged in by collecting societies.

Collective Trade Mark

A trade mark that belongs not to the trader who uses it but to an association whose members use it to declare their membership of the association and therefore their adherence to certain standards. Registrable in the UK since 1994 and in the European Community trade marks system. Collective trade marks do at least a similar job to **certification trade marks**, which have been protected in UK trade mark law for much longer (though they are not registrable under EC trade mark law). In the *Parma Ham* case [1991] RPC 251 the Consorzio del Prosciutto di Parma sued for passing off to protect their unregistered collective mark, something that could now amount to infringement of a registered mark.

Collective Work

A work in which a plurality of contributions, each a separate and independent work in itself, are assembled into a single whole. Includes periodicals, anthologies, encyclopedias and many legal text books. Although there might be a number of contributors, the result is not a work of joint authorship: rather, each contributor is the author of their own contribution and the compiler might in some countries also own copyright (and possibly database right or its equivalent) in the compilation.

Collins, Phil

English rock musician, drummer and vocalist with the well-known musical combination, Genesis and subsequently a solo artist. In Joined cases C-92/92 and C-326/92, *Phil Collins v Imtrat Handelsgesellschaft mbH and Patricia Im- und Export Verwaltungsgesellschaft mbH and Leif Emanuel Kraul v EMI Electrola GmbH*. That case originated in an action brought against a German company which was marketing records of a concert Collins had given in the US. German law gave German performers the right to prohibit the distribution of recordings made without their consent, regardless of the place where the performance had occurred; but, applying the comparison of terms rule, granted the same right to foreign performers only for their performances that had occurred in Germany. The Court of Justice decided that this violated the non-discrimination provision of Article 7 of the EC Treaty (as it then was).

Collocation

An inventor may create something new by bringing together what a patent lawyer would refer to as a plurality of elements that have not previously been brought together in the same way. The requirement in patent law for an invention to involve an inventive step may be satisfied by this collocation. UK patent jurisprudence (the **Windsurfing** case) suggested that the inventor only had to show that the elements had been put together in a way that would not be obvious to the skilled person. But the EPO Guidelines for Substantive Examination (citing decision T 389/86, OJ 3/1988, 87) and recent cases like *Sabaf SpA v MFI Furniture Centres Limited* [2004] UKHL 45 have rejected this approach, applying a new less favourable criterion to identify the inventive step. This 'law of collocation' stipulates that where the invention comprises nothing more than the juxtaposition or association (even if that is non-obvious) of known devices or processes functioning in their normal way and not producing any non-obvious working interrelationship, it is not patentable.

Colour

May be an important element in a trade mark, and might even be the trade mark itself. While a monochrome representation of a trade mark will generally give the widest protection, colour might be a distinctive element. Applying to register a trade mark in colour could overcome objections that it is inherently non-distinctive.

Commerce Clause (US)

Article 1, Section 8, clause 3 of the US Constitution gave Congress power to legislate: 'To regulate Commerce with foreign Nations, and among the several States, and with the Indian Tribes'.

This clause underpins the trade mark laws of the United States, which replaced legislation made under the *intellectual property clause* (clause 8) of the same section but which had been held to be unlawful. The fact that the regulation of interstate commerce is the justification for trade mark laws explains why states still have their own trade mark laws in addition to the Federal ones.

Commercial Success

See **secondary indications of inventiveness**.

Common Field of Activity

In the past, a requirement in the UK and Commonwealth countries for a passing-off action to lie. If the parties were not engaged in a common field of activity, there would be no likelihood of confusion and consequently no passing-off. The principle received its classic formulation in *McCulloch v Lewis A May* (1947) 65 RPC 58, the Uncle Mac case, in 1947. In *Irvine v Talksport* [2002] EWHC 367 (Ch) (on appeal [2002] EWCA Civ 95), Laddie J clearly thought the time had come to dispense with this requirement – passing-off could take place in circumstances (in suit, unauthorised celebrity endorsements) where confusion or deception could be caused notwithstanding that the parties were engaged in very different fields of activity.

Common General Knowledge

Information which, at the priority date of the patent in question, was generally known and accepted by the skilled person in the field to which the alleged invention relates. In essence, it is the knowledge which the addressee of the specification can be expected to have as part of their ordinary technical knowledge, and it plays an important role in considering anticipation and obviousness. It is a peculiarly British concept, not found in the European patent system (nor in the US).

The law about what constitutes common general knowledge is set out in the decisions of the Court of Appeal in *General Tire & Rubber Co v Firestone Tyre & Rubber Co Ltd* [1972] RPC 457 at 482–3 and *Beloit Technologies Inc v Valmet Paper Machinery Inc* [1997] RPC 489 at 494–5. As Laddie J explained in *Raychem Corp's Patents* [1998] RPC 31 at 40:

The common general knowledge is the technical background of the notional man in the art against which the prior art must be considered. This is not limited to material he has memorised and has at the front of his mind. It includes all that material in the field he is working in which he knows exists, which he would refer to as a matter of course if he cannot remember it and which he understands is generally regarded as sufficiently reliable to use as a foundation for further work or to help understand the pleaded prior art. This does not mean that everything on the shelf which is capable of being referred to without difficulty is common general knowledge nor does it mean that every word in a common text book is either. In the case of standard textbooks, it is likely that all or most of the main text will be common general knowledge. In many cases common general knowledge will include or be reflected in readily available trade literature which a man in the art would be expected to have at his elbow and regard as basic reliable information.

In addition, a further concept of secondary common general knowledge is used to describe that extra knowledge that the skilled person would routinely obtain or be provided with before trying to tackle the technical problem which his or her invention claims to solve. The first case expressly to refer to this type of knowledge is *Activis v Novartis* [2009] EWHC 41 (Ch).

Common Law

The system of precedent-based law found in those countries which derive their laws from the common law of England – those countries that were at one time or another part of the British Empire, including the United States. They typically have common law protection for trade marks (see **common law trade mark, passing off**). Common law copyright existed in England before the **Statute of Anne**, but in *Donaldson v Becket* 2 Brown's Parl. Cases 129, 1 Eng. Rep. 837; 4 Burr. 2408, 98 Eng. Rep. 257 (1774) it was decided that the statute had completely supplanted common law protection.

Common Law Trade Mark

A trade mark (not necessarily in the narrow statutory sense of the expression) which is protected without registration under the law of **passing off**. As the name suggests, such trade marks are only available in the common law countries although many civil law jurisdictions have **unfair competition laws** which tend to do a similar job. UK trade mark law states that there is no action for infringement of a common law mark, only an action for passing off: in the US, on the other hand, an infringement action is precisely what is used to protect a common law mark.

This distinction between the common law and civil law systems originally informed the way their trade mark registration systems worked, with the common law world using registration (very broadly speaking) as a record of marks actually used in commerce while the civil law systems made registration the act that created legal rights in the mark.

Commonplace Design Features

Features excluded from protection under UK **unregistered design right** (UDR). Sub-section (4) adds a further limitation, requiring that a design not be commonplace, thus excluding designs which, while they are not copies, are no more than an expression of what is widely known in the design field in question. In the **Pig fenders** case the judge described the 'commonplace' provision as imposing a requirement akin to novelty but in *Amoena v Trulife* [1996] IPD 19006 the court considered novelty unnecessary.

In *Farmers Build Ltd v Carier Bulk Materials Ltd and others* [1999] RPC461 (CA) (see *Slurry Seprator*) the defendant claimed that the individual parts of the machines, and the machines themselves, were commonplace in the design field at the time of their creation. The court considered that the correct approach was to compare the design of the article in which UDR is claimed with the design of other articles in the same field, including the alleged infringing one. The material time for this exercise is when the design is created. A design copied from the design of an earlier article will not be original, and it is not necessary to consider whether it is commonplace or not.

Whether it is commonplace is determined by ascertaining the degree of similarity to the design of similar, independent articles in the same design field. This is to be done objectively, in the light of the evidence (including expert evidence) but is a question of fact and degree for the court. If there are aspects of the plaintiff's design not found in other designs in the field, except the defendant's, the court can conclude that the design was not commonplace. In *Scholes Windows v Magnet Ltd* the horn design had been used on windows for many years and was therefore commonplace. In the case of a decorative design where there is greater design freedom, as was the case there, the *Farmers Build* guidelines will be less help.

The guidelines were applied by the High Court (Rattee J) in *Round Imports v PML Redfearn Ltd.* [1999] CIPA 725. This concerned UDR in a tall-necked bottle designed for the plaintiff for its Red Eye beverage. The design of the Red Eye bottle was original in that it was not a copy of another design: it was however very similar to a Miller bottle which the plaintiffs had provided to the defendant as a model, and although there were minor variations in shape and dimension they were not in the judge's view sufficient to make the bottle significantly different from the Miller bottle or any other tall-necked bottle available at the time. Glass designers have always considered small differences sufficient, but it seems that the law differs from their view and their designs will now be open to copying.

The guidelines were also applied in *Jo-Y-Jo v Matalan* (1999, unreported), where expert evidence showed that the cardigan designs in question were 'classic'. Embellishing the garments with embroidery and edging did not prevent the designs being commonplace. In *Fulton v Barnett* [2001] RPC 16, a claim to unregistered design right in the handle and case of a folding umbrella was upheld: to enable functional designs to enjoy any protection, the judge (Park J) said a narrow interpretation of what is commonplace was needed. Merely because references to two designs of close similarity could be shown was insufficient. Very minor changes of line or angle can have a significant effect on a design (as happened in *Scholes*).

In *Spraymiser Ltd. v Wrightway Marketing Ltd.* [2000] ECDR 349 the judge took the view that the field was extremely small, consisting as it did of only two designs. There were sufficient differences between them that the claimant's design was not commonplace within the field. Had there been a greater number of candidates, more differences may (it is submitted) have been needed.

Commons

In the world of real property, commons are areas of land available for all to use. By extension, in the copyright world 'commons' designate property whose owner is prepared to allow them to be used liberally by others, leading to a general increase in creative activity. See **Creative Commons**. See also **anticommons**.

Communication to the Public

An act restricted to the copyright owner (or others acting with the copyright owner's consent). Article 8 of the WIPO Copyright (see **WIPO Treaties**) treaty required:

> [A]uthors of literary and artistic works shall enjoy the exclusive right of authorizing any communication to the public of their works, by wire or wireless means, including the making available to the public of their works in such a way that members of the public may access these works from a place and at a time individually chosen by them.

Easier said than done, because this tends to conflict with existing rights to control broadcasting and inclusion in cable programme services. In the UK, these concepts have been subsumed into one another.

Controversial, too, because while European countries could readily accommodate a communication right, the US law was based on a different approach and relied on the rights of distribution, public performance, public display, and digital audio transmission. As a compromise – the 'umbrella solution' – the Treaty provides for the right of **making available** to the public. (See Yu, Peter K., 'Digital Copyright Reform and Legal Transplants in Hong Kong' (January 18, 2010). *University of Louisville Law Review*, Vol. 48, 2010. Available at SSRN: http://ssrn.com/abstract=1538638.)

Community Registered Design

A design registered under the Community Designs Regulation, which gives monopoly protection throughout the European Union to designs that are novel and have individual character. The fee for registration is €230, and there is an additional fee for publication of €120 (and if publication is deferred, a fee of €40 is payable).

Applications are examined for formalities (whether it is a design application, whether contrary to public policy and morality), but there is no search for earlier designs. It is up to third parties to challenge the validity of a Community design once it has been registered.

Invalidity proceedings are heard in the Office for Harmonisation in the Internal Market and an appeal lies to OHIM's Boards of Appeal. From there an appeal may lie to the Court of First Instance as it was then called (it is now called the General Court). Deferment preserves secrecy for up to 30 months. It can be cancelled at any time by the applicant asking OHIM to publish.

Applications may be filed electronically, by fax (with confirmation by mail), by mail or courier delivery, in person, via national IP offices or through WIPO. The application must contain views of the design, a maximum of seven different ones. What is seen is what is protected so views from different angles make protection stronger. They may be in black and white or colour, or a combination. At least one view of a complex product must show it assembled. For a set of articles, at least one view must show the set together. Dotted lines may show parts of articles that are not protected or which are not visible in that particular view.

For typefaces, the representation must show a complete set of upper- and lower-case letters and Arabic numerals, and five lines of text in size 16 type.

See also *Community Unregistered Design Right.*

Community Patent

A pipedream that might be coming to reality at last. The Community Patent Convention (CPC) was drafted in the 1970s and signed, in the form of the Luxembourg Convention, in 1975 by all nine members of the European Community. However, it was never ratified by a sufficient number of countries – some having problems with giving an overseas court jurisdiction over matters that were within its own national competence, with Ireland having to put the matter to a referendum.

Since the demise of the CPC, the European Patent Convention – created on the foundations built for the CPC – has filled the void, and does most of the things that a Community patent could do. The CPC was doomed to failure because it was not a creature of the European Community, so issues of supranational jurisdiction could not be resolved in the context of the Treaty, but since 1975 the Community (and now the Union) has found ways to carve out a role for itself in the intellectual property world. A Community patent regulation was proposed in 2000, availing itself of the mechanisms of the EPC and providing that once a European patent had been granted and published in one official language, with the claims translated into the two other official languages, it would be valid without the need for more translations. It might be necessary to translate into the language of an alleged infringer, who would be considered to be an innocent infringer until the patent was available in his language, and so protected from claims for damages.

The regulation also envisaged a single Community patent court, attached to the present Community courts in Luxembourg, to deal with matters of infringement and validity. But the proposal foundered, in 2005, on disputes about the time limits for making translations, in particular the authentic translations that would be needed before an infringer could be liable for damages.

Further consultations led to the issue of a White Paper in 2007, and in October of that year the Portuguese presidency announced a new proposal based on the rejected **European Patent Litigation Agreement**. In December 2009 it was announced that the Swedish presidency had engineered an agreement on a single patent court, and on the principle that the EU should join the EPC so that a granted European patent would have unitary effect throughout the territory of the European Union.

Community patent review, peer-to-patent

Nothing whatsoever to do with the European Community, or the Community patent: a peer review system for patents, founded by Prof. Beth Noveck and developed in the mid-2000s by the USPTO and at the time of writing (May 2010) being tried out in other places. It offers a neat and democratic way to deal with a backlog of unexamined patent applications by recruiting a potentially large number of experts to 'examine' them, based around a website at http://www.peertopatent.org/.

Community Trade Mark (CTM)

A single, unitary trade mark valid throughout the Member States of the European Community (now Union). Usefully, though subject to earlier national registrations, it is proof against enlargement of the Community, extending automatically into new Member States. Administered from the Office for Harmonisation in the Internal Market (no problems of descriptiveness with a name like that) in Alicante, the CTM system is now governed by Council Regulation (EC) No 207/2009 of 26 February 2009 on the Community trade mark (which replaced Regulation 40/94) and subordinate legislation.

Maintenance of a Community trade mark requires it to be used in a substantial part of the Community, but the case-law indicates that this might be only one Member State – in which case, calling it a Community trade mark is a little unrealistic. At the time of writing (May 2010), the question of how extensive the use of a CTM must be is perhaps the most contentious issue in this area.

Community Unregistered Design Right

A short-lived form of automatic protection given to designs that qualify for registration as Community designs. Lasting for a mere three years, the right protects against copying only, and given that a design must be novel and have individual character before it will have protection it is unlikely to protect much. Nevertheless, it is attractive to those whose needs for protection are limited in time (fashion designers, for example), and it also has the merit of covering the period of grace given to designers before they have to file an application for registration. In addition, it is often used as a last straw by those who wish to protect something but have no other rights on which to base a claim, even a spurious one.

Company Names

Company names often function as trade marks, and indeed are frequently registered as such. It has however been very easy in the UK (which, for company formation purposes as for many others is three jurisdictions: England and Wales, Scotland, and Northern Ireland) to incorporate a company with a name very close to another company's, a proposed company's or a trade mark. Now section 69 of the Companies Act 2006 creates a right to object to a company name, and section 70 empowers the Secretary of State to appoint adjudicators to form the Company Names Tribunal.

Comparative Advertising

The practice of referring in advertising material to the goods or services of one's competitors in order to draw comparisons, rarely favourable to the competitor, between those goods and services and those offered by the advertiser. Because this inevitably involves the use of the other business's trade mark – which, after all, is what it is for – issues of infringement may arise. Section 10(6) of the 1994 Act permits comparative advertising – or, rather, it permits the use of a trade mark to identify the goods or services of the proprietor of the trade mark – provided that the use is in accordance with honest practices in industrial and commercial matters and that it neither takes unfair advantage of the repute of that trade mark nor is otherwise detrimental to it.

Comparative advertising is also the subject of specific legislation, in the misleading advertising directive (and the related regulations in the UK). These set out criteria against which comparative advertising must be judged, and in the UK the Office of Fair Trading is empowered to take action to prevent comparative advertising that fails to meet the criteria. However, the regulations have no part to play in considering whether a trade mark infringement has taken place (per Jacob J in *British Airways v Ryanair* [2001] FSR 541).

Comparison of Terms Rule

The principle, often found in international conventions, that as a derogation from the 'national treatment' rule, one country may decide to limit the protection given to rights holders from a second country (or, in some cases, to works or performances connected with that country) to match the protection given by the law of that second country to rights holders from the first country. Thus in the Phil Collins case (see **Collins, Phil**) German law on performers' rights purported to exclude performances given in the United States from protection, because US law failed to protect performances given in Germany (or anywhere else, for that matter: there are no rights in performances in the US). However, the German law did protect performances by German performers wherever they took place, and this was held by the CJEC to discriminate unlawfully against nationals of other Member States (such as Mr Collins).

Competition Law

A body of law designed to promote or maintain the operation of markets by prohibiting anti-competitive practices, and therefore having a sometimes uneasy relationship with intellectual property rights. Known as antitrust law in the United States (and increasingly elsewhere, though in the European Union it is a subdivision of competition law). The Treaty of Rome, the founding treaty of the European Economic Community, prohibited restrictive agreements and the abuse of a dominant position (Articles 85 and 86, now Articles 101 and 102 of the Treaty on the Functioning of the European Union). All EU Member States (and Turkey, as a candidate) now have domestic competition laws based on these same prohibitions, so within the European Union competition law forms a seamless web composed of domestic and EU rules which can be brought to bear as appropriate, depending on whether there is an effect on trade between Member States or only within a single Member State.

The original work on the EU rules owes much to US jurisprudence, and there are similarities between the EU rules and the US legislation (principally the Sherman and Clayton Acts). In the post-war period when European integration was first being pursued the influence of American thinking is not surprising. Now, the EU rules are in turn influencing emerging competition laws beyond the frontiers of the Union – for example, in the Russian Federation.

See **monopoly, technology transfer agreement, Magill**.

Competitiveness and Innovation Framework Programme

A Framework Programme of the European Union, 2007–13, divided into three operational programmes: the Entrepreneurship and Innovation Programme (EIP), the Information and Communication Technologies

Policy Support Programme (ICT-PSP) and the Intelligent Energy-Europe Programme (IEE).

Compilation

A type of literary work, for the purposes of the Copyright, Designs and Patents Act 1988, and therefore protectable if it is original. Any originality that there might be in a compilation must lie in the selection and arrangement of the contents, for the contents themselves have not been created by the activity of making the compilation – they might, however, be protected in their own right.

The English courts have upheld claims to copyright in railway timetables, football pools coupons, and directories of solicitors, but in *Greyhound Racing Association v Challis* [1923-28] Macg CC 370 protection was denied to a list of runners in a greyhound race – six dogs, selection being by drawing numbers out of a bag. Jacob J suggested (in *Ibcos v Barclays* [1994] FSR 275) that 'compilation' might be an appropriate rubric under which to place computer programs, which are assemblages of pieces of code rather than outright works of authorship, but this approach has not yet been adopted by the judges.

The 1988 Act includes tables and compilations in the definition of literary works, but excludes the possibility that databases would fall under the same heading, before adding databases to the list as a discrete element – implying that somehow there is a difference between a table or compilation on the one hand and a database on the other. One day a judge will do us the service of explaining what this difference is.

Complete Candor

The standard of disclosure required of an applicant for a patent in the United States. All prior art known to the applicant must be disclosed to the USPTO within three months of it coming to the applicant's notice.

Compliance Date (UK)

The period, four years and six months, from the declared priority date (or 12 months from the date of the first s.18(3) report) in which a UK patent application must comply with the requirements in the Act and Rules.

Compositional Claim

A patent claim to a specific composition, for example:

> gasoline with a RVP less than 7.5 psi, T50 greater than 215 degrees, T10 less than 140 degrees, T50 less than 215 degrees, T90 no greater than 315 degrees, paraffins greater than 65 percent, olefin content less than 8 percent, aromatics of at least 4.5 and octane value of at least 87.

US Patent 5 837 126: see *In the Matter of Union Oil Company of California,* Docket No. 9305 (Federal Trade Commission, 2003).

Comprising

A word encountered frequently in patents, but one that should be used with great care. It is usually employed to mean 'including' – that is, the invention must have A and B but can also have C and D – which is the way the EPO interprets it. It can however also mean 'consisting of' (a sense which features along with a surprising number of others in the *Oxford English Dictionary*), in other words must have A, B and C but no D or anything else.

Compulsory Licensing

A means to avoid harmful effects arising from the grant of monopolies in the form of intellectual property rights. In the UK Patents Act 1977, there are provisions allowing licences of right to be made available if an invention is not being **worked** in the UK, and in the unregistered designs field there are provisions with similar effect enabling the Secretary of State to make licences available of right if the Competition Commission reports that unregistered design right (UDR) is being exercised in a manner that is contrary to the public interest. The Paris Convention sets out provisions relating to compulsory licensing, but some countries have more stringent rules though **TRIPS** does serve to limit the extent to which rights can be derogated from in this way, which it refers to as 'use without Authorisation of the Right Holder'.

Compu-Mark

A commercial provider of trade mark related services, including in particular computerised searches. Part of the Thomson Reuters group of companies.

Computer Associates v Altai

A US copyright case in which the **'three-step' test** for analysing the extent of copyright protection, and accordingly determining whether an infringement had been committed, was formulated.

Computer-Implemented Invention

See **CII**.

Computer Patent Annuities

A company, originally set up in 1969 by a number of UK patent agents, to provide a renewals service initially for patents (which require annual fees to be paid, hence the name) but later including also trade marks and designs. It is said to control 60 per cent of the global patent annuities market (*The Times*, 13 September 2009). The main company is now called CPA Global Limited, and the group includes subsidiaries in a number of countries and territories and in different sectors: the group has diversified into domain name services, trade mark watching, searching, software (FoundationIP, a web-based intellectual property management software solution) and more recently legal service outsourcing. In 2010 Intermediate Capital group acquired a substantial shareholding.

Computer Program

A set of instructions created to control a computer. The process of creating a computer program is described at length in the judgment of the late Pumphrey J in *Cantor Fitzgerald v Tradition* [2000] RPC 95. Commonly, a program will start life in the form of an algorithm which is translated into one of several computer languages and thence into source code, which by the process of compilation is translated in turn into object code, the machine-readable form of the program that when processed by the appropriate equipment will cause the computer to perform certain tasks.

Conception

One of the criteria used in the USA in determining who has the right to an invention – who was first to invent? Often verified by signed and witnessed statements of invention or laboratory notebooks.

Conceptual Similarity

A factor taken into account in European Union trade mark law when comparing two signs, either in an infringement action or for relative grounds for refusal.

Conclusie

Dutch, '**claim**'.

Concurrent Use Proceeding

Proceeding before the **TTAB** in which a party alleges that it has common law rights in a mark that are geographically limited and that territorial rights within the US should be carved out between the parties to the proceeding

Conditional Access

The subject matter of Directive 98/84 of the European Parliament and of the Council of 20 November 1998 on the legal protection of services based on, or consisting of, conditional access. It defines 'conditional access services' as television or radio broadcasts or internet services to which 'access . . . in an intelligible form is made conditional upon prior individual authorisation' and payment. Includes pay-per-view and encrypted television, and Internet sites which charge for access.

Confidence

The essential characteristic of information the disclosure or use of which someone hopes to be able to control. The first of the **Coco criteria** stipulates that the information must have the necessary quality of confidence: it must not be available to the public. See the following entry.

Confidential Information

'Information', wrote Stanley Berwin, without his usual elegance, 'not readily available to the public which there is a duty not to disclose or exploit.' That duty might arise whenever information is given in confidence or obtained through a position of trust. It may even arise where the information is obtained improperly.

Specific statutes such as the Official Secrets Act (described by Berwin as 'a blunderbuss whose notorious section 2 is indiscriminate in its scope, but permits leaks authorized by Ministers of the Crown') and the Financial Services and Markets Act 2000 aimed at preventing insider dealing also impose confidentiality obligations.

Confidentiality Agreement

An agreement that imposes express obligations of confidence on one or more parties: the obligations are commonly mutual, but there is no need for them to be. Such agreements are useful in a very wide range of situations, including pre-application disclosures relating to inventions. See also **non-disclosure agreement**.

Confidentiality Club

A group of people who share some secret, whether an addiction to *The Archers* or something of greater commercial value, bound together by implied or expressed mutual obligations of confidentiality.

Confirmation, Patent of

A patent, usually a short-term one, granted on the basis of an existing patent in another country. It was a common device in colonial times, when a local patent would be granted to the holder of a patent in the colonial power; see H.E. Grundmann, Patent Laws in New African States, *Journal of the Patent Office Society*, 50, p. 486, 1968.

Confusion

That of which there must be a likelihood before trade mark infringement can be established based on mere similarities between either the claimant's trade mark and the defendant's sign, or between the respective goods and services, or both. See **likelihood of confusion**.

Consent

A concept that is important in trade mark law for two reasons. First, the consent of the owner of an earlier trade mark is a way to overcome a refusal of an application on grounds relating to the existence of that prior registration. Second, trade mark rights are commonly exhausted when goods bearing the trade mark have been placed on a market (especially the European Economic Area) by or with the consent of the trade mark owner. This has given rise to a significant body of EU case law exploring when consent can be said to have been given. See **exhaustion**.

Consistory Clause

A type of clause in a patent description that, predictably, sets out what the invention comprises. It is a generalised description of the invention, and it will reflect or be reflected in the first independent claim in the patent. It has no connection with any of the assemblies found in various churches known as consistories, though the sense of meaning is not entirely different.

Construction, Interpretation of Patent Claims

The process of working out what the claims in a patent mean, usually in order to determine whether something falls within the scope of the monopoly. The task has generated a huge amount of case law and controversy over the years, and that is just in the UK. For the UK, see **pith and marrow, Catnic, Improver, Protocol on Interpretation of Article 69**, and **Kirin Amgen**. For the US, see **equivalents, doctrine of**.

Content

A trendy, postmodern expression denoting material (particularly digital material) contained in some medium, usually online: so, arguably synonymous with copyright work. *A Shropshire Lad* (1896) by A.E. Houseman (1859–1936) contains the lines:

Into my heart on air that kills
From yon far country blows:
What are those blue remembered hills,
What spires, what farms are those?

That is the land of lost content,
I see it shining plain,
The happy highways where I went
And cannot come again.

This reference to 'content' is too early to have any connection with this definition of the word, but in a usage that appears to be closely related to this modern meaning the Land of Lost Content has been adopted as the name of a museum of twentieth-century popular British culture located, of course, in Shropshire (www.lolc.org.uk).

Content Owner

A trendy expression designating the proprietor of rights in the material contained in some media product. Synonymous with 'copyright holder', which is a much more precise and lawyerly expression.

Continuation

Where an applicant for a patent wishes to add claims where an application has already been filed in respect of the invention, and that parent application has not yet been issued or abandoned, a continuation application may be filed. It uses the same specification as the pending parent application and claims that application's priority.

Continuation in Part

A continuation application that claims the priority of the parent application for the common matter, but with alterations or additions that do not enjoy that priority. It enables the applicant to add subject-matter not disclosed in the parent while repeating substantial portions of the parent's specification. In the US, it must share at least one inventor with the parent application. Such an application enables the applicant to claim enhancements developed after the initial filing. It replaces the earlier concept of additional improvement patents in the US system. See also **addition, patent of**.

Continuing Application, Continuing Prosecution Application

A divisional application, a continuation application or a continuation-in-part application See **request for continued examination**.

Contribution

Patent law rewards a contribution to human knowledge, but this important principle rarely finds expression in the governing laws. In Canada, however, the *Manual of Patent Office Practice* defines a contribution as 'new and unobvious matter which constitutes what the inventor has added to human knowledge' [Ch. 13.05.03]

Contributory Infringement

An infringement committed not directly but by a party doing something that leads to an infringement, for example supplying something that is not itself an infringement but the only use for which is an infringing one; or by supplying it with instructions on how to use it in manner that will infringe. For patents, see 35 U.S.C. S271(c) for the US law on this matter and Section 60(2) of the Patents Act 1977 for the UK law. Also applicable in other areas of IP law. See also **secondary infringement**.

Convention on Biological Diversity

An international convention adopted in Rio in June 1992. It has a broad agenda, and several areas in common with the world of intellectual property. These include:

- Regulated access to genetic resources and traditional knowledge, including prior informed consent of the party providing resources.

- Sharing, in a fair and equitable way, the results of research and development and the benefits arising from the commercial and other utilization of genetic resources with the contracting party providing such resources (governments or local communities that provided the traditional knowledge or biodiversity resources utilized).
- Access to and transfer of technology, including biotechnology, to the governments or local communities that provided traditional knowledge or biodiversity resources.

A formal link between the Convention and the TRIPS Agreement is likely, which will make the Convention still more important in the IP world.

Convention Priority

See **priority**.

Conversion (EPC)

The EPC contains a mechanism for the conversion of applications into national applications in the unlikely event that a national office, acting as a receiving office for European applications, fails to pass on an application in time. National laws often require, for reasons of national security, that all applications are filed through the national IP office. If the application is not passed on within the time limit set by the EPC, some way is needed to save the application and this provision is it.

Conversion Damages

Before the Copyright, Designs and Patents Act 1988 came into operation a copyright infringer ran the risk of an award of conversion damages, which treated infringing articles made by him as the property of the copyright owner. The amount of damages awarded would therefore reflect the full ill-gotten gains from the infringement, without deduction of the costs of manufacture and so on.

Cooling-off Period

A period allowed prior to the formal commencement of opposition proceedings, to allow the parties to settle the dispute without incurring liability for the other's costs. The applicant might choose to withdraw the application. Found in UK and Community trade mark procedure.

Copy Protection

An omnibus expression for a range of techniques that can prevent the copying of copyright material – though the techniques are notoriously incapable of determining whether the material is in fact not protected, or the act being perpetrated on it permitted. Usually means technology used to prevent copying of digital sound recordings, films or computer programs, but may be wider than this. Copy prevention and copy control are near-synonyms, and as far as the use of such techniques in the digital world is concerned 'technical protection measures' is another synonym, and 'digital rights management' is a broader concept that includes these techniques.

Copycat Packaging

Why are cats universally associated with copying? See **lookalike product**.

Copyleft

A technique which uses the protection given by copyright laws to subvert their usual purpose, using them to remove restrictions on distributing copies and modified versions of a work for others and requiring that the same freedoms be preserved in modified versions. The open-source movement is based on the notion of copyleft, and the GNU General Public Licence embodies the principles. So too are the various Creative Commons licences. It does not amount to a complete surrender of copyright, which is legally impossible, but by contrast to the traditional position of the copyright owner who states 'all rights reserved', copyleft can be (and often is) characterised as 'some rights reserved'.

Copyright

A personal property right, created by statute, that protects the exclusive right of **authors** of **literary**, **dramatic**, **musical** and **artistic works** to carry out (or permit, or **licence**, others to carry out) certain defined restricted acts in relation to those works. Separate copyright also subsists in secondary works such as films, sound recordings and broadcasts.

Copyright comes into existence automatically, with no need for registration – except in the United States of America (for works of US origin) and some other jurisdictions. Even in the US, though, the grant of copyright is independent of the act of registration, which confers additional benefits on the copyright holder (including the right to recover **statutory damages** and attorneys' fees). However, works of US origin must be registered before an infringement suit can be filed.

Because copyright is concerned with protecting a person's works, there is no copyright in mere ideas. They must be reduced to some material form – it is the expression of the underlying material that copyright protects, for that is where the creative work of the author is to be found. Neither does copyright confer a monopoly (as a patent or registered design does): there must be a causal connection between the claimant's (plaintiff's) work and the alleged copy – independent creation is a defence to an infringement action.

The **Copyright, Designs and Patents Act 1988**, as much amended, is the latest restatement of copyright law in the United Kingdom. The European Community has taken an active interest in the copyright area since the late 1980s, and several directives harmonise copyright laws among the Member States. The UK had the earliest copyright law in the world, the **Statute of Anne** (1709), although the common law had previously recognised similar rights. The common law copyright system still pertains (despite EC harmonisation and the effects of international conventions, principally the **Berne Convention** and the **Universal Copyright Convention**) throughout the countries of the former British Empire, including the United States: most of the rest of the world subscribes to the **droit d'auteur** system, originating in revolutionary France.

Copyright Clearance Center

A US-based (but globally active) organisation that deals with licensing and permissions for the use of copyright(ed) material.

Copyright, Designs and Patents Act 1988 (UK)

A large piece of legislation to restate the law of copyright; to make fresh provision for the rights of performers and others in performances; to confer a design right in original designs; to amend the Registered Designs Act 1949; to make provision with respect to patent agents and trade mark agents; to confer patents and designs jurisdiction on certain county courts; to amend the law of patents; to make provision with respect to devices designed to circumvent copy-protection of works in electronic form; to make fresh provision penalising the fraudulent reception of transmissions; to make the fraudulent application or use of a trade mark an offence; to make provision for the benefit of the Hospital for Sick Children, Great Ormond Street, London; to enable financial assistance to be given to certain international bodies; and for connected purposes.

- Part I contains the law on copyright (although there are related bits elsewhere).
- Part II deals with rights in performances.
- Part III deals with unregistered design right and Part IV contains the amendments to the Registered Designs Act.
- Part V deals with patent and trade mark agents.
- Part VI sets up the *Patents County Court*, and has some miscellaneous amendments to patent law.
- Part VII – miscellaneous and general – touches on some copyright-related areas such as circumvention of copy-protection measures.

Since 1988 there have been numerous amendments to the Act, many of them imposed by EC Directives.

Copyright Management Information

See **rights management information**.

Copyright Tribunal

A body established under Sections 145 to 148 of the Copyrights, Designs and Patents Act 1988. It replaced the old Performing Rights Tribunal: its new name reflected the increase in collective licensing activities encouraged by the new legislation. The tribunal has a chairman and two deputy chairmen, plus two to eight ordinary members. In the field of copyright and related rights, it decides the terms of licences offered by, or licensing schemes operated by, collective licensing bodies, if the parties are unable to do so themselves. It performs an extremely important function, because the collecting societies whose activities it regulates are monopolies. It has to determine the facts and decide what is reasonable in the light of them. An appeal lies on points of law to the High Court (the Court of Session in Scotland).

The Tribunal's biggest recent case was *Universities UK (formerly the Committee of Vice Chancellors and Principals of the Universities of the United Kingdom) v Copyright Licensing Agency (CLA)* (2002).

Anyone who has been unreasonably refused a licence, or who believes that the terms of a licence are unreasonable, may bring the matter before the Tribunal. It also has power to deal with other matters referred by the Secretary of State – including the royalties paid by publishers of television programme listings to broadcasters (a consequence of the contretemps that led to the Monopolies and Mergers Commission's report on the subject and the *Magill* case in the CJEC: the Broadcasting Act 1990 made provision to deal with these matters).

Could–Would Approach

An approach to deciding whether inventiveness is present, used by the EPO. If a person skilled in the art could have done something, that does not necessarily mean that it is not inventive. The important question is whether he or she would have done so. This is assessed in the light of the known art and what it teaches. See also **'obvious to try'**.

Counteraction

The principle, applied for example in Case C-16/06 P *Les Éditions Albert René Sàrl v Office for Harmonisation in the Internal Market, Orange A/S* that the similarity between the trade marks in suit (MOBILIX and OBELIX) was effectively offset by the fact that everyone knew Obelix as a fictional character.

Counterfeiting, Counterfeit Goods

An imitation of a product made to look identical (or as nearly identical as possible, or necessary) with the original. This might involve copying designs, copyright material, and possibly patents, but it is the use of trade marks or get-up that usually completes the deception. It is not even necessary, in some cases, for the trade marks to be copied very closely: when it first became a problem, counterfeiting was a greater problem in the developing world than in the developed one, and if prospective customers are not familiar with the Latin alphabet the words inside a familiar logo can be complete gibberish.

The expression has sometimes been used to hyperbolic effect by businesses whose complaint was in fact that someone had simply copied their designs, rather in the way that the expression copyright or intellectual property **theft** has been used to the point of tedium.

Court of First Instance (CFI)

Since December 2009, when the Lisbon Treaty came into operation, known (rather unspecifically) as the General Court. An independent court attached to the Court of Justice of the European Communities, created in 1989 to hear disputes about certain matters including now Community trade marks and designs, where it acts as a court of appeal from the Boards of Appeal of OHIM. Originally, it was designed to provide a venue for the proliferating staff cases brought by employees of the Community institutions, which under the Treaty of Rome were heard by the Court of Justice. It also took on a large body of competition cases. Appeals lay from the CFI (as it was universally known) to the CJEC, and now lie from the General Court to the CJEU.

Court of Justice of the European Union

Before 1 December 2009, the Court of Justice of the European Communities. The institution known by that name also includes the General Court (called the Court of First Instance from its establishment in 1988 until the Lisbon Treaty came into operation) and the Civil Service Tribunal (2004). Often called the European Court of Justice, but as an institution of the European Communities (its name did not change with the merger of the original three Communities) its remit never ran to that diminishing number of countries that remain outside the Community, who ought to be appalled by the implied assumption of jurisdiction over them. The transformation into a Union makes no difference to this point.

The title Court of Justice identifies the senior tribunal of the institution.

The Court of Justice does not even have jurisdiction over the three

European Free Trade Area (EFTA) members of the **EEA**: that is for the EFTA court, which is also based in Luxembourg. The court hears appeals from decisions of the General Court, which include Community trade mark and design cases, and also entertains references from the courts of Member States seeking a preliminary opinion on the meaning of a piece of Community legislation – hence Jacob LJ's phrase, 'expedition to Luxembourg', in his judgment in *Budejovicky Budvar Narodni Podnik v Anheuser-Busch Inc* [2009] EWCA Civ 1022.

Covetousness and Delay (UK)

The ability to amend a granted patent is strictly limited so as to avoid abuse. Section 75 of the Patents Act 1977 (very similar to section 30 of the 1949 Act) gives the court discretion to allow amendment. In *Kimberly-Clark Worldwide Inc. v Procter & Gamble* [2000] FSR 235 the Court of Appeal (Aldous LJ) remarked:

> the grounds upon which the courts had refused amendment in the past arose from a desire to protect the public against abuse of monopoly. The courts were slow to allow a patentee to validate an invalid claim by amendment when he had for many years inflicted upon the public a monopoly of a width which he knew to be unjustified. I can find nothing in the 1977 Act which would suggest that the legislature intended to restrict the court's discretion to prevent such covetousness from being a ground of refusal of amendment.

This is an area where the concurrent jurisdiction of the EPO and national courts has created problems, arising mainly from the unexpected length of proceedings in the EPO. EPC 2000 introduced a new procedure under Article 123 for the amendment of European patents centrally at the EPO, and amendments to the Patents Act require the Comptroller or the court to have regard to the relevant principles in EPO 2000, and guidelines and decisions of the Boards of Appeal when dealing with amendments. This has been predicted to herald the demise of the old UK law relating to covetousness and delay.

CPA

Chartered Patent Attorney, **Computer Patent Annuities** or **continuing prosecution application (continuing application)**, as the case may be.

CREATE Act (US)

Cooperative Research and Technology Enhancement (CREATE) Act of 2004. The CREATE Act broadens the scope of the 35 U.S.C. Section 103(c) exception – a safe harbour for inventions the product of collaborative efforts of co-inventors within a single entity – by encouraging and rewarding joint research and collaborative efforts among inventors in separate research organizations. Prompted by a 1997 Federal Circuit decision, *OddzOn Products, Inc. v. Just Toys Inc.*, 122 F.3d 1396 (Fed. Cir. 1997), which ruled that confidential, non-public prior art may serve as evidence of obviousness.

Creative Commons

1. A non-profit organisation, established in the USA in 2001, dedicated to increasing the range of creative works available for others to use, share and build upon. It starts from the premise that creativity will be served if copyright works are licensed on a liberal basis, and promulgates licences designed to do this. Copyright owners who use Creative Commons licences (indicated by an encircled double-c symbol) can choose what rights they wish to retain under their control. It uses the techniques of **copyleft** for this purpose. The co-founders of Creative Commons were Larry Lessig, Hal Abelson, Professor of Electrical Engineering and Computer Science at Massachusetts Institute of Technology (MIT), and Eric Eldred.
2. Licences, and the licensing technique they embody, using this approach.

Creative Spark

A colloquial expression that describes the inspiration for a copyright work or an invention, invariably characterised in graphic works by a light bulb illuminating in a character's head.

Criminal Offences

Although intellectual property law creates private property rights which the owner enforces through infringement actions, criminal offences have become depressingly ubiquitous in the IP field in recent decades. There is some justification for public enforcement of private rights: the rationale for creating criminal offences might be found in public safety considerations, the need to fight organised crime, consumer protection, or (least defensible) the inconvenience, expense and unpopularity of suing myriad small infringers. Making the small infringers criminals is, however, often even less popular.

Cross-Licensing

When two parties have patents that overlap, and they are not able to work their own patents without permission from the other, they might license each other. This is a problem that can arise particularly with **selection patents**, where by definition there is a degree of dependency between the two parties.

Cross-Undertaking in Damages

An undertaking demanded from a claimant who seeks an interim (or interlocutory) injunction. The claimant must agree to compensate the defendant for the loss the defendant will suffer from complying with the injunction, should it later emerge that the injunction should not have been granted.

Crown Copyright (UK)

Crown copyright subsists in a work made by or under the direction or control of Her Majesty or a government department (Copyright, Designs and Patents Act 1988, section 163). This begs the question of whether a commissioned work is made under such direction or control. The bill that eventually became the 1988 Act originally dealt with this problem by giving to the Crown copyright in works it commissioned, but this put the Crown in a much more favourable position than other commissioners. For the sake of consistency the government concluded that the Crown should be placed in the same position as any other commissioner, having to rely on contract if it wanted the rights.

As for the application of the rules about employee authors, servants of the Crown are not employed under contracts of employment, being servants at will, so section 163 is the sole basis on which Crown copyright stands.

Copyright in parliamentary papers vests in the House concerned, not as previously (under the 1956 Act) in the Crown. All works made by officers or employees of the House in the course of their duties are included.

Parliamentary copyright extends to any sound recording, film, live broadcast or cable programme of Parliamentary proceedings. Although the Houses of Parliament are not legally bodies corporate, the Act deems that they are such for copyright purposes. The Speaker exercises the rights of the House of Commons, and the Clerk of the Parliaments exercises those of the House of Lords. The Act provides for the situation where there is no incumbent in one of these positions, and for the exercise of the rights during dissolutions.

Crown copyright subsists for a period of 125 years from the end of the year in which the literary, dramatic or musical work was made, or, if it was published commercially before the end of 75 years from the end of the year of making, for 50 years from the end of the year in which publication took place (Section 163(3)). 'Commercial publication' is defined in section 175(2) as:

- issuing copies of the work to the public at a time when copies made in advance of the receipt of orders are generally available to the public, or
- making the work available to the public by means of an electronic retrieval system . . .

Publication is not other than commercial merely because it is not done for gain. Clearly, publication by Her Majesty's Stationery Office (HMSO) causes the shorter period to apply.

Copyright in Acts and Measures runs for 50 years from the end of the year in which Royal Assent is given (Section 164), and Parliamentary copyright for 50 years from the end of the year in which the work was made (Section 165). Copyright in Parliamentary Bills only subsists for the life of the bill, so it expires when Royal Assent is given or on the withdrawal of the bill or at the end of the session.

If copyright vests in an international organisation by virtue of section 168 and any Orders made under that section it subsists for 50 years from the end of the year in which the work was made. This period may be extended by Order in Council if necessary to comply with the UK's international obligations.

Crown Use

In the UK, intellectual property statutes contain extensive provisions allowing the Crown (for which readers outside the UK might read 'the state') to avail itself of the private rights it has granted.

CSS

Content Scramble System, a Digital Rights Management (DRM) scheme used on almost all commercially produced DVDs. See also **DeCSS**.

Cybersquatting

The practice of registering as a domain name, or as part of one, a word or words that serve to distinguish someone's goods or services, or business, from those of others. In other words, it is the act of hijacking someone else's trade mark to register as a domain name. The second stage is to offer to transfer the domain name to the person whose business reputation attaches to it. The consideration demanded for doing so was often substantial, though often cybersquatters would try to justify their actions by claiming that they had found the domain name unregistered and had generously and public-spiritedly registered it to ensure that the trade mark owner was fully protected. This story might be contradicted by a declared willingness to sell the registration to the highest bidder.

Dispute resolution procedures including the **UDRP** now make cybersquatting less of a threat to trade mark owners than formerly.

D

Damages (Inquiry As To)

The monetary compensation awarded by a court for loss, damage or injury suffered by someone following a breach of contract or of statutory duty (such as an infringement of an author's moral rights) or the commission of a tort, such as infringement of an intellectual property right or a breach of confidence. The purpose of the award is to place the injured party in the same position as if the tort had not been commmitted. Aggravated damages may sometimes be awarded, and exemplary damages may be awarded for example where the defendant has calculated to make a profit from his wrongdoing that may exceed the amount of damages that would be awarded. In the intellectual property field, statute provides for awards of additional damages.

Nominal damages may be awarded where the tort is actionable per se but the injury caused is minimal and the judge (or jury) wishes to indicate their contempt for the plaintiff's case.

The plaintiff must take reasonable steps to mitigate his loss. The award of damages will take this into account. However, the plaintiff is under no obligation to take steps that would harm his commercial reputation.

In *Gerber Garment Technology Inc v Lectra Systems Ltd* [1995] R.P.C. 383 the court awarded damages which exceeded turnover in the infringing articles because it was directly foreseeable that the patentee would lose profits in related areas of its business as a result of the infringement taking place so shortly before patent expiry. See also **springboarding**.

Database

According to Directive 96/9/EC, a collection of independent works, data or other materials arranged in a systematic and methodical way and individually accessible by electronic or other means. Contrast with the concept, in UK copyright law, of a compilation or table. To be protected by copyright, it is necessary to show that by reason of the selection and arrangement of its content a database is its author's own intellectual creation. Database right was created by the same directive to compensate by the same directive for the inevitable loss of most copyright protection in the field.

Database right (UK)

The right given to the makers of databases under Directive 96/9/EC, which refers to it as '*sui generis*' protection. The Council of the European Community adopted the Directive on the legal protection of databases in 1996. It seeks to harmonise the laws of the Member States relating to copyright in databases, and in particular the degree of originality required of them: it also introduces a new *sui generis* right for database operators. The Directive was implemented in the UK from 1 January 1998 by the Copyright and Rights in Databases Regulations 1997, SI no 3032.

The Regulations insert a new definition of database in the 1988 Act. The term means:

A collection of independent works, data or other materials which –
(a) are arranged in a systematic or methodical way, and
(b) are individually accessible by electronic or other means.

Databases are no longer treated for copyright purposes as a type of compilation, but remain a type of literary work. (This raises the intriguing possibility that there are databases that are not compilations, and compilations that are not databases.)

Databases only receive copyright protection if they are their author's own intellectual creation. This is a much higher standard (taken from Dutch and German law) than previously applied in the UK: non-database compilations (should such things exist) are still subject to the lesser test, so should more easily obtain protection. A collection of data not arranged in a systematic or methodical way might fit through this loophole.

New section 50D of the Act permits certain acts that would otherwise be restricted by copyright in the database: 'anything which is necessary for the purposes of access to and use of the contents of the database'. Section 296B makes void any contractual term that purports to prohibit or restrict a permitted act.

The effect of the increased standard of originality is that databases will be hard to protect by copyright. The new database right (as the EC's **sui generis** right has become in the UK legislation) will however give database operators valuable new rights. The definition of a database for these purposes is the same as in the copyright provisions, but there is no originality requirement: the mere fact that there has been a substantial investment in the database is sufficient.

The new right enables the database operator to control two activities:

- Unauthorised extraction of material from the database; and
- Unauthorised reutilisation of material from the database.

DBA

Doing business as. A DBA name is a style under which a business trades, which differs from its actual name. Mostly an expression in US usage: in the UK, it would be referred to as a trading name, which makes this another illustration of the way US lawyers use much more colourful language than their counterparts elsewhere.

De-branding

An activity undertaken by parallel importers, who may remove references to the original manufacturer of the goods in which they are trading: a particular problem in the European Union, where pharmaceuticals may also be overstickered, co-branded or repackaged so as to cause damage to the reputation of the brand or the proprietor. See *Boehringer Ingelheim (and others) v Swingward Ltd* [2004] EWCA Civ 757.

De minimis

1. A shortened version of the Latin maxim, *de minimis non curat lex*, 'the law cares not for small things'. Applicable in all manner of legal situations, including the application of **competition law** to agreements of minor importance.
2. A defence to a copyright infringement claim, under the new Israeli law.
3. The approach adopted in some countries to the registration of trade marks comprising surnames. The rarity of a surname may be judged by the number of times it appears in the telephone directory or on the electoral roll.

Deception

The essential element of an action for **passing off**.

Deceptiveness

An undesirable quality in a trade mark. Generally, if a trade mark will deceive consumers about the nature or origins of the goods to which it is applied it will be unregistrable. Offences may also be committed under consumer protection legislation, but that is another matter.

Declaration of Continued Use (Section 8 Declaration) (US)

A declaration required during the sixth year of a US trademark registration and with each ten-year renewal. The proprietor must submit a declaration and evidence that the mark is in use.

Declaration of Non-infringement

A declaration, available in the UK from the Patent Office or the court under section 71 of the Patents Act 1977, confirming that an activity does not infringe a patent. The person seeking the declaration has to have asked the patentee for an assurance that they are not infringing first. A similar declaration can be obtained in the case of a trade mark or registered design.

In the US, a declaratory judgment serves the same purpose.

Decompilation

The process of working back from the object code form of a computer program (the form that is distributed to users) to the source code (the form that is useful to programmers). The object code is created from the source code by a process known as compiling, using a program known as a compiler. In the closed-source universe, decompiling is an undesirable activity and the source code is often treated by software houses as confidential information. On the face of it the process of decompilation requires the copyright owner's consent, being a form of adaptation of a copyright work, and involving the making of incidental copies, but many copyright laws (including those of the European Union Member States) permit such activities in limited circumstances. This is a necessary safeguard to prevent **overreaching**. Cf. **reverse engineering**.

In the open-source universe, of course, problems with decompilation do not arise.

DeCSS

A computer program for decrypting the content of a commercially-produced DVD, protected by the Content Scramble System (**CSS**). It was a necessity for anyone wishing to watch such disks on a Linux computer, but as it had been created without a licence the one author (out of three) who could be identified, Jon Lech Johansen, was prosecuted by the Norwegian authorities. Eventually, the court of appeal upheld his acquittal by the trial court and the authorities decided to take no further action, though the controversy has rumbled on in the US.

Defensive Patenting

The activity of obtaining patent protection not for what one is actually doing, but for other matter so as to make it difficult for a competitor to come close.

Defensive Registration

A type of trade mark registration available in the UK from 1938 until 1994 (and in other systems based on UK law, and in Japan) allowing the registration of a well-known trade mark to be maintained without the need to use it for the goods or services for which it was registered. The utility of this provision was severely limited in the UK because it was available only for invented word trade marks (as in, for example, the key case on the UK law, *Ferodo* (1945) 62 RPC 111: but, although the trade mark was an invented word, it was not sufficiently well known).

Delivery Up

A court order requiring the defendant to hand over infringing articles to the owner of the intellectual property, who might wish publicly to crush them under a steamroller.

Dependent Claim

A patent claim that refers to an earlier claim and adds one or more additional features, thus making the claim somewhat narrower and possibly overcoming an allegation that it lacks novelty or is obvious. See also **independent claim**.

Deposit, Micro-organism Deposit

The **Budapest Treaty** provides for the international recognition of the deposit of micro-organisms for the purposes of patent procedure. The written disclosure of an invention of a new micro-organism must be supplemented by the deposit of that micro-organism in a recognised culture collection, and for this purpose the Budapest Treaty recognises **International Depositary Authorities**.

Derivative Work

A work based on an earlier copyright work that is changed in some way. It includes translations, musical arrangements, screenplays made from plays or novels, and the like. The **Gowers** Review (2006) recommended that there should be an exception in UK copyright law to permit the creation of derivative works (and also transformative and creative works, though the latter category should pose no problems for copyright law as it stands).

Derwent

Derwent World Patents Index, a service offered by Thomson Reuters, claims to be the most comprehensive enhanced patent database in the world.

Description

Part of the specification that has to be filed in support of a patent application, comprising a description of the claimed invention in sufficient detail to enable a hypothetical skilled person (person skilled in the art – (UK); person having ordinary skill in the art – US) to put the invention into practice (or, in the case of a PHOSITA, practise).

In the preferred PCT and USPTO format, the description is broken down into the following sections (which may be presented in whatever order the applicant chooses):

- title;
- technical field of invention;
- background art;
- disclosure of invention (which will usually be in terms identical to those of the main claim);
- description of figures (if any);
- description of best mode of performing the invention, including examples;
- reference to industrial applicability.

Descriptive, Descriptiveness

Given that the purpose of a trade mark is to distinguish the goods or services of one undertaking from those of others, a descriptive word, device or other sign will not make a good one and (unless it has acquired distinctiveness or a secondary meaning) it will not be registrable. The standards applied in different jurisdictions can vary widely. A sign which is merely **suggestive** – a **skilful and covert allusion** to, or one that hints at the characteristics of the goods or services – will stand a better chance.

Design

Usually refers to the appearance of an **article** or **product** (often, but not always, one produced industrially). The word may also be used to refer to the legal rights protecting such subject-matter. There are four different uses of the word in the Copyright, Designs and Patents Act 1988; one in the copyright provisions, another in the provisions on (UK) unregistered design right, another in the amendments to the Registered Designs Act 1949 (subsequently replaced) and yet another in the provisions concerning patent agents. The first three of these uses each has its own definition; it is not clear which, if any, of the definitions fits the fourth.

Design Copyright (UK)

The rather unfortunate name by which the right given by registration under the original Registered Designs Act 1949 was known. It bore no resemblance to copyright, being a monopoly right granted after an application and examination process and lasting for a mere 15 years. Abolished in 1989. The expression could now logically refer to copyright in a design, but to avoid ambiguity it is probably best not to use it.

Design Document

In UK law, if a copyright artistic work is a design document there are restrictions on what activities will constitute an infringement of copyright in it. This is intended to exclude copyright, to a great extent, from the field of design protection (and therefore to leave the field to UK unregistered design right). Whether an artistic work should be considered a design document or not depends on the intention of the creator at the time of making it.

Design Freedom

A concept of considerable importance in some design laws, including the UK and EU systems, for both subsistence and infringement. A design is more likely to be considered to be novel and to have individual character if the designer's freedom to create something very different from what had gone before was constrained by some external factor. If the designer starts with a blank sheet, they will be expected to produce something further removed from designs already in the field. When considering an infringement, the question whether the design produces a different overall impression on the informed user or not will also be judged in the light of the degree of freedom enjoyed by the designer. In a crowded field, smaller differences will suffice to show non-infringement.

Extreme cases of lack of design freedom are covered by the **must-fit** and **must-match** exceptions, in certain legal systems including the UK and (in part) the EU.

Design Patent

In the United States, design protection is part of the patent system. The law there distinguishes between what in other countries is simply called a patent (and in the US is referred to as a utility patent) and a design patent (which an English lawyer, for example, would recognise as a registered design or something very similar to one). A US design patent lasts for 14 years and is issued for visual ornamental characteristics embodied in, or applied to, an article of manufacture.

Designation, Designated State

There are myriad contexts in which the verb 'to designate' and its derivatives might be encountered, and most have an international dimension to them. In the European Patent System, applicants designate those countries for which they wish to have patents (and incidentally must also designate the inventor). States are also designated in a **PCT** application. The expression is used in a similar way in the international trade marks system under the Madrid Agreement and Protocol.

Detriment

Article 5(2) of the Trade Marks Directive (89/104/EEC), which gives the owners of certain trade marks a remedy for **dilution**, indicates that an action will lie where the use of the defendant's sign takes unfair advantage of the reputation of the claimant's trade mark or is otherwise detrimental to its distinctive character or repute. There is no need to prove likelihood of detriment in an action based on unfair advantage, though if there is detriment it will help the case.

Device

A slightly archaic expression denoting a class of signs that are not merely words (although words may be included) and that might be used and registered as trade marks. Still found in countries whose laws are based on the old British law, synonymous with the word 'design' in the EC Directive and the UK's 1994 Act: perhaps also synonymous with the more colloquial 'logo'.

Diamond v Chakrabarty

Diamond v Chakrabarty 447 US 303, 309 (1980) is a key US Supreme Court case involving the patentability of micro-organisms. The applicant had developed a bacterium that was capable of breaking down crude oil – a very useful creature, given the propensity of the oil industry to spill the stuff (coincidentally, I write this definition as a huge oil slick threatens the United States' Gulf Coast). The Supreme Court found in favour of Prof. Chakrabarty, holding: 'Respondent's micro-organism constitutes a "manufacture" or "composition of matter" within that statute.'

Diamond v Diehr

Another key US Supreme Court patent case, 450 U.S. 175 (1981): Sidney A. Diamond was the Commissioner for Patents, not a habitual litigant in his own interest. The Court held patentable the execution of a physical process (in suit, curing synthetic rubber) controlled by running a computer program that implemented the Arrhenius Equation. The Court reiterated its earlier holdings that software algorithms could not be patented, but held that the mere presence of a software element did not make an otherwise patentable machine or process unpatentable.

Diehr is the third of a trilogy of Supreme Court decisions on the patentability of computer software related inventions: see also ***Gottschalk v Benson***, 409 U.S. 63 (1972) and *Parker v Flook*, 437 U.S. 584 (1978).

Digital Millennium Copyright Act

A US copyright statute, which includes provisions implementing the **WIPO Treaties** and creates a '**safe harbor**' for online service providers provided they respond to claims that they are hosting infringing material (see **DMCA takedown**). The Act also creates exceptions from normal copyright rules to enable computer repairers to carry on their business and creates a specialised type of *sui generis* protection for boat hull designs.

Digital Rights Management, Digital Rights Management Information

The automated management of rights in digital material and the technology used by content owners to control the use of their material. The information that enables rights owners to track and control the use of their material is protected from removal under the laws of a number of countries.

Dilution

A wrong perpetrated on trade mark owners when a sign identical with or similar to theirs is used for goods or services that are not similar at all. Long recognised by state laws in the US, though very rarely successfully enforced.

The Kodak bicycles case (*Eastman v Griffiths Cycles* (1898) 15 RPC 105) and the **Odol** case (1924, 25 Juristische Wochenschrift 502) convey a flavour of what the law is trying to control here. The EC directive on trade marks offered Member States the option of adopting anti-dilution provisions in their national laws, and the Community trade marks regulation protected CTMs against this type of harm. There has been much controversy in the EU about 'dilution' theory, as summarized in Case C-408/01 *Adidas v Fitness World* [2004] FSR 21 where the Court of Justice said (emphasis added):

> the protection conferred by Article 5(2) of the Directive is not conditional on a finding of a degree of similarity between the mark with a reputation and the sign such that there exists a likelihood of confusion between them on the part of the relevant section of the public. *It is sufficient for the degree of similarity between the mark with a reputation and the sign to have the effect that the relevant section of the public establishes a link between the sign and the mark.*

Anti-dilution laws have existed in individual states in the USA for many years without making much of a mark on the trade mark scene. The Federal Trademark Dilution Act of 1995 (since supplanted by the Trademark Dilution Revision Act of 2006) introduced the concept of dilution at Federal level: its expected revolutionary effect was such that it acquired the nickname Federal Lawyers' Welfare Act, though it rather failed to live up to the billing.

Dilution is actually a number of different wrongs, including tarnishment, detriment, blurring and **unfair advantage**.

Directive

A type of legislative instrument in the European Union (and before it the European Communities): it is binding on the Member States as to the effect to be achieved but not as to the means for achieving it. Much used to harmonise or approximate the laws of the Member States in a variety of fields, including trade marks, copyright and neighbouring rights, and designs. Member States must implement the requirements of the Directive in national law. The experience of the UK shows that unless the domestic legislation uses precisely the same words it risks being found inadequate, but if the words are faithfully reproduced it can be difficult to assign a meaning to them.

Disclaimer

1. A statement in a trade mark application that the applicant claims no rights in a descriptive element in a composite mark – for example, in

descriptive or non-**distinctive** words that accompany a **figurative trade mark**. See also **limitation**.

2. A technique for avoiding prior art during examination of a patent application – for purposes of novelty, but not of inventive step. It is used mainly in the EPO. The applicant may claim, for example, a range of compounds one of which is disclosed in the prior art. A proviso can state that that compound is not included. However, the anticipation must be accidental – the disclosure must have been in a different field altogether, such that the skilled person would not have taken it into account.

Disclosure

1. The making available to the public of information about an invention, such that its novelty might be compromised and a patent for it refused (or, if granted, prove to be invalid).
2. What an inventor must give to the public in consideration of the grant of a patent: the learning embodied in the patent is placed into the common pool of knowledge. Some patent laws impose an express duty of disclosure: See **complete candor**.

Disclosure Requirement

The requirement that an invention be described in sufficient detail in a patent application, such that the teaching of the patent is fully available to the public. This requirement manifests itself in different ways in different patent laws. Also, the proposed art. 29 bis in TRIPS put forward by six developing countries led by India, and a Swiss proposal to amend the PCT Regulations, imposing specific requirements for disclosure of from where biological material in patent applications has been obtained.

Discovery

1. 35 USC 100 says that 'invention' means invention or discovery, but a mere discovery is not patentable. In the European system, a discovery is not patentable as such. In most other common-law countries discoveries are not patentable, which makes second-use medical claims non-starters too, and in India the concept of a discovery is taken so far as to preclude most chemical patents – section 3(c) of the Patents

Act 1970, as amended by the 2002 Act, excluding 'the discovery of any living thing or non-living substances occurring in nature'.
2.   In common law systems, the name for the duty of both sides in a civil law suit to reveal evidence to the other: now known in England as disclosure.

Discrete Element

In Canadian patent practice, a feature or set of features whose role in achieving the objects of an invention can be considered independently of other features. *Canadian Manual of Patent Office Practice* Ch. 13.05.03a.

Distinctiveness

The defining feature of a trade mark; that which differentiates it from other types of signs. A sign might have it from the moment of creation (if, for example, it is an invented word, like Kodak) or it can be acquired through the use made of the sign by its proprietor, largely as a result of advertising. It might be necessary to provide a trade mark registry with evidence of distinctiveness to support an application to register, and advertising expenditure is likely to be a significant element in such evidence.

Divisional

A new patent application with a priority claim based on the filing date of the parent application and which contains matter divided out from the parent. Differs from a continuation application in that it claims a distinct or independent invention carved out of the parent application. In US practice, a divisional application does not need to name any of the inventors named in the parent application – it can name a different set of inventors. Often filed at the request of the examiner, because a patent can only claim a single invention (cf. **unity of invention**).

Divulgation, Droit de

One of four moral rights recognised in French law: the author has complete control over whether their work is made public. Once the author has demonstrated a wish that the work should be available to the public (by sending a manuscript to a publisher, for example) the right ceases to have any effect in relation to that work. See repentir, droit au.

DMCA, DMCA Takedown

The **Digital Millennium Copyright Act**, and the name of the notice given under the Act to online service providers where websites using their services contain allegedly infringing material.

Docket

A log recording developments in a case, whether in a court's file or in the records of the lawyers dealing with the matter (including a patent or trade mark application). Hence 'docketing', and specialist computer software to facilitate it: patent and trade mark applications, like litigation, are replete with important time limits and a docketing system is an important part of meeting them. In common use in the US, but encountered also in other countries.

Accelerated legal proceedings are often referred to in the US as a 'rocket docket'.

Doctorow, Cory

A Canadian blogger, journalist, science fiction author and copyright activist, proponent of **Creative Commons**.

Domain Name

Domain names act as electronic addresses for websites, so they are commonly used to identify the sites with which they are associated. If you say you are visiting amazon.com, for example, what you mean is that you are visiting the website at that address – or more precisely downloading some of the web pages that make up that site to your computer.

Domain names act as indications of origin, which is exactly what trade marks do too. They often reflect a business's identity (indeed, in the case of amazon.com and other online businesses they might actually be the business's identity) and serve to attract customers, just like trade marks do.

Because they perform this function, domain names (like trade marks) have a value to the businesses that use them – perhaps a considerable value. Many domain names incorporate the trade marks of the businesses that use them. However, one significant difference between domain names and trade marks is that the most valuable domain names are generic ones, such as sex.com and business.com. Neither of these would work very well as a trade mark (although having said that, there are two SEX trade marks on the UK register and another two Community trademarks, registered for a range of goods and services for which the word is not descriptive).

Unlike trade marks, which are registered at a national or regional level, domain names operate in a global marketplace. The domain name system relies on each domain name being unique, so once someone has registered it they have exclusive rights throughout the world. If they are only doing business in a small part of the world, this effectively means that a part of commercial speech has been enclosed and denied to other would-be users, something that the trade mark system would not tolerate.

The domain name registration system also differs from the trade mark system because it cannot accommodate more than one user of a particular identifier. In the trade mark world, because trade marks are registered for specific goods or services, it is perfectly possible for several businesses to use the same trade mark for different goods or services – think of Polo. The lack of such flexibility in the domain name system has unfortunate results for trade mark owners: see **cybersquatting**. The domain name system does offer some flexibility, because it includes myriad **top-level domains** (on which, see the entry for that topic).

Internet Protocol (IP) addresses are related to and often confused with domain names. They are numerical addresses which identify devices attached to a computer network. Uniform Resource Identifiers (URIs) are numerical addresses for particular resources, for example files. They are often confused with Uniform Resource Locators, which are much more technical, and which are not numerical – for example http://www.bailii.org/ew/cases/EWCA/Civ/1998/1272.html. A hostname is a special type of domain name that has an IP address associated with it and starts with the host, for example www. URIs preface the hostname with the appropriate protocol e.g. http://www.IPsojure.co.uk.

Double Dipping

Claiming payment twice for the same use of a copyright work. In the UK, this is a concept used by the Copyright Tribunal, referred to in the parallel imports and trade mark case *Honda Giken Kogyo Kabushiki Kaisha & Anor v Neesam & Ors* [2009] EWHC 1213 (Pat).

Double Identity

Identical trade mark and sign, identical goods or services. Nothing to do with the **triple identity test** in US patent law.

Double Patenting

Something that is not permitted.

Douglas

See **Zeta Jones**.

Dramatic Work

One of the categories of works capable of being protected under the Copyright, Designs and Patents Act 1988, which provides no further guidance save to tell us that it includes a work of dance or mime.

DRM

See **digital rights management**.

Droit d'auteur

The equivalent of copyright law among the civil law countries, originally a creature of French law. As the name suggests, it recognises the rights of authors rather than those of the commercial interests who exploit the creations of others. By contrast, the common law world has tended historically to stress the interests of printers and publishers and by extension record producers, film producers and broadcasting organisations.

Many other countries call these rights by the same name in their respective languages: *urherrberrecht, Auteursrecht, diretto d'autore, derecho de autor, ophavsret, opphavsrett, upphovsrätt, авторское право, prawa autorskie, autorsko pravo* (Croatian), 着作权 (Chinese), 著作権 (*chosakuken*) (Japanese).

Droit de Suite

See **artist's resale right**.

Druckexemplar

German, the approved text of a patent (which is then printed).

E

Early Publication

Most patent offices in the world publish applications 18 months after the application date or priority date. The USA used not to, but now publishes early all US applications that have equivalent applications in early publishing countries.

Earth Closet Order

In the course of an attack on the validity of a patent, the party attacking it might find out about prior art that had previously escaped its attention. If it then seeks leave to amend its grounds of invalidity to include new prior art, the court may grant it but give the patentee a limited period within which it may elect to abandon its patent in the face of the new prior art. If the patentee so elects, the attacker has to bear some of the patentee's costs, generally from the date of service of the unamended grounds of invalidity to the date of election. Named after *Baird v Moule's Patent Earth Closet Company Limited* (1881) 17 Ch.D, 139.

In *CIL International v Vitrashop* [2002] FSR 67 Pumphrey J declined to make such an order, because the late discovery of the additional prior art was not due to any failure of due diligence by the applicants. This is consistent with a tendency in recent years for the courts to decline to give such orders, though most of the cases are unreported.

Also called a *See v Scott Paine* Order.

Eastern District of Texas, US District Court for the

A jurisdiction regarded as particularly friendly to **trolls**.

ECJ

See **Court of Justice of the European Union**.

Economic Rights

A subset of copyright. The transferable rights that enable the owner of copyright to earn revenue from the exploitation of the work. The expression is not used in statutes, but is employed when these rights need to be distinguished from moral rights. Also called pecuniary rights.

ECTA

The European Community Trademark Association: an organisation of trade mark owners that does within Europe what **INTA** does worldwide (on a more manageable scale).

EEA

The European Economic Area, comprising the **European Union** and most of the non-EU countries that make up the European Free Trade Association (but excluding Switzerland). The non-EU members are Norway, Iceland and Liechtenstein. The EEA agreement imposes many of the obligations on these three countries that apply in the EU, including in the intellectual property field (though Community intellectual property rights do not extend to them). References to the common market or the internal market now mean the EEA, which is the territory relevant to considerations of **exhaustion** of rights.

EESR

See **Extended European Search Report**.

EEUPC

The proposed European and EU Patents Court system, part of the project for a Community (or EU) patent system which may one day come to fruition. See **Unified Patent Litigation System**.

Einspruch

German, 'opposition'.

EISPE

Enhanced International Search and Preliminary Examination, under the Patent Co-operation Treaty. This system will ensure that all applications receive an examination, not only those that request an international preliminary examination as formerly, and get an international preliminary report on patentability.

Election

In the demand for an international application filed under the Patent Co-operation Treaty, the applicant's indication of the contracting states in which it intends to use the results of the International Preliminary Examination.

Electronic Frontier Foundation

A digital rights advocacy and legal organisation, based in the US and with accredited observer status at WIPO. Founded by Mitch Kapor, who previously founded Lotus Development Corporation, and John Perry Barlow, retired cattle rancher and lyricist with The Grateful Dead.

Electronic Rights Management Information

According to the Copyright, Designs and Patents Act 1988, as amended:

> 'rights management information' means any information provided by the copyright owner or the holder of any right under the copyright holder which identifies the work, the author, the copyright holder or the holder of any intellectual property rights, or information about the terms and conditions of use of the work, and any numbers or codes that represent such information.

This appears in section 296ZG(7)(b). See **digital rights management**, Z sections.

Embodiment

In patent drafting, a device used to introduce a particular implementation or method of performing or carrying out the invention. Embodiments may feature in the description of the invention or in dependent claims.

Employee

1. A class of author to whose works special ownership rules tend to apply. The English courts are clear that there is no special meaning of the word for intellectual property purposes. It has been considered at great length in employment cases, and the meaning it has in employment law is the one the courts apply in intellectual property cases.
2. In the case of inventions, the usual approach (taken in the UK law) is for the invention to be the property of the employer if it could reasonably be considered part of an employee's remit to invent things. The contract of employment will normally reinforce this situation. Employees may be entitled to compensation for the use of their inventions under the Patents Act 1977.
3. In UK copyright law, rights in works made by an employee in the course of his or her employment vest automatically in the employer. To avoid arguments about whether something was done in the course of the employment (perhaps because it was done off the premises, or out of hours) the contract of employment will usually supplement the statutory provisions.
4. In the case of designs, the provisions about ownership of an employee's work are of similar effect to those relating to copyright (or, for registered designs, patents).

Enablement

See **enabling disclosure**.

Enabling Disclosure

A disclosure of an invention in sufficient detail to enable a skilled person to work the invention. There is no requirement in statute that a novelty-destroying disclosure be an enabling one, but the courts have read such a requirement into it. See Article 83 EPC. Insufficient disclosure is a ground for opposition and also a ground for invalidity under section 72 of the Patents Act 1977 (UK).

End User Licence Agreement

An agreement permitting the end user of a computer program to do certain acts restricted by copyright with that program. The most commonly encountered type of licence, given that we are all end users; other varieties include Value Added Retailer licences and Original Equipment Manufacturer licences.

Enforcement Directive

Directive 2004/48/EC of the European Parliament and of the Council of 29 April 2004 on the enforcement of intellectual property rights (known familiarly as IPRED). It requires all Member States to apply 'effective, dissuasive and proportionate' remedies and penalties (but not criminal offences,which were dropped from early drafts) against those engaged in counterfeiting and piracy. All Member States will therefore have a similar set of measures, procedures and remedies available for rights-holders to defend their intellectual property rights. A second directive (IPRED2) reintroducing criminal sanctions was proposed in 2005, but whether the founding Treaties allow the Community (or now the European Union) to legislate in this area has been questioned.

Enlarged Board of Appeal

An appeal board of the EPO which is charged with ensuring uniform application of the EPC. It does not hear cases, but gives decisions on points of patent law which arise in other proceedings in the EPO or are referred to it by the President of the EPO.

Enola Bean, Yellow Bean

US Patent No. 5,894,079 was granted in 1999 to John Proctor, the president of seed company POD-NERS, LLC, who brought the bean seeds back from Mexico. The claims cover a wide range of yellow beans and can exclude the importation or sale of any yellow bean exhibiting the yellow shade of the Enola beans. Highly controversial, a paradigm case of the alleged detriment that patents can cause to development, led to the **ActionAid Chip** patent application. In 2009, the Proctor patent was revoked by the **CAFC**, but not before it had allegedly caused immense damage to the interests of Mexican farmers.

Enveloppe Soleau

A means for establishing the date of an invention, not unlike the time-honoured method of posting a copy of a copyright work to oneself or one's lawyer (see **Poor Man's Copyright**). It involves submitting a description of the invention to the Institut National pour la Propriété Intellectualle in two envelopes, which are stamped before one is returned to the sender. It may not be opened until there is a dispute over inventorship. It works only in France, though similar procedures are followed in some other countries.

EPC 2000

See **European Patent Convention 2000**.

Epilady

The trade name of the product, launched in 1986 in Israel, involved in a notorious and important European patent case between the patentee, Improver Corporation, and Remington. The British and German courts came to opposite conclusions about whether or not a claim calling for a rotating helical spring was infringed by a rotating rubber bar with slits in it, which performed the same function. See **Improver**.

EPO

See **European Patent Office**.

Equivalent

A patent or patent application in country B that is the same as one in country A, from which it might (but does not have to) claim priority.

Equivalents, Doctrine of

A judicial doctrine which is used to assess whether an alleged infringement is indeed an infringement. It seeks to exclude any trivial variations that have no bearing on the working of an invention. The United States has the best-known and most complicated such doctrine, but other countries such as China and Japan also have them.

The problem is that once the scope of the monopoly has been allowed to exceed the bounds of the claims, as it is acknowledged has happened in the USA, it is difficult to know where to stop. In the leading US case of *Graver Tank & Manufacturing Co Inc v Linde Air Products Company* 339 US 605, 607 (1950), Jackson J said that the American courts had recognised:

> that to permit imitation of a patented invention which does not copy every literal detail would be to convert the protection of the patent grant into a hollow and useless thing. Such a limitation would leave room for – indeed encourage – the unscrupulous copyist to make unimportant and insubstantial changes and substitutions in the patent which, though adding nothing, would be enough to take the copied matter outside the claim, and hence outside the reach of law.

In *Royal Typewriter Co v Remington Rand Inc* (CA2nd Conn) 168 F2nd 691, 692 Learned Hand J said that the purpose of the doctrine of equivalents was 'to temper unsparing logic and prevent an infringer from stealing the benefit of the invention'. The doctrine deliberately extends protection to matters outside the claims which perform substantially the same function in substantially the same way to obtain the same result.

The EPC 2000 introduced a doctrine of equivalents in Europe, although the *Protocol on the Interpretation of Article 69* might be thought to have suggested that there was already one in place:

> For the purpose of determining the extent of protection conferred by a European patent, due account shall be taken of any element which is equivalent to an element specified in the claims.

But that does not amount to extending protection beyond the claims – something which Article 69 itself clearly prohibits. In *Kirin-Amgen Inc & Ors v Hoechst Marion Roussel Ltd & Ors* [2004] UKHL 46, Lord Hoffmann (at para 36ff) reviewed the development of the doctrine and made clear that there was no such thing in the UK. The English courts had not gone outside the claims to catch equivalents: rather, they had approached the problem identified by Learned Hand J by abandoning literality.

Erfindungshöhe

German, 'inventive height'. A concept encountered in German patent law, which requires that an invention must not only be inventive but must possess a minimum degree of inventiveness.

esp@cenet

The EPO's free online patent service. It covers most of the world's patents, and scanned original texts can be downloaded. Very useful.

Essential Features

Objections may be raised against a patent application in the European Patent Office that the description and claims fail to describe the essential features of the invention. Case T 32/82 decided that:

> Article 84 EPC requires, amongst other things, that the claims, which define the matter for which protection is sought . . . be clear. The Board of Appeal considers that this has to be interpreted as meaning not only that the claim from a technical point of view must be comprehensible but also that it must define clearly the object of the invention, that is to say indicate all the essential features thereof.

Essential Function

See **specific subject matter**.

Essential Means

The supplier of essential means for working a patent commits a form of contributory infringement (for example, UK Patents Act 1977, section 60(2)).

Essentially derived variety

A plant variety predominantly derived from another plant variety which retains the essential characteristics that result from the genotype or combination of genotypes of that other variety, and does not exhibit any important (as distinct from cosmetic) features that differentiate it from the other variety.

Estoppel

A legal bar to a right of action that arises from a person's own actions. In the intellectual property world, it is most important in the form of **file wrapper estoppel** in the US.

EULA

See **end user licence agreement**.

Eurasian Patent

Like the European Patent Convention, the Eurasian Patent Convention (EAPC) is a regional special arrangement under the Paris Convention and a regional patent treaty within the meaning of the PCT. The EAPC was signed on 9 September 1994 by the prime ministers of ten Commonwealth of Independent States (CIS) countries – former USSR republics – and came into force on 12 August 1995. It created the Eurasian Patent Organization and the Eurasian Patent Office, based in Moscow and with Russian its official language. Unlike the EPC, it grants unitary patents.

There are currently 12 signatories but only nine of those countries have ratified the Convention, for political reasons – Georgia, the Ukraine and Uzbekistan are the non-signatories. The others cover most of the territory of the former USSR. The Baltic states are not signatories.

Euro-Defences

A colloquial term used to denote defences to intellectual property infringement claims based on European Community principles of competition law or free movement. For example, a defendant might argue that the intellectual property rights owner is abusing a dominant position by enforcing its rights. See **Magill**.

Euro-PCT Route

Filing a European patent application by means of the PCT. For a European applicant, this has the advantage that it keeps the process in the hands of one agent from application until grant. At that point, national **validation** is needed.

Euroace

A database of descriptions of goods and services acceptable to OHIM. Using terms found in the database will minimise the time taken to process a **Community Trade Mark** (CTM) application.

European Community

Created in 1992 by the Maastricht Treaty, the European Community was one of the three pillars of the European Union (the others being Foreign Policy and Defence, and Police and Judicial Co-operation). The Lisbon Treaty did away with the 'three pillars' concept in December 2009 and the **European Union** became the single supranational organisation.

The Community was created out of the three original Communities that were set up in the 1950s: the European Economic Community, the European Coal and Steel Community, and the European Atomic Energy Community.

European Patent

A misnomer. There is really no such thing as a European Patent, although the national patents granted under the European Patent Convention are called by that name, supplemented by the two-letter code identifying the relevant country (DE for Germany; FR for France; GB, oddly, for the United Kingdom).

After grant, each of the national patents has an independent life. Infringement and revocation proceedings can only be taken in national courts, which leads to odd results. The *Improver* litigation (*Improver Corp v Remington Consumer Products Ltd* [1990] FSR. 181) is the classic example of how things can go wrong, with the English and Italian courts finding that there was no infringement while the German, Austrian and Dutch courts reached the opposite conclusion. More recently, in *SEB*

SA v De'Longhi SpA [2002] EWHC 1556 (Pat Ct), [2003] EWCA Civ 952 (Court of Appeal) the English court found that the patent was infringed but invalid for obviousness: the courts in France and Germany found it valid and not infringed.

European Patent Attorney

An individual who has been successful in the European Qualifying Examinations and has been recognised as fit to act as a professional representative before the European Patent Office.

European Patent Convention (EPC)

Properly, the Convention on the Grant of European Patents, signed in Munich on 5 October 1973. One thing it does not provide for, however, is a European Patent – the system is designed to produce bundles of national patents, depending on which countries the applicant has designated. There is a single harmonised procedure leading to the grant of this bundle of national patents, carried out by the European Patent Office.

European Patent Convention 2000

A substantial revision to the EPC, which came into force in December 2007. Its main aim was to bring the EPC into line with the requirements of **TRIPS**, including ensuring that priority may be claimed from an application in any **WTO** member state.

European Patent Litigation Agreement

A dead duck, superseded by the **Unified Patent Litigation System**. It did, however, seem to be a good idea at the time. An excellent idea, indeed. A proposed single European patent litigation system, EPLA would have created a protocol to the EPC allowing for an integrated judicial system and a common European Patent Court, with a court of first instance and an appeal court, working in the three official EPC languages.

European Patent Office

The institution, based in Munich with offices also in Rijswijk (The Hague), where the searching is done, and sub-offices in Berlin and Vienna, which receives applications for and grants European Patents.

European Patent Organisation

An intergovernmental organisation, set up on 7 October 1977 under the **European Patent Convention**. It has two bodies, the **European Patent Office** and the **Administrative Council**, which supervises the Office's activities.

European Qualifying Examination (EQE)

An examination touching upon the competence and aptitude of the candidate to represent applicants before the European Patent Office. See **grandfather**.

European Search Report

The report prepared by the Search Divisions of the **European Patent Office** on a European patent application. See also **Extended European Search Report**.

European Union

Originally created in 1992 by the Maastricht Treaty, based on the three pillars of the European Community, Foreign Policy and Defence, and Police and Judicial Co-operation. In December 2009 the Lisbon Treaty reformed the European Union structure, abolishing the three pillars and making the European Union the key supranational institution in the field.
   See **Directive** and regulation.

Evergreening

The practice of extending patent protection, particularly for pharmaceutical products, by obtaining new patents for improvements, buying up competitors' patents, or simply using trade marks to continue the monopoly after the basic patent has expired.

Ex parte

Civil proceedings brought before a judge by one party alone, without notice to the other. Used in emergency cases where there is no time to go through the normal notification procedures and where an urgent and immediate remedy is required. Common in English intellectual property cases before the Civil Procedure Act, when the grant of an interlocutory injunction would frequently determine the outcome of the litigation without the need for a trial – having been given a clear indication of the relative strengths of the respective parties' cases a settlement was often reached before the matter came to trial some months later.

Ex Post Facto

Latin: literally, 'from that which is done afterwards'. Formulated, enacted or operating retroactively; having retrospective effect.

Examination

The stage of the registration process following the submission of an application for a patent, trademark or registered design. The purpose and extent of the examination varies greatly, between the different rights and from one country or office to another. In trade marks, France conducts the briefest examination, considering only basic formalities, while other offices carry out extensive searches of prior rights and communicate the results of them to both applicant and prior rights owners, and yet others (for example the USA) will refuse applications following a detailed examination. In patents, Italy carries out no examination, Switzerland raises only formal objections, and the USA carries out a very tough formal examination. See also **substantive examination**.

Excluded Matter

Not an expression actually used in the Patents Act, but it is often used to refer to the matters mentioned in section 2(2) which are not inventions for the purposes of the Act. There are four parts to the list, which comprises:

- a discovery, scientific theory or mathematical method;
- a literary, dramatic, musical or artistic work or any other aesthetic creation;
- a scheme, rule or method for performing a mental act, playing a game or doing business, or a program for a computer; or
- the presentation of information.

These matters are however only excluded from the patent system as such, and those two words open up a world of possibilities for securing patent protection for inventions that involve discoveries, scientific theories, computer programs or business methods.

Excusable Non-use

The owner of a US trade mark registration may file a sworn statement or affidavit explaining that the mark is not in use in commerce because of special circumstances that excuse that non-use, and that it is not due to any intention to abandon the mark. The statement must be filed by the current owner and received by the end of each successive ten-year period after the date of registration, with a six-month period of grace. Failure to meet these deadlines results in cancellation.

Exhaustion

1. The doctrine that holds that intellectual property owners cannot, once they have enjoyed the advantage conferred by ownership of the intellectual property by placing goods on the market, take action to prevent their resale, usually in another market where prices are rather higher. This is the phenomenon commonly referred to as parallel importation, and it is an important issue in many parts of the world but particularly in the European Union where IP rights might be used to partition the common market. The key question is whether the goods have been put into free circulation on the market (for example, within the European Economic Area) by the rights owner or with

its consent, and cases in the European Union focus on the question of what amounts to consent for this purpose. Other important cases explore the circumstances in which the rights are not exhausted, including where a trade mark owner can oppose further marketing of pharmaceutical products that have been repackaged to suit the prescribing habits of doctors in other national markets.

In the European Union, it is well established that exhaustion happens at the level of the European Economic Area – the fact that goods have been placed on the market outside the EEA does not mean that rights are exhausted. The UK government, sensing potential for electoral advantage in persuading electors that they were being 'ripped off' as a result of price differentials, sought briefly in the mid-1990s to convince other Member States that international exhaustion was a better rule (so first marketing anywhere would exhaust the rights). It did not prevail.

International exhaustion, though it does not run in the EEA, does run in other parts of the world. In the BBS aluminium wheels case, the Japanese Supreme Court recognised the doctrine.

2.   The sensation experienced part-way through reading any judgment of the Court of Justice of the European Union.

Exhibition Priority

A rule found in some but not all patent and design laws (the **EPC** being a notable exception) providing that disclosing matter at an exhibition (usually a limited range of international exhibitions) does not destroy novelty. Given the fact that many systems have no such rule, it is unwise to rely too much on it. Grace periods have similar effect.

Experimental Use

Patent systems throughout the world require a full disclosure of the invention – a complete contribution of the inventor's learning to the common pool, where others can draw on it, though not to compete with the inventor. Accordingly, patent laws generally make clear that experimental use is not an infringement, while containing rules to prevent **springboarding** – developing a competing product under the guise of experimental use.

Section 60(5)(a) of the Patents Act 1977 allows researchers to conduct experiments without fear of infringing someone's patent rights, but only in relation to the subject-matter of the invention. The scope of the exception is far from clear, and there is no case law to provide guidance on how far the statute goes. As **Gowers** noted:

> uses in relation to the subject matter of a patent are generally covered by the exception, while uses relating to different subject matter are not covered by the exception. Confusion arises because there is no definition of what is in relation to, and what is different from the subject matter. (Para 4.5)

The possibility of facing expensive litigation deters many researchers from taking advantage of the exception ('Patents for Genetic Sequences: the Competitiveness of Current UK Law and Practices', Intellectual Property Institute for the DTI, 2004; and see the **Manchester Manifesto**) and apart from the exception Gowers quotes reports that show high fees being demanded and access to research material being refused.

See also **Bolar exemption**, which deals with the special area of pharmaceuticals and clinical trials.

Section 7A(2)(b) of the Registered Designs Act 1949 (as amended, reflecting Article 13(1)(b) of Directive 98/71/EC) provides that the rights in a registered design are not infringed by any act done for experimental purposes, which is less comprehensible in a system of law that protects appearence, not function.

Expert Option, Expert Solution

Where an applicant for a European Patent relating to a micro-organism has deposited a sample with the International Depositary Authority under the Budapest Treaty, it can specify that until the patent is granted, samples can be released only to an appointed independent expert.

Extended Collective Licence

Known in the Scandinavian countries, a form of statutory collective licence which extends to the works of copyright owners who are not members of the collecting society that administers the scheme. It applies only to works of the same description as those covered by the voluntary licence and the terms are the same for ordinary members and non-members. Authors may refuse permission for the reproduction of their work, but non-members are entitled to receive remuneration for the use of their works on the same basis as members of the society.

In the UK, the Digital Economy Bill initially contained provisions that would have made extended collective licensing widespread. When the bill became the Digital Economy Act 2010, however, these provisions had been dropped. See **orphan work**.

Extended European Search Report

The sum of the **European Search Report** and the opinion based thereon. Before 1 April 2010 it was not compulsory to respond to the opinion, but it is now. The time limit is six months from when the European Patent Bulletin announces the publication of the search report, which also happens to be the time limit for requesting examination. Now that the search opinion has the status of a conventional (see **official or office action**), failure to respond in time will result in the application being deemed to be withdrawn.

Extension of Patent Term

The duration of certain patents (commonly pharmaceutical patents) can be extended in many countries to reflect the long time it may take for a product to obtain the necessary approvals and come to market. This is often in the form of a **supplementary Protection Certificate**, a creature of European Community law in one manifestation, which is strictly speaking not an extension of the patent term but is rather hard to distinguish from one. In the US, an extension can be secured for the time between the date of grant of the patent and the date of the Food and Drug Administration (FDA) marketing approval, provided that the sum of this period and the patent term remaining at the approval date is at least 14 years.

In the old British law, it was possible to obtain an extension on grounds of inadequate remuneration, but it was necessary to go to court for it and to present a very compelling case with a great deal of evidence. In *Fairey Aviation's Patent* [1969] RPC 281, [1969] FSR 526, a ten-year extension was given for Concorde's droop-snoot.

Exxon

Not a literary work, in UK copyright law. The Court of Appeal held in *Exxon Corporation and others v Exxon Insurance Consultants International Limited* [1982] Ch 119 that there could be no copyright in the invented word 'Exxon', which the oil company tried to argue was a literary work, because of its very modest extent. Referring to the judgment of Davey L.J.

in *Hollinrake v Truswell* [1894] 3 Ch. 420, 428, where he said: 'Now, a literary work is intended to afford either information and instruction, or pleasure, in the form of literary enjoyment', the Court decided (in the words of Oliver LJ as he then was):

> that for which protection is sought in the instant case does not appear to me to have any of the qualities which commonsense would demand. It conveys no information; it provides no instruction; it gives no pleasure that I can conceive; it is simply an artificial combination of four letters of the alphabet which serves a purpose only when it is used in juxtaposition with other English words, to identify one or other of the companies in the plaintiffs' group. Whether, as might perhaps be the case if one followed up the suggestion made in the judgment of Graham J, the insertion of the extra 'x' was to avoid the risk of involving the Bishop of Exeter in proceedings for infringement every time he wrote to *The Times* newspaper, I do not pause to inquire.

The plaintiffs did however succeed in a passing off claim, so the lack of copyright protection did not seriously inconvenience them.

F

Faccenda

Faccenda Chicken Ltd v Fowler [1985] 1 All ER 724 is an English breach of confidence case involving information about customers and the best route to follow in order to make deliveries to them. At first instance Goulding J divided information into three classes:

- information that, because of its trivial character or its easy accessibility from public sources, cannot be regarded as confidential;
- information that an employee must treat as confidential, but which, once learned, reasonably remains in the employee's head and becomes part of his skill and experience; and
- specific **trade secrets** so confidential that a continuing duty of confidence applies even beyond the termination of the employment or the service contract.

There was no restrictive covenant in the contract of employment in this case, so the question was how far an implied obligation of confidentiality would run. The Court of Appeal held that the information in suit did not constitute trade secrets and the defendant had not breached his obligation. The judgment remains of great importance.

Fair and Reasonable Conditions

Appropriate conditions according to the European Commission's Seventh (Research) Framework Programme (2007–2013) (FP7) rules. These include possible financial terms taking account of the specific circumstances of the request for access: for example, the actual or potential value of the foreground or background to which access is requested, or the scope, duration or other characteristics of the proposed use. See also **FRAN**.

Fair Dealing

The rubric under which a number of specific activities are permitted under UK copyright law. Fair dealing is permitted for purposes of private study and non-commercial research, reporting current events, and criticism and review. Such permitted acts must conform to the classic **three-step test**.

The UK law concept is confusingly similar, in name at least, to that of **'fair use'** in US copyright law. As between themselves, publishers operate their own 'fair dealing rule', under which there is no charge for a single quote of up to 400 words, or several quotes of up to 800 words, any one not exceeding 300 words.

Fair Use

US copyright law allows fair use of copyright works. Unlike the equivalent provisions in UK copyright law, which permit certain types of fair dealing, this is not limited to specific situations or activities.

When Congress codified the fair use doctrine in 17 USC. § 107, it set out a list of four, non-exhaustive, factors that determine whether a use is fair:

1. the purpose and character of the use, including whether the use is commercial or for nonprofit educational purposes;
2. the nature of the copyrighted work;
3. the amount and substantiality of the portion used in relation to the copyrighted work as a whole; and
4. the effect of the use on the potential market for or value of the copyrighted work. Courts have added several additional factors.

These factors appear in copyright laws in Hong Kong (section 38 of the Copyright Ordinance), Singapore (Copyright Act, section 35), and Israel (Copyright Act 2007, section 19).

False Attribution, Right Against

Under UK copyright law a person has the right not to have a work falsely attributed to him or her. The right covers a false statement about the authorship of a literary, dramatic, musical or artistic work or about the directorship of a film. It makes no difference whether the statement is express or implied. In *Moore v News of the World* [1972] 1 QB 441 the divorced wife of a well-known television and film star had attributed to her an article which appeared in the *News of the World* about her former marriage. The late Alan Clark MP invoked the provision in his action against the *Evening Standard* which was running a spoof diary column attributed to him: he also took action for passing off (*Clark v Associated Newspapers Ltd* [1998] RPC 261). To widespread surprise, he succeeded in both claims.

False Suggestion (US)

A ground for revoking a patent, where the patent was obtained on a false suggestion or representation. Cf. **fraud on the USPTO**.

Famous

A famous trade mark obtains protection under US laws from dilution. In the European Union, it is marks with reputations that enjoy this extra protection, though this implies the existence of trade marks with no reputation whatsoever, which seems illogical. Not to be confused with **well-known trade marks** – though it would be very easy to do so.

Fanciful

A quality that is likely to make a trade mark more registrable than one that is not fanciful. See also **arbitrary**.

Farmer's Rights

Rights held by local and indigenous communities and farmers of all regions, including:

(a)   protection of traditional knowledge relevant to plant genetic resources for food and agriculture;
(b)   the right to equitably participate in sharing benefits arising from the utilization of plant genetic resources for food and agriculture; and
(c)   the right to participate in making decisions, at the national level, on matters related to the conservation and sustainable use of plant genetic resources for food and agriculture.

(See Article 9.2 of the Food and Agriculture Organization of the United Nations International Treaty on Plant Genetic Resources for Food and Agriculture which is responsible for the split infinitive). See also farmers' exception.

Farmers' Exception

Article 15(2) of the **International Convention for the Protection of New Varieties of Plants** allows (but does not oblige) contracting parties to restrict the breeder's right in relation to any variety in order to permit farmers to use for propagating purposes, on their own holdings, the product of the harvest which they have obtained by planting, on their own holdings, the protected variety.

Feist

The abbreviated name of the case (*Feist Publications, Inc., v. Rural Telephone Service Co.*, 499 US 340 (1991)) in which the Supreme Court of the US held that copyright did not subsist in a white pages (alphabetical) telephone directory, and drove a nail into the coffin of the '**sweat of the brow**' test.

Festo

The doctrine of equivalents (see equivalents, doctrine of) and file wrapper estoppel came together in *Festo Corp v Shoketsu Kinzoku Kogyo KK*, 535 US 722 (2002) – the last in a long series of cases in the dispute. If the patentee accepts a restriction in order to obtain a patent (which is revealed on the file wrapper or prosecution history), does the restriction apply to all equivalents? The Supreme Court held (in a unanimous opinion given by Justice Kennedy) that the question was not whether the estoppel applied to amendments, but to what extent the amendment surrendered coverage of the claim. The inventor's rights should not be reduced if the amendment were made to clarify a translation, but if the change were made to deal with an overlap with another patent the applicant should be assumed to have given up the right to complain about matters broader than the patent claim. The decision to narrow a claim to comply with the Patent Act assumes the surrender of the territory between the original claim and the amended claim – in other words, all the equivalents to the limitation are assumed to be surrendered. The burden of showing which equivalents were not surrendered falls on the applicant.

There may however be cases where the amendment cannot be considered a surrender of a particular equivalent:

The equivalent may have been unforeseeable at the time of the application; the rationale underlying the amendment may bear no more than a tangential relation to the equivalent in question; or there may be some other reason suggesting that the patentee could not reasonably be expected to have described the insubstantial substitute in question. In those cases the patentee can overcome the presumption that prosecution history estoppel bars a finding of equivalence.

Field of Activity, Common

See **common field of activity**.

Field of Use

An expression often encountered in connection with patents, and especially in patent licensing arrangements. A licence might be granted allowing the licensee to work the patent within a carefully defined field of use. There might then be room for other licensees to be granted exclusive rights in other fields of use, or for the patent owner itself to continue to work the patent.

Figurative Trade Mark

The expression used in the Community trade mark system to denote what is referred to elsewhere as a **device** or design trade mark, or more colloquially as a logo.

File Wrapper Estoppel

The file wrapper contains the entire prosecution history of an old-style US patent. On grant, this would become available to the public, and would reveal admissions and concessions made during the prosecution. In subsequent litigation, the patentee would be estopped from arguing contrary to the evidence of the file wrapper. The idea applies not only in the US but also in other countries where access to files is allowed.

Filesharing

The activity of allowing other people to have access to computer files, usually involving the use of the Internet. Although it can be a perfectly innocent activity (as when the author of this *Dictionary* uploads monthly intellectual property updates for anyone interested to download) it can also involve the sharing of unauthorised copies of copyright works. In the classic case, the shared file is a sound recording or film.

Dealing with such activities is a major challenge for copyright laws. Litigation against the peer-to-peer filesharing site Napster foundered because the offending website did not actually offer copies of the files: it merely introduced those seeking files to others who had them on their computers (hence, peer-to-peer). Rights owners then started suing the people doing the sharing, a tactic that was never likely to make them popular.

Film

A recording on any medium from which a moving image may by any means be produced (Copyright, Designs and Patents Act 1988 section 5B).

Film Rights

A colloquial name given to the rights protected by copyright that control the right to make a film (or, perhaps more accurately, a screenplay) from a literary or dramatic work. The film or screenplay will be an adaptation (in UK copyright parlance) or a derivative work (US) requiring the consent of the owner of the literary or dramatic copyright. Frequently the subject of the grant of options to purchase the copyright at a future date (when the arrangements necessary for making the film have been put in place, and production is 'greenlighted' or 'greenlit').

First Medical Use Claim

A claim to the use of a known substance as a medicament, in the form 'use of a compound [formula] as a therapeutic substance', or similar words. Such claims are found particularly in the EPO.

First Sale Doctrine

A limitation on copyright in the United States, recognised in *Bobbs-Merrill Co v Straus* 210 US 339 (1908) and subsequently codified in the copyright law (see now 17 USC § 109). A purchaser may transfer a lawful copy of a copyright work without infringing the copyright owner's rights. A similar doctrine applies in trade mark law, and in patent law. Equivalent to the doctrine of **exhaustion**.

First to File, First to Register

The principle on which most registered intellectual property systems operate: the first person to file an application gets the rights. The most important exception to this general rule is the US patent system, which works on a **first to invent** basis. However, it is still possible in any system that the person who files the first application was not entitled to do so, and laws provide for the resolution of disputes about such matters.

First to Invent

The principle, found in the US patent system, that the person entitled to a patent is its inventor (referring to the first inventor of something is surely a tautology). An application might be filed by someone who thinks they devised the invention, unaware of the claim of another who has not made his invention public. This leads to what are known, in that wonderfully graphic way in which the English language is often used in the United States, as interference actions, or just interferences.

First to Use

In common law countries, the principle that governs entitlement to a registered trade mark – except that, under the malevolent influence of European Community law, the UK and Ireland have moved towards a first to file system.

Flexibilities

A term of art in the context of the discretionary policy space now built into international treaties like TRIPS. Formerly such treatics merely set minimum standards.

Fong Kong

Something that is very obviously fake, plastic or unbelievable, and therefore by extension **counterfeit goods (counterfeiting)**. Originated among South African youth in the early 2000s. **Zhing-zhong** has the same meaning.

Footprint

Of a communications satellite, the ground area within which its transponders offer coverage. Replete with copyright problems, especially if the footprint crosses national frontiers. See **Bogsch theory**.

Foreground Intellectual Property

Intellectual property generated by a joint venture of some sort. It is called by this name in the joint venture's documents to distinguish it from background intellectual property, which is brought to the joint venture by the parties.

Foreign Filing

The filing of an application in countries other than the country of first filing, which normally takes place towards the end of the 12-month **priority** period but can be done later. On the latter point, see **non-con filing**.

Formal Examination

The examination of an application for compliance with formalities, as opposed to the later substantive examination (if performed) which judges whether the rights requested in the application can be granted.

Formalities, Formalities Officer

IP applications, particularly patent ones, generate a considerable volume of purely formal correspondence. Patent attorneys often employ staff specifically to deal with these matters, as opposed to the substantive questions about patentability that are proper to qualified practitioners.

Format Rights

An imaginary form of intellectual property, the non-existence of which (under the copyright law of New Zealand, at least) was confirmed in *Green v New Zealand Broadcasting Organisation* [1989] RPC 700 (Privy Council). Hughie Green unsuccessfully claimed copyright in scripts and the dramatic format of the TV show *Opportunity Knocks*.

Such rights are however recognised at law in some jurisdictions: in Brazil, a claim that an unauthorised version of *Big Brother* infringed copyright succeeded in 2004. Passing off and unfair competition laws may also assist, and clearly there is scope for using registered trade marks and perhaps registered designs to protect elements of the format of a TV show. However, the International Format Lawyers Association states that there is no specific, tailored, legal format right in any country that they know of.

The most important element in the legal protection of formats is peer pressure, or the simple fact that format rights are extensively traded and licensed and make a great deal of money for the owners of the non-existent rights in them – which means that the rights, adopting a realist perspective, do exist.

Bournemouth University has carried out research into the subject of format rights, including analysing 59 legal decisions from around the world. The results of this work are summarised at http://tvformats. bournemouth.ac.uk/index.html.

Format Shifting

The activity of converting digital files – usually, but not necessarily, music or video – from one format to another, for example from CD to MP3. It is not permitted under UK copyright law, though the BPI (formerly the British Phonographic Industry Limited) acknowledges that it would be unreasonable to try to control it. The urban myths that substitute in many people's minds for a proper grasp of copyright law hold that this activity is permissible, based on the principle that people have already 'bought' what they refer to as 'their' music and should be entitled to transfer it from one format to another. **Gowers** supported this view.

Often used interchangeably with the expression 'media shifting', which more expressly includes the notion of moving the file from one type of storage device to another.

Formstein Defence

A defence closely related to the UK's *Gillette* defence and the US *Wilson* case. In the landmark *Formstein* ('moulded kerbstone') case, 28 IIC 795 (1987) the *Bundesgrichtshof* (Federal Supreme Court of Germany) confirmed that Section 14 of the Patentgesetz (1981), which corresponds to Art. 69 of the European Patent Convention, also covers equivalents. The Court limited the application of this theory by the following principle: 'The defence that the embodiment alleged to be an equivalent would not be patentable over the prior art is admissible.'

So, in other words, it is open to the defendant to argue that the equivalent element, notwithstanding that it might fall within the scope of protection of the patent, cannot be regarded as an infringement if it does not in itself constitute a patentable invention. The reasoning behind this defence is the simple proposition that prior art may not be taken away from the public and protected by patent law.

Fox

See **hedgehog**.

FRAN

Fair, reasonable and non-discriminatory, a concept of importance in certain licensing transactions, in particular where patented technology is essential for compliance with a technical standard (on which, see for example *Nokia v Interdigital* [2007] UKHC (Pat) 445).

Fraud on the PTO

Obtaining a patent or trademark by concealing or misrepresenting facts.

Free Beer Claim

A claim in a patent to a solution to a known problem that does not define the means used. In effect, the claim is to the desired result with only a narrow disclosure (if any) to support it – it invites the skilled person to make the invention, then claims ownership of it. If the claim is a free beer claim, it will be invalid for insufficiency, so the fact that it is one is a ground for objection.

John Richards links the expression to the alcoholic reward given to operators of Newsham's patented improved 'New Water Engine for Quenching and Extinguishing fiers [*sic*]' (1725) (see his paper 'Firefighting and Intellectual Property', at http://www.ladas.com/generallantepest/firefighting.html), but as he says this is mere conjecture on his part – and the means seems to be clearly set out in the Newsham patent, which would not have been examined very carefully back in 1725. See also David Musker's hugely entertaining (though somewhat controversial) article 'The Great Free Beer Debate: Or, What Ales the Patent System', *Journal of Intellectual Property Law and Practice*, 2, pp. 799–804, 2007.

Free Software Foundation

A body set up by **Richard Stallman** in 1985 to oversee the **GNU Project**, based on four freedoms:

- the freedom to run the software for any purpose;
- the freedom to study how the software works and to adapt it;
- the freedom to redistribute copies of the software; and
- the freedom to improve the software, and to release those improvements.

It will be seen that free software is unconstrained by legal restrictions, not necessarily gratis.

Freedom to operate (FTO)

The ability to perform a process or make a product without infringing someone else's patent; a patent search (and associated report) directed to the question whether there are any existing patents or applications that might be infringed if the person commissioning the search does what he hoped to be able to do. See also **clearance search.**

Freeze plus Compromise

A fudge devised by the Commission and the European Parliament to allow the Directive on the legal protection of designs to be adopted. The degree of protection given to designs for certain spare parts was highly contentious: UK legislation addressed the problem with a '**must-match**' exception that effectively denied protection to designs for visible parts of a complex product (in practice, this concerned car body panels, windows and lamps) whereas some other Member States were quite unaware that there was a problem. The compromise allowed Member States to retain their existing rules ('freeze') and to amend them, but only in the direction of reducing protection ('plus'; although some might think 'minus' would have been the better word to use). The Directive also required the Commission to return to the issue after a period of reflection to try once again to achieve the impossible. It was not successful.

Fuliginous Obscurity

The description applied to section 4 of the Trade Marks Act 1938 by Mackinnon LJ in *Bismag v Amblins*. 'Fuliginous' – a word perhaps known only to trade mark lawyers – comes from the Latin, *fuliginosus*, meaning full of soot.

Full Title Guarantee

The Law of Property (Miscellaneous Provisions) Act 1994 provides, in section 1, that certain covenants will be implied in any disposition of property (including **things in action**: note that this does not include patents, although they are property so are probably swept up by the wider expression). Full title guarantee implies that:

- The disposing party has the right to dispose of the property (section 2(1)(a)).
- The disposing party will do all it reasonably can to give the title it purports to give, at its own cost (section 2(1)(b) and (2)).
- If the property being disposed of is registered, there is a presumption that the whole of the property in the registered title is being disposed of (section 2(3)).
- The disposal is free from all charges, encumbrances and adverse rights, except any charges, encumbrances or adverse rights about

which the seller does not know and could not reasonably be expected to know, that is, free from all known encumbrances (section 3(1)).

See also **limited title guarantee.**

Functional

Aspects of the design of an article that make it work, and are generally matters for patent protection if they can be protected at all. Design law being concerned with the appearance of articles, it commonly excludes protection for features dictated solely by function. This unfortunate wording appears in the UK Registered Designs Act. Few features of a design do not leave the designer with a tiny bit of freedom, so the scope of this exclusion is far from clear. Protection was also limited to designs with eye-appeal, but now designs are protected without such a requirement throughout the European Union.

Further Processing

The EPO allows applicants to miss deadlines, giving two months from the date of a communication reporting the lapse of the application within which to respond. If the applicant responds to the notice of lapse, the lapse is withdrawn and the application proceeds. The fee is modest, and no questions are asked (unlike the procedure for **restoration**).

Fysh, Michael (1940–)

The second judge to be appointed to the Patents County Court (2001). He has now retired and Colin Birss QC appointed in his place. He also became Chairman of the Copyright Tribunal. Some have suggested that two poison chalices at once is more than anyone should have to deal with.

G

GCC Patent

A form of regional patent within the Gulf Co-Operation Council, like **ARIPO**, **OAPI**, Eurasian or European.

Gebrauchsmuster

A patent-like intellectual property right known to German and Austrian law, which provides protection for product inventions only. The term of protection is only ten years. The right is known in English (but not in England) as a **utility model**.

In German law, under the *Gebrauchsmustergesetz* and the V*erordnung zur Ausführung des Gebrauchsmustergesetzes* novelty and inventive step are still necessary, but the prior art does not include oral disclosures, only written ones. Prior use in public is not taken into account unless it was in Germany. There is a six-month grace period, covering written disclosures or prior public use by the applicant or their predecessors in title.

In the German system, they become available to the public from the date of entry in the *Register of Utility Models* (*Eintragungstag*), which precedes the date of announcement in the *Patent Bulletin* (*Bekanntmachung im Patentblatt*)

In Austria, a search report is prepared within six to eight months after filing, without payment of an additional fee. Protection can be given to computer programs, processes and methods of treatment of animals. Otherwise the law is similar to the German.

Gene Patents

Nothing can be relied upon to stir up greater controversy, although patents for gene sequences, or for all possible uses of the gene, are not available. Patent laws require a degree of utility or industrial application, and while a gene sequence may be central to the invention the patent will protect something other than the gene sequence itself.

General Exclusion Order (s 337)

From section 337 ITC Proceeding (US); see **ITC**.

General Public Licence

Probably the most important open-source licence, and one of the most extreme. The current version is GPLv3. See **copyleft**.

Generic, Genericide

1. A trade mark will be refused registration (or, if registered, will be invalid) if it is generic. In the 1994 Act and the Directive, this means that it consists exclusively of signs or indications which have become customary in the current language or in the bona fide and established practices of the trade, hence 'genericide'.
2. A generic drug is one that is an exact duplicate of an earlier patented one, the patent having expired (or being due to do so shortly). Generics are not sold by reference to a brand. Pharmaceutical companies try to stretch their exclusive rights by **evergreening** or **life cycle management**.

Geneva Conventions

A series of four international agreements (with associated protocols) dated between 1864 and 1849 dealing with humanitarian concerns in times of war. The expression 'Geneva Convention' indicates the 1949 consolidating Convention, which deals *inter alia* with the red cross, red crescent, red crystal and red lion with sun symbols (the last, peculiar to Iran, no longer in use but maintained as a protected symbol as that country reserves the right to resume using it) in their protective use: they also serve as signs to identify the organisations that are members of the International Red Cross and Red Crescent Movement. Because their protective function would be compromised, the use (not merely the registration) of the symbols as a trade mark is prohibited by the Conventions and by provisions in many national and regional trade mark laws.

See also **International Convention for the Protection of New Varieties of Plants**.

Genuine Use

A trade mark may be revoked if it has not been used by the trade mark owner (or, usually, with its permission) for five years. To save a trade mark from a non-use challenge, the use to which it is put must be genuine use and not 'merely colourable' or token use. The trade mark owner must be prepared to meet demand for its goods or services if such demand should arise: non-use resulting from a lack of demand, however, does not in itself count against the registration.

Geographical Indication

A right that protects geographical names used as signs to identify goods originating in a specific territory where a given quality, reputation or other characteristic of the goods is essentially attributable to their geographical origin. See **Protected Geographical Indication.**

Geographical Name

A word not very suitable for use as a trade mark, but since *York TM* the law in the UK has changed to allow the possibility of such names being registered.

Geschmacksmuster

An 'aesthetic model' (cf. *Gebrauchsmuster*, or **utility model**) protected under German law for 20 years. It protects the visual design of objects that are not purely functional or utilitarian.

Get-Up

The visual appearance of a product, part of the image or overall impression created by the product or its packaging in the marketplace: one of the indicia that a passing off action is apt to protect. The **Jif** case is a classic instance of a passing off action being used for this purpose. See also **trade dress**.

Gillette Defence

A rather elegant defence to a patent (or by extension other intellectual property) infringement action first deployed in (and named after) *Gillette Safety Razor Co v Anglo-American Trading Co Ltd* [1913] RPC 465: if the act complained of is indeed an infringement of the patent, then the patent is invalid – if the the claim is wide enough to catch the alleged infringement, the claimed invention is obvious.

The defence is not limited to obviousness. In *Hickman v Andrews* [1983] RPC 14 (CA), Goff LJ said:

> If a defendant to an infringement action can show that he has merely developed an existing article other than the patentable article itself with no more than non-patentable changes of size or substitution of mechanical equivalents, then he shows that the alleged infringement is not novel, from which it must follow, without even reading the specification, that the plaintiff is impaled on one or other of the horns of dilemma. Either his invention is also not novel and the patent is invalid, or there is no infringement.

See, for a more recent example, Jacob J in *Mabuchi Motor KK's patents* [1996] RPC 1995.

Global Assessment

What is needed in EU trade mark law to determine whether there is a likelihood of confusion. Only when all other components of a complex mark are negligible is it permissible to make the comparison on the basis of the dominant element. See for example the **CJEU** decision in Case C-334/05P, *Shaker/Limoncello* 12 June 2007.

Global Patent Warming

A phrase coined by Alison Brimelow, then president of the **European Patent Office** on 8 September 2008 to describe the phenomenon of dramatic increases in the volume of patent applications, consequent backlogs in examining them and delays in granting.

GNU Project

A mass collaboration to create free software and in the first place a free operating system, launched in 1983 by **Richard Stallman**. The name is a reverse acronym for Gnu's Not Unix. The collaboration used a form of licence called the **General Public Licence**.

Going National

Entering the national phase of an international patent application.

Goodwill

'An intangible asset of a business', according to Stanley Berwin, 'which can take years to develop and minutes to destroy.' Or: 'An elusive compound, which includes personal goodwill, goodwill of site, goodwill of name and/or reputation and, to further confuse the issue, the somewhat metaphysical goodwill adopted by accountants, who lump together as "goodwill" any potential future gain which may be derived from assets not otherwise identifiable', according to Mr P. Gerber, Deputy President of the Administrative Appeals Tribunal, Taxation Appeals Division, in appeal No. QT95/14 AAT No. 10536 Income Tax (Brisbane, 1995). The paucity of authority from the UK courts justifies raiding the Australian law reports, though Mr Gerber's review of the authorities and his own delightful contribution to the jurisprudence of goodwill makes any further justification unnecessary.

First, though, according to HM Revenue and Customs 'Corporate Intangibles Research and Development Manual' (CIRD30535), 'Intangible assets: notes on accounting practice: definition and when to capitalise: goodwill': 'Goodwill is the difference between the consideration payable for a business and the aggregate fair value of its identifiable assets less liabilities' (www.hmrc.gov.uk/manuals/cirdmanual/cird30535.htm).

This may be a useful definition for a tax inspector or an accountant, but for an intellectual property lawyer the famous definition put forward by Lord Macnaughton in *IRC v Muller and Co's Margarine* [1901] AC 217 at 223 might be more helpful:

> the benefit and advantage of the good name, reputation and connection of a business. It is the attractive force which brings in custom. It is the one thing which distinguishes an old-established business from a new business at its first start.

The nineteenth-century Lord Chancellor, Lord Eldon, was a pioneer in this area of law (see 'Lord Eldon's Goodwill' by Ian Tregoning, *King's Law Journal*, 15 (1), pp. 93–116 (2004)). In *Cruttwell v Lye* (1810) 17 Ves

335 at p. 346, Lord Eldon observed: 'The good-will, which has been the subject of sale is nothing more than the probability, that the old customers will resort to the old place.'

In *Churton v Douglas* (1859) Johns 174; 70 ER 385 Sir W Page-Wood VC noted (at p. 188) that Lord Eldon's view of goodwill was 'too narrow' and substituted his own view:

(I)t appears to me that, when the defendant parted with the good-will of the business to the Plaintiffs, he handed over to them all the benefit that might be derived from holding themselves out as the persons interested in that particular business, which business has been identified as being carried on by the particular firm.

Trego v Hunt (1886) AC 7 involved the extent to which a vendor of a business may compete with the purchaser absent a restraint provision in the contract of sale, to which may be added the observation of Warrington J who, in *Hill v Fearis* (1905) 1 Ch 466, after noting the speeches of Lords Herschell and Macnaghten in *Trego*, stated (at p. 471):

the goodwill of a business is the advantage, whatever it may be, which a person gets by continuing to carry on and being entitled to represent to the outside world that he is carrying on a business which has been carried on for some time previously.

Mr Gerber thought that:

the bulk of these early cases do little more than reflect a 19th century view of free trade, reflecting a laissez-faire philosophy, Lord Macnaghten observing in *Trego* that Sir George Jessel MR (in *Ginesi v Cooper* 14 ChD 599) 'went too far' in holding 'that a person who had sold the goodwill of his business could not even deal with his former customers'. Indeed, searching through the Year Books for cases dealing with the rights and wrongs of restraint of trade, that is, having sold the 'goodwill', may the vendor continue in the very kind of business he has sold – 'to withdraw from the purchaser the benefit of his purchase', do little to help me in determining whether a taxi licence contains an element of goodwill for purposes of capital gains tax.

The *Margarine* case turned on two questions: (1) was the agreement to sell the manufacturing business (carried on abroad) 'made' in England? and (2) was the goodwill of this business property 'locally situate out of the United Kingdom' for purposes of the Stamp Act 1891? Lord Macnaghten observed:

Goodwill is composed of a variety of elements. It differs in its composition in different trades and in different businesses in the same trade. One element may preponderate here and another element there. To analyse goodwill and split it up into its component parts, to pare it down as the Commissioners desire to do until nothing is left but a dry residuum ingrained in the actual place where the business is carried on while everything else is in the air, seems to me to be as useful for practical purposes as it would be to resolve the human body into the various substances of which it is said to be composed. The goodwill of a business is one whole, and in a case like this it must be dealt with as such. For my part, I think that if there is one attribute common to all cases of goodwill it is the attribute of locality. For goodwill has no independent existence. It cannot subsist by itself. It must be attached to a business.

Lord Brampton asked himself (at p. 230):

Was the goodwill in this case, when it was purchased by the company, 'property locally situate out of the United Kingdom'? The answer to this depends, in my judgment, upon whether at the time of the making of the written contract, the goodwill was attached to and incorporated with the business premises and formed in the hands of the then vendor an inseparable property, very valuable in its combination as giving to the premises a character and an increase of the value which, stripped of the goodwill, they would not have possessed and which represents the value of the profit-earning quality of those premises, when and so long as they are used by the then occupier, for carrying on in them the business he had created within them by reason of the attraction of customers from any of those causes which tend to make a prosperous business.

Finally, Lord Lindley (at p. 235), noted:

Goodwill regarded as property has no meaning except in connection with some trade, business, or calling. In that connection I understand the word to include whatever adds value to a business by reason of situation, name and reputation, connection, introduction to old customers, and agreed absence from competition, or any of these things, and there may be others which do not occur to me. In this wide sense, goodwill is inseparable from the business to which its adds value, and, in my opinion, exists where the business is carried on.

Quoting Mr Gerber, *Whiteman Smith Morton Co v Chaplin* (1934) 2KB 35 'resuscitated the somewhat obscure monograph on goodwill by Mr SPJ Merlin (Butterworth and Co 1907) in which the author divided goodwill, like Gaul, into three parts, one part ruled over by the cat, another governed by the dog and the third by the rat.' This epigram, described by Mr Gerber as 'charming, if somewhat simplistic', appealed to Scrutton LJ, who noted (at p. 42) that:

(T)he cat prefers the old home to the person who keeps it, and stays in the old home though the person who has kept the house leaves. The cat represents that part of the customers who continue to go to the old shop, though the shopkeeper has gone; the probability of their custom may be regarded as an additional value given to the premises by the tenant's trading. The dog represents that part of the customers who follow the person rather than the place . . . There remains a class of customer who may neither follow the place nor the person, but drift away elsewhere. They are neither a benefit to the landlord nor the tenant, and have been called 'the rat' for no particular reason except to keep the epigram in the animal kingdom.

Mr Gerber concluded his review of the English cases by saying: 'The inadequacy of dividing goodwill into only three parts was already obvious to Maugham LJ, who in the same case felt compelled to add the rabbit (at p. 50). I am tempted to add the Falcon (*falconis australis*), that bird of prey which hovers over its marked territory hunting for its daily fare.' Far from being the preserve of accountants, perhaps it is zoologists to whom we should look for guidance on the subject.

Gottschalk v Benson (US)

A key Supreme Court decision (409 US 63 (1972)) on the patentability of computer software, where it held that a process claim directed to a numerical algorithm, as such, was not patentable because 'the patent would wholly pre-empt the mathematical formula and in practical effect would be a patent on the algorithm itself'. That would amount effectively to allowing a patent over an abstract idea. The Court added, however: 'it is said that the decision precludes a patent for any program servicing a computer. We do not so hold.'

Government Use

It is common to find provisions in intellectual property statutes that permit governments to use patented inventions or registered designs without having to ask, and without infringing the exclusive rights. Compensation might have to be paid, depending on what the law says. The provisions will probably only be capable of being invoked for reasons of national security or some other crisis. See also **Crown use**.

Gowers, Andrew

Former editor of the *Financial Times* who was commissioned by HM Treasury in 2005 to review the intellectual property system in the UK, to widespread surprise given that the form of the UK's laws on the subject are largely dictated by European Community Directives and international treaties.

The review was published in December 2006. Its main substantive recommendations included introducing a fast-track application procedure for trade marks (and enhancing the existing fast-track patent application), increasing penalties for counterfeiting and piracy (including removing the difference in penalties for online and real-world infringements) and clarifying the rights of users under copyright law. An extension of the term of protection for sound recordings was rejected, as was the introduction of petty patents. The opportunity to consider whether the action for passing off had developed (as Lord Justice Aldous had suggested in *Arsenal v Reed* it had) into a full-blown unfair competition law was not taken.

Several proposals relating to the work and organisation of the Patent Office were also made, including its renaming as the United Kingdom Intellectual Property Office. In *EI Du Pont Du Nemours & Co v United Kingdom Intellectual Property Office* [2009] EWCA Civ 966 Jacob LJ referred to 'the trendy but pointless "operating name" of "UK Intellectual Property Office"'. It has since been re-rebranded again, dropping the 'UK' part.

GPL

See **General Public Licence**.

Grace Period

See **period of grace**.

Graduated Response

See **three strikes**.

Graham Factors, *Graham v John Deere*

The key US case on obviousness, a decision of the Supreme Court (383 US 1 (1966)). The principles by which obviousness should be assessed are:

- determine the scope and content of the prior art;
- determine the difference between this art and the disputed claims;
- ascertain the level of ordinary skill in the art; and

- determine the obviousness or non-obviousness against this background.

See also ***KSR v Teleflex,*** and cf. ***Windsurfing International v Tabur Marine.***

Grand Right(s)

The right to put on a dramatico-musical performance which must be obtained directly from the publishers of the music, as these rights have not been assigned to a collecting society (the Mechanical-Copyright Protection Society – MCPS, in the UK, would otherwise be the appropriate collecting society). Collecting societies deal in what are known, logically, as 'small rights'. In a rather poorly written note, MCPS says:

> A grand rights licence is always required when performing or recording dramatico-musical works (for example, a ballet, opera, musical, musical play or work of a similar nature).

In the USA, the expression bears essentially the same meaning.

Granddaughter Divisional

A divisional application divided from an application which itself is a divisional application.

Grandfather, Grandfather Clause, Grandfathering

Generally, to exempt from new legislation or regulations, usually because of some prior condition or previously existing privilege. See (for example) the Patented Medicines (Notice of Compliance) Regulations in Canada, the treatment of the Novell/Microsoft patent settlement in version 3 of the **General Public Licence**, and the (US) Interior and Related Agencies Appropriations Act of 1994, Section 113 (which permits the Department of the Interior to process certain patent applications filed on or before the date of enactment of the Act for vein or lode claims). Grandfather patent attorneys under the European Patent Convention, Article 163, are those who were qualified or experienced Patent Attorneys at the entry into force of the EPC in their state. In December 1998, the ratio of registrations under the grandfather clause to those having passed the European Qualifying Examination (EQE) was two to one (D. Visser, *The Annotated European Patent Convention 2000*, 15th edition, Veldhoven, The Netherlands: H Tel, 2007, p. 321.

Graphic Work

A subset of artistic works for (UK) copyright purposes, which will enjoy protection (provided other conditions are met) irrespective of artistic quality. It includes (the list is not exhaustive) any painting, drawing, diagram, map, chart or plan, and any engraving, etching, lithograph, woodcut or similar work.

Green Channel

By analogy with customs channels at ports and airports, the UK Patent Office introduced a special channel for environmentally friendly patent applications in May 2009. The applicant may make a written request stating that the patent relates to green or environmentally friendly technology and requesting that any of the search, combined search and examination, publication, and examination be accelerated.

Green Patents

Patents contained in a database produced by the EPO in which patents are reclassified in 160 different green categories. See also **green channel**.

Gregory Report

The Report of the Gregory Committee (Cmnd 8662 (1952) – not, as the Intellectual Property Office seems to think, Cmnd 8662: the Cmnd series of Command Papers began in 1956) laid the groundwork for the UK's Copyright Act 1956.

Grey Goods, Grey Market Goods

See **parallel imports**.

Grey Literature

Documents produced by government, academia, or business and industry, in print or electronic form, but not published commercially. May include technical reports, standards and specifications, and translations. Difficult to access because of inconsistent methods of publication and dissemination, but potentially fatal to a patent application if the examiner finds it.

Groundless Threat

Registered intellectual property rights might well be invalid, for the simple reason that examiners have limited resources (including time) and will inevitably sometimes miss something that should have prevented a patent being granted, or a trade mark or design being registered. Indeed in the trade mark system many countries and regional systems do not purport to deal with conflicts with other trade marks, thus leaving the possibility that a granted trade mark might turn out to be invalid against an earlier one. To guard against this, it is common to find provisions in legislation dealing with registered IP rights (and some unregistered ones, such as UK and Community unregistered design right, but not copyright) dealing with groundless threats.

The approach, in broad terms, is to give remedies to anyone aggrieved by groundless threats of infringement proceedings. A person might be aggrieved even though the threats have been directed against someone else – for example, a manufacturer would be aggrieved if no one would sell its products because a competitor threatened them with legal action if they dealt in those products.

GRUR

Gewerblicher Rechtsschutz und Urheberrecht, Internationaler Teil, a monthly journal published in German by Verlag C.H. Beck, Munich, Germany, edited by the **Max Planck Institute for Intellectual Property, Competition and Tax Law**, covering European, foreign (to Germany) and international intellectual property law. It has been published since 1952.

Guarantee of Origin

What a trade mark provides, although this appears to be an increasingly old-fashioned view. Nowadays it seems that the origin-indicating function of a trade mark is only one of several jobs done by it – others including the advertising function and the communication function. The list is not exhaustive, and like particle physics the field is growing as new items are identified to make the theory work.

Gutta Percha

A tropical tree, *Palaquium gutta*, and its sap which forms a latex with some desirable qualities lacking in rubber. Used for many applications until the middle of the twentieth century, including particularly golf balls (which were known for that reason as 'gutties', as for similar reasons were plimsolls in Scots dialect). In modern times it is a substance known almost exclusively to trade mark lawyers, on account of its inclusion in class 17 of the Nice classification.

H

HABM

German, Harmonisierungsamt für den Binnenmarkt, or Office for Harmonisation in the Internal Market (**OHIM**).

HADOPI

Haute Autorité pour la diffusion des œuvres et la protection des droits sur Internet. French government agency with responsibilities for the Internet.

Hague Agreement

A special arrangement under the Paris Convention, permitting international applications for registration of designs. Three Acts of the Hague Agreement are currently in force, the 1999 Act, the 1960 Act and the 1934 Act.

Membership is limited (there are 57 contracting parties) and the Agreement is of little practical importance as it stands, although with the European Union having become a party in 2008 the Agreement's best days are almost certainly ahead of it.

Harare Protocol

See **ARIPO**.

Hatch–Waxman Act

The Drug Price Competition and Patent Restoration Act 1984. An amendment to the Food, Drug and Cosmetics Act in the USA to expedite the approval of generic pharmaceuticals while protecting the interests of patent owners. A therapeutic equivalent can be approved under an **ANDA**, piggybacking on the safety and efficacy information in the original New Drug Approval (NDA). The ANDA must include certification (for example Para IV certification) that the patents listed in the Food and Drugs Administration's Orange book are either invalid or not infringed, and must show the bioequivalence of the generic drug with the patented one.

The Act also extends the term of patent protection for pharmaceuticals (see **extension of patent term**).

Heart of the Work

In US copyright law, a formula that defines what it can never be **fair dealing** to take. Impossible to predict with much certainty.

Hedgehog

In *The Fox and the Hedgehog*, Sir Isaiah **Berlin** quotes the Greek poet Archilochus: 'The fox knows many things, but the hedgehog knows one big thing.' He notes that '[s]cholars have differed about the correct inter-pretation of these dark words', and offers one possible meaning, but for the scholar of intellectual property the reference to the original quota-tion in Lord Hoffmann's judgment in *Designers Guild Limited v Russell Williams Textiles Limited* [2002] 1 WLR 2416 is the interesting thing. Comparing the protection given by copyright and unregistered design right, his Lordship remarked:

> Generally speaking, in cases of artistic copyright, the more abstract and simple the copied idea, the less likely it is to constitute a substantial part. Originality, in the sense of the contribution of the author's skill and labour, tends to lie in the detail with which the basic idea is presented. Copyright law protects foxes better than hedgehogs.

By contrast, hedgehogs fare better under the law on unregistered design right, which looks at the overall appearance of the article rather than its manifold features: this appears to be the import of the judgment of Lady Justice Arden in the Court of Appeal, overturning the judgment of H H Judge Fysh in the Patents County Court, in *L Woolley Jewellers Limited v (1) A & A Jewellery Limited (2) A & A Jewellery (London) Limited* [2002] EWCA Civ 1119.

Hello!

See **Zeta Jones**.

Heraldry

The profession, study, or art of devising, granting and blazoning arms and ruling on questions of rank or protocol. Not entirely unconnected with trade mark law: indeed, in some countries the only way to protect a coat of arms is to register it as a trade mark – something that the UK's Trade Marks Act 1994 prohibits. See **Chivalry, High Court of**, and **Manchester Palace of Varieties**.

Hire, Work Made for

In US copyright law, a work created by an employee within the scope of his or her employment, or a commissioned work that the parties agree in writing to treat as a work made for hire. The legal or natural person for whom the work was made is considered to be not only the owner of copyright from the moment of creation of the work but also its author. See for example *Cmty. for Creative Non-Violence v Reid*, 490 US 730 (1989).

Hoffmann of Chedworth, Lord

As Lennie Hoffmann, had a highly successful career at the Bar before becoming a High Court judge, in which capacity he formulated the so-called **Improver** questions (*Improver Corp v Remington Consumer Products* [1990] FSR 181, 192) which he then, 15 years later, consigned to history in his influential judgment in *Kirin-Amgen Inc v Hoechst Marion Roussel Ltd* [2005] RPC 169, 191. Regarded as the cleverest of the law lords, and once described by *Legal Business* magazine as 'the most dominant [*sic*] personality in the Lords by a mile', he was also reputed to be the most daunting member of the judicial committee before whom to appear. In 1998 he set an unfortunate precedent when he neglected to declare his links with Amnesty International before sitting on the Pinochet appeal, with the result that the Lords' judgment had to be set aside.

Holdup

'[T]he danger', described by Carl Schapiro (in the work quoted below under '**thicket**'), 'that new products will inadvertently infringe on patents issued after these products were designed.'

Honest Concurrent Use, Honest Concurrent User

Formerly, under the Trade Marks Act 1938, a person who enjoyed the privilege of being able to register a trade mark identical to that of another already on the register for the same goods or services. If the two marks had coexisted in the marketplace, there was no reason for the Registry to prefer one over the other. In the 1994 Act, because this approach was incompatible with the Directive, the honest concurrent user was spared *ex officio* rejection because of the conflict between their sign and an earlier registered trade mark, and it was left to the proprietor of the earlier mark to oppose the application. More recently, the UK system has left all trade mark applications to be dealt with in this way. The last privilege of an honest concurrent user is to be permitted to continue using the sign in the locality, a rather indeterminate expression.

Honest Practices in Industrial and Commercial Matters

The standard demanded in European Community trade mark law (the Directive and the Regulation) if one is to be able to avail oneself of certain exceptions to what would otherwise be infringements. Analogous to **nominative use** in the US. In the UK, the test also forms one limb of a proviso to the exception for comparative advertising.

Human Rights

A crucial area of legal scholarship, practice and campaigning, now somewhat debased and mundane especially in the UK since the advent of the Human Rights Act, which imported the European Convention on Human Rights into domestic law. The Act has been in large part responsible for the emergence of a law of privacy in the UK as purported celebrities have invoked Article 8 of the Convention. The Convention has also featured in some intellectual property cases, notably *Anheuser Busch Inc v Portugal* (1 October 2005).

I

ICANN

The Internet Corporation for Assigned Names and Numbers, which manages domain names and IP addresses. It is a California not-for-profit corporation which was set up to take over responsibility for the domain name system from the US government. The Internet Assigned Numbers Authority (IANA) carries out the technical work of ICANN.

ICANN administers the **Uniform Domain Name Dispute Resolution Policy (UDRP)**.

Idea–Expression Dichotomy, Idea–Expression Merger (US)

It is axiomatic in copyright law that ideas are not protected, only original expression. This principle has statutory weight in the US but is not expressly stated in the UK. The dichotomy can be traced back at least to *Baker v Seldon* in the US Supreme Court 101 US 99 (1880). See Samuels, 56 Tenn. L. Rev. 321 (1989). The idea–expression dichotomy was codified for the first time in Section 102(b) of the Copyright Act of 1976 which provides:

> In no case does copyright protection for an original work of authorship extend to any idea, procedure, process, system, method of operation, concept, principle, or discovery, regardless of the form in which it is described, explained, illustrated, or embodied in such work.

Problems arise where ideas and expression are not easily distinguished – in many situations they are said to merge. This can be a particular problem where the copyright work in question is a computer program: see ***Whelan v Jaslow***, ***Computer Associates v Altai***. In *Baker*, the Court formulated it like this:

> Where the art [that the book] teaches cannot be used without employing the methods and diagrams used to illustrate the book, or such as are similar to them, such methods and diagrams are to be considered as necessary incidents to the art, and given therewith to the public.

So where there is only one way (or there are a limited number of ways) to express a particular idea, the expression is dictated by the underlying idea, the idea and the expression merge, and the expression does not qualify for copyright protection. And the more banal the work, the more likely that idea and expression will merge – a proposition well illustrated by *Kenrick v Lawrence*, (1890) LR 25 QBD 99, where the work in question was a graphic representation of a human hand designed to assist illiterate voters in the polling station. In *Ibcos Computers Ltd v Barclays Mercantile Highland Finance Ltd* [1994] FSR 275 **Jacob J** (as he then was) said that copyright subsisted in the program as a whole, because looked at as a whole it was the original work of the first programmer; far from excluding ideas from copyright protection, English copyright law has always given protection to elaborated ideas.

It should be noted that the software Directive stipulates that there can be no copyright in the underlying ideas of a computer program, and that these ideas include interfaces. This is not implemented in UK copyright law, so the Directive is likely to be given direct effect in any case in which the point arises.

Image Rights

The rights that enable one to prevent the unauthorised use of one's name, image or personal attributes. The desire to exercise such rights may be connected with a simple wish to be left alone, or a more complex desire to exploit those matters commercially. In England, image rights are a motley collection: the right to privacy under the Human Rights Act 1998 (and the European Convention on Human Rights), the law on breach of confidence, the Data Protection Act 1998, and the action for passing off. In *Douglas & Ors v. Hello! Ltd & Ors* [2007] UKHL 21 (2 May 2007) an action for breach of confidence protected celebrity wedding photographs, which had been the subject of a very lucrative commercial arrangement; in *Irvine & Ors v Talksport Ltd* [2003] EWCA Civ 423 (1 April 2003) the common law action for passing off was used against an unauthorised celebrity endorsement. See also **personality rights**, **publicity** rights.

Implementing Regulations

Legislation in (for example) the European Union that may be almost as important as the primary legislation but rather more obscure, and made by an administrative process. The Community trade mark system provides a good illustration: the Community Trade Mark Regulation (Council Regulation (EC) No 207/2009 of 26 February 2009 on the Community trade mark) is ineffective without Commission Regulation (EC) No 2868/95 of 13 December 1995 implementing Council Regulation (EC) No 40/94 on the Community trade mark (the original CTM Regulation).

Implied Consent

A concept that might be encountered in many contexts, but of particular interest to intellectual property lawyers because of the arguments that have raged about how, if at all, a trade mark owner might be said impliedly to have consented to goods bearing the trade mark being in free circulation on the internal market. The short answer is not at all. See **parallel imports, exhaustion**.

Implied Licensing

Permitting someone to do something that one could prevent, such as using one's intellectual property, but without recording that permission (and the detailed terms and conditions on which it is given) in writing, or even proclaiming them orally. An implied licence may arise in many situations, for example where a commissioner of a copyright work has not received express permission to use it.

Importation, Patent of

A patent granted not for something that has been invented but for something that has been imported. In the early days of the English patent system the majority of patents were patents of importation, and they continued to be granted until the nineteenth century. Nowadays, many national laws (for example in Georgia and Iran) permit patents of importation, but these are now co-terminous with (and entirely dependent on) a foreign patent. See also **confirmation, patent of, revalidation**.

Impoundment Order (US)

A rough equivalent of an **Anton Piller** order. Section 503(a) of the Copyright Act (17 U.S.C, § 503(a)) provides for the impounding of allegedly infringing copies of works and equipment for making them. In recent years, as a result of doubts about the constitutionality of such orders and a certain amount of abuse, the courts have tended to insist that impoundment be necessary and reasonable, and comport with the requirements of due process.

Improvement, Improvement Patent

A patent issued following an application filed later than a prior application, which builds upon the previously disclosed invention. Such a patent is independent of the earlier one, though it might be that a licence to use the earlier one is needed too.

Improver

In *Improver Corp v Remington Consumer Products Ltd* [1990] FSR 181 Hoffmann J (as he then was) had the opportunity to apply the **purposive** approach to patent claims construction taken in *Catnic Components v Hill & Smith* to a 1977 Act patent (see **Epilady**). He reformulated Lord Diplock's test, putting it into three questions known as the Improver questions:

- Does the variant have, in fact, a material effect on the way the invention works? If yes, it falls outside the claim.
- If no, would it have been obvious to the informed reader at the date of publication of the patent specification that the variant had no material effect? If no, the variant falls outside the claim: the patentee is assumed to have limited the claim deliberately.
- If yes, is it apparent to any reader skilled in the art that strict compliance with the primary meaning of the claim was intended to be an essential requirement? If yes, the variant is outside the claim, but if no it is an infringement.

Later the questions became known as the Protocol Questions, following Aldous LJ's suggestion that they provided exactly the right guidance in applying the Protocol on Interpretation of Article 69 of the European Patent Convention. In **Kirin Amgen** Lord Hoffmann (as he had by then become), finally consigned the Improver questions to the dustbin of history, acknowledging that the Protocol on the Interpretation of Article 69 was the definitive statement of how to interpret patent claims.

Incontestability

The owner of a US trademark registered on the Principal Register may file a sworn statement or affidavit, claiming 'incontestable' rights in the mark for the goods and services specified. There is however no obligation to do so.

An incontestable registration is conclusive evidence of the validity of the registered mark, of the registration of the mark, of the owner's ownership of the mark and of the owner's exclusive right to use the mark with the goods and services, subject to certain limited exceptions. Known as a Section 15 Declaration.

The mark must generally have been in continuous use in commerce for at least five consecutive years from the date of registration and the affidavit must be executed and filed within one year following a five-year period of continuous use of the mark in commerce.

Incorporeal Property

A term employed in civil law jurisdictions, equivalent to intangible property and therefore including many intellectual property rights.

Independent Claim

A patent claim that does not refer back to another claim. A patent may have one or several independent claims. See also **dependent claim**.

Individual Character

A design will be registrable if, in addition to being new, it exhibits individual character. This means that the overall impression it produces on the informed user differs from the overall impression produced on the informed user by any design which has been made available to the public before the relevant date: Registered Designs Act 1949, section 1B(3), and Article 6 of the Community Design Regulation. The informed user is a user of the product to which the design is applied: *Bailey v Haynes* [2007] FSR 10.

Industrial Application, Capable of

A requirement under the Patents Act 1977 and the European Patent Convention: an invention, to be patentable, must be capable of industrial application. Under the previous legislation (going back to the Statute of Monopolies in 1623) an invention was defined as a manner of manufacture, which achieved a similar result. A perpetual motion machine is the paradigm case of something that offends against this principle (though the fact that it offends against scientific principles is perhaps more important:

in *Blacklight Power Inc v The Comptroller-General of Patents* [2008] EWHC 2763 (Pat), the UK Patent Office refused a patent based on an unproven scientific theory). US patent law requires that an invention have **utility**, which achieves much the same thing.

Industrial Design

Features of the appearance of an article that is made by (or has the design applied to it by) industrial means. Not an expression actually used in any UK intellectual property statute, the sense is important in the field of copyright (from which since 1989 industrial designs have, by and large, been excluded) as well as registered designs and unregistered design right (UK and EC, in both cases).

Industrial Property

The subject-matter of the **Paris Convention**: patents, trade marks, industrial designs, utility models, unfair competition and some other matters. When the Convention was written, copyright had no place in industry – even what we now think of as the copyright industries (publishing) were considered professions, copyright had not yet invaded the field of industrial designs and the invention of computer software was a long way off. The distinction between industrial and intellectual property is nowadays of relatively little importance.

Inequitable Conduct (US)

A defence to allegations of patent infringement. Even if the patent is valid and infringed, the court may exercise its equitable discretion not to enforce the patent if the patentee has engaged in inequitable conduct. This occurs when a patent applicant breaches his duty of **complete candor** and good faith to the US Patent and Trademark Office (Rule 56).

Information Disclosure Statement

A submission of background art or relevant information to the USPTO in connection with a patent application, required under the applicant's duty of **complete candor** and good faith: see **inequitable conduct**.

Information Society Directive

A shorthand reference to Directive 2001/29/EC on the harmonisation of certain aspects of copyright and related rights in the information society.

Informed User

The hypothetical person upon whom a design must produce an impression different from that produced on the same person by any other design, if that design is to be considered to possess the necessary individual character to be registered (under the Registered Designs Act or the Community designs regulation) or to be protected by Community unregistered design right.

In *Woodhouse (UK) plc v Aquila Design* [2005] ECPCC 25, [2006] RPC 1 the Patents County Court considered who the informed user should be. The case concerned street lamps. The court took the view that the informed user should be a regular user of articles of the sort covered by the design, a customer or user but not a manufacturer of them nor an average man in the street. Being informed, the user would be aware of what is and has recently been in the market. As design law is concerned with appearance not function, the informed user will consider whether it makes a different impression on him by considering only appearance and not technology. Moreover, the comparison was to be carried out with the articles in situ, 8–10 metres above the viewer's head, notwithstanding that a buyer would inspect them at ground level.

Infringement

An actionable wrong committed against some form of intellectual property. Copyright, trade marks, patents, the various design rights and a range of lesser *sui generis* rights are infringed if another carries out one of the acts reserved to the owner without permission, provided whatever conditions the relevant legislation imposes are met. One must not talk of breaching these rights (per the **IPKat**, 19 March 2006). One must be careful about talking of infringing an unregistered trade mark, too, as there is no action for infringement of such a right in the UK (but there is in the US): an unregistered trade mark is, however, protected in the UK and many common law countries by an action for passing off.

In US usage, the verb 'to infringe' usually takes the preposition 'on'. In British English no preposition is used.

Inherency

The problem for an invention of disclosure by prior use. In *Merrill Dow v Norton* [1996] RPC 76 the patentee of a drug found later that it worked by producing a substance in the liver, and sought to patent this effect too. The House of Lords held the second patent invalid, because the production of the substance was an inevitable consequence of working the first patent.

Initial Interest Confusion

See **bait and snatch**.

Injunction

An equitable remedy ordering a person to refrain from doing, or threatening to do, an act of some kind, or, more rarely, to require him to do something. Being an equitable remedy, it is granted, at the discretion of the court, only if it is just and convenient to do so. It will be refused where the applicant is not suffering much inconvenience, or damages would be an adequate remedy, or greater hardship would be caused by its grant than by a refusal.

The courts can deal with urgent cases very quickly *ex parte*. A temporary or interlocutory injunction may be given, often *ex parte*, pending the full hearing of the dispute. The claimant must normally give a **cross-undertaking in damages** which acts as a considerable disincentive to the capricious applicant.

A perpetual injunction, which relieves the applicant from having to seek relief on each fresh infringement of his rights, may be granted after a full hearing. A breach of the terms of an injunction is a contempt of court.

INN

International non-proprietary name for pharmaceutical products, which cannot be registered as trade marks. These are decided on by the World Health Organization. Under the (UK) Trade Marks Act 1994, they are 'reserved words'.

Innocent Infringement

An infringement committed by someone who did not know, and had no reason to believe, that there were any intellectual property rights to worry about. Generally, an innocent infringer will escape a claim for damages but not an injunction. Easily prevented from arising at all, by judicious marking of the relevant articles.

Innovation Patent

An Australian utility model, granted without examination but not enforceable until it has been examined.

INPADOC

The International Patent Documentation Centre in Vienna: part of the EPO.

Inquiry as to Damages

See **damages, inquiry as to**.

Insubstantial Change (US)

The doctrine in patent law that holds that matter is deemed equivalent if there is only an 'insubstantial change' between each of the elements of the accused device or process and each of the elements of the patent claim. Laid down in *Warner-Jenkinson Co. v. Hilton Davis Chem. Co.* (1997), the doctrine is limited primarily by **prosecution history estoppel**.

Insufficiency

A patent will be invalid if 'the specification of the patent does not disclose the invention clearly enough and completely enough for it to be performed by a person skilled in the art': section 72(1)(c) of the Patents Act 1977. Insufficiency is a single objection to validity, though it might arise in several different ways. The purpose underlying the objection is to stop the patentee laying claim to products or processes not fully taught by the patent.

INTA

The International Trademarks Association, known commonly by the acronym but officially prefers to be known by its initials (that is, I-N-T-A rather than 'inta'). Formerly the US Trademarks Association (on which see **Lanham Act**). Most famous for its annual meeting, a gathering of (now) some 8000 trade mark owners and lawyers from virtually every country in the world.

Integer

The word comes from the Latin, meaning 'whole' or 'untouched', and in mathematics signifies a natural number (that is, one that includes no decimal or fraction): by extension, any whole or complete entity. In the terminology of patent practitioners, it means an element that makes up an invention, or perhaps an invention by itself. In interpreting the claims in a patent, the court will often have to reduce it to its component integers. In the *Catnic* case the point at issue was an integer that set out a 'rear support member' that extended 'vertically'. The alleged infringer had the member inclined at 6 or 8 degrees from the vertical. The inclination had very little effect on the function and the House of Lords found infringement.

By way of illustration, in *Dyson v Hoover* [2001] R.P.C. 26, the first claim was divided into its integers thus (the numbers referring to drawings have been deleted):

(a)   A vacuum cleaning appliance including
(b)   cyclone units of successively higher efficiency, in the capability of depositing fine dust,
(c)   in series connection,
(d)   the highest efficiency cyclone having a frusto-conical part tapered away from its entry and
(e)   means for generating an airflow from a dirty air inlet sequentially through the cyclone units
(f)   characterised in that a lower efficiency cyclone unit upstream of the highest efficiency unit has a body without the taper away from the air entry, being either cylindrical or having a reverse taper.

Integrated Circuit Topography

The pattern, shape and configuration of the three-dimensional disposition of the elements of an integrated circuit, and sometimes the maskworks used to make them. Protected in many countries by copyright or design laws, and in others by *sui generis* legislation such as **topography right**. The Washington Treaty defines an integrated circuit as:

> a product, in its final form or an intermediate form, in which the elements, at least one of which is an active element, and some or all of the interconnections are integrally formed in and/or on a piece of material and which is intended to perform an electronic function . . .

and the layout design or topography of an integrated circuit as:

> the three-dimensional disposition, however expressed, of the elements, at least one of which is an active element, and of some or all of the interconnections of an integrated circuit, or such a three-dimensional disposition prepared for an integrated circuit intended for manufacture.

Integrity Right

The right not to have their work subjected to derogatory treatment given to authors of copyright works and directors of copyright films by Article 6 bis of the Berne Convention (implemented in the UK in section 76 of the Copyright, Designs and Patents Act 1988).

In this context treatment means any addition to, deletion from, or alteration to or adaptation of the work. It does not include a translation of a literary or dramatic work or an arrangement or transcription of a musical work which involves no more than a change of key or register. The treatment will be regarded as derogatory if it amounts to a distortion or mutilation of the work, or if it is otherwise prejudicial to the honour or reputation of the author or director.

Intellectual Property

'A generic term', according to Stanley Berwin, 'which includes letters patent, trademarks [*sic*], copyright and registered designs, all of which can be described as products of the intellect rather than hand, hammer or sickle. Commonly, though less correctly, used to include rights in know-how'.

The use of the expression 'intellectual property' is therefore at least potentially misleading, and in recent history has probably created the impression that the law will protect more than it actually does. Intellectual property is not a unitary area of law: it is a combination of several areas of law that had existed for years, and had often been practised by the same people and which have long been studied together, but which did not form a single body of law.

The expression has, however, been in use since at least the early nineteenth century when the French liberal thinker and politician, Benjamin Constant, argued (in 'Esquisse de Constitution', in *Collection complète des ouvrages publiés sur le Gouvernement representatif et la Constitution actuelle de la France*, Paris: P. Plancher, 1818, p. 296) against the recently introduced idea of 'property which has been called intellectual'. 27 years later Circuit Justice Woodbury, in the Massachusetts Circuit Court, in *Davoll v Brown* C.C.Mass. 1845.Case No. 3,662, 1 Woodb. & M. 53; 2 Robb, Pat. Cas. 303; 3 West. Law J. 151; Merw. Pat. Inv. 414 said:

> Only thus can ingenuity and perseverance be encouraged to exert themselves in this way usefully to the community; and only in this way can we protect intellectual property, the labors of the mind, productions and interests as much a man's own, and as much the fruit of his honest industry, as the wheat he cultivates, or the flocks he rears.

In the UK, there is no single intellectual property code to which to refer (as there is, for example, in France). The UK statute book does however contain a couple of definitions of intellectual property, though in unexpected places – first, section 72(5) of the Senior Courts Act (formerly the Supreme Court Act) 1981:

> 'intellectual property' means any patent, trade mark, copyright, design right, registered design, technical or commercial information or other intellectual property

Great caution should be exercised with any definition that includes the term it is supposed to be defining. The other is in the Companies Act 2006, section 861 (re-enacting section 396(3A) of the 1985 Act):

- any patent, trade mark, service mark, registered design, copyright or design right, or
- any licence under or in respect of any such right.

These definitions omit express reference to rights in performances and plant varieties protection as well as more recent innovations such as database right and publication right.

The treatment of a right to use intellectual property – the benefit of a licence – as itself a property right is not to be taken too seriously. For the purpose of registering company charges (which is why the second definition is on the statute book) it is perhaps an appropriate analysis, but it is plain from the case law that a licence will not be considered property. This is true of the right to use a patent, per Lord Diplock in *Allen & Hanburys Ltd v Generics* [1986] RPC 203 at 246: 'A licence passes no proprietary interest in anything, it only makes an action lawful that would otherwise have been unlawful.' It is true of copyright, per Browne-Wilkinson J in *CBS Records v Charmdale* [1980] FSR 289 at 295:

> I would not expect a licensee to be treated as having a property interest in the copyright. Under the general law a licensee is a person who enjoys contractual rights as against the property owner. I can find nothing in the [1956 Copyright] Act which conflicts with the principle that the licensee's rights rest in contract and are not proprietary.

And it is true of trade marks, per **Jacob J** (as he then was) in *Northern & Shell Plc v Condé Nast* [1995] RPC 117 at 127: 's.30(3) [of the Trade Marks Act 1994] is the provision enabling a licensee to sue. Just as before, no proprietary right is conferred.'

Trustees in the *CB Simkin Trust v Inland Revenue Commissioner of New Zealand* [2004] UKPC 55 might be thought to indicate otherwise, but the Privy Council had little alternative given that the statute, the Income Tax Act 1994, like the UK Companies Act quoted above, made it a foregone conclusion. In that Act, 'intangible property' is defined to include 'the right to use a trade mark', so the Privy Council was quite right in its decision (which disallowed the trustees' application for depreciation allowance because the exclusive licensee, not the trustees, owned the right to use the trade mark in question).

Intellectual Property Clause

The US constitution empowered Congress to enact legislation (*inter alia*): 'To promote the Progress of Science and useful Arts, by securing for limited Times to Authors and Inventors the exclusive Right to their respective Writings and Discoveries' (Article 1, Section 8.) On the strength of this, laws have been created to protect copyright and to grant patents. In 1870 the same constitutional basis was used for trade marks legislation, and following an amendment in 1878 it was ruled unconstitutional. This crisis led directly to the creation of the US Trademark Association – now the International Trademark Association (see **INTA**) – which worked to produce the Trade-Mark Act 1881, based on the clause of the constitution that allowed Congress to legislate to regulate interstate commerce (see **commerce clause**).

Intellectual Property Enforcement Co-ordinator (US)

An office, known informally as the IP Czar, created by the Obama administration under the Prioritizing Resources and Organization for Intellectual Property Act ('Pro-IP Act') of 2008, the holder of which is Victoria Espinel. Mostly concerned with fighting the trade in counterfeit and pirate goods, which is entirely laudable, but too ready to resort to meaningless slogans about intellectual property **theft**.

Intellectual Property Regulation Board (IPREG)

The body set up by the Chartered Institute of Patent Attorneys and the Institute of Trade Mark Attorneys to undertake the regulation of the two professions. The two Institutes will be Approved Regulators under the Legal Services Act 2007, and as required by the Act have set up Boards to take on the regulatory functions, which must be kept separate from the representational functions the Institutes perform.

Interference

Another wonderfully graphic expression from the United States – meaning a type of proceeding to determine who among several claimants to the same invention (or overlapping ones) is entitled to it. A by-product of the first to invent system, applicants can prove their entitlement by 'swearing back' to the date of conception of the invention, referring to records made before the application was filed. Hence the need for meticulous record keeping, and for having the records witnessed.

Intermediate Citation

Relevant prior art against a patent application of the same nationality, which was filed before but published after the patent application. In European practice, it is known as a 54(3) citation. Such prior art can usually only be cited against the novelty of the alleged invention, but in the US it can be cited against inventiveness too.

Intermediate Generalisation

Explained by the EPO Board of Appeal in T-879/09:

> [2.1.2] A patent application describes an invention in general terms together with one or more detailed embodiments. In order to overcome an objection of lack of novelty and/or inventive step the applicant often adds some but not all the features from the detailed embodiments to the general disclosure. This results in an object that lies between the original general disclosure and the detailed embodiments. This is called an 'intermediate generalization' in the patent jargon, although a more proper naming would be 'intermediate restriction' to make clear that it is in fact a restriction from the more general original disclosure (T 461/05 [2.3]).
>
> [2.1.3] Such an intermediate restriction or generalization is permissible under A 123(2) only if the skilled person would recognize without any doubt from the application as filed that characteristics taken from a detailed embodiment were not closely related to the other characteristics of that embodiment and applied directly and unambiguously to the more general context (T 962/98 [2.5]).

See also *Teva UK Ltd v Merck & Co, Inc* [2009] EWHC 2952 (Pat) (20 November 2009)

Internal Priority

Many national laws provide for claims to priority from earlier-filed national applications in the same country. Such claims fall outside the international priority system of the Paris Convention. Note that a later patent application in the USA may only claim priority from an earlier application if that earlier application is a **provisional**.

International Application

An application made under the Patent Co-operation Treaty for patents in a number of contracting states.

International Classification for Industrial Designs

The classification set out in the **Locarno Agreement**.

International Convention for the Protection of New Varieties of Plants

Convention signed in Geneva on 2 December 1961, revised in 1972, 1978 and 1991. Provides for plant varieties protection internationally, on the basis of national treatment. Establishes **UPOV**, and referred to as the UPOV Convention.

International Depository Authority

An institution designated under the Budapest Treaty for the purpose of receiving deposits of samples as disclosure of biotechnology inventions.

International Exhibition

An exhibition at which an invention or design may be shown without destroying its novelty and making protection impossible. Generally, documentation must be obtained from the exhibition organisers, and presented in support of the application which must be filed within six months.

International Extension

Under the **Madrid Agreement** and the **Madrid Protocol**, the effect of an International Registration may be extended territorially to countries not included in the International Registration, including countries that have joined the Madrid System subsequently. Extension is also the word used to describe the addition of new goods or services in an existing international registration.

International Patent Classification (IPC)

A hierarchical system in which the universe of technology is divided into sections, classes, subclasses and groups: a language-independent tool for the retrieval of patent documents in the search for prior art. There are eight sections, broken down into classes and subclasses. Documents are classified by function and by application.

International Phase

The part of the procedure under the PCT where the application is in the hands of the International Bureau of WIPO. This phase lasts for up to 30 months from the application date or the priority date: some countries still follow the old rules which stipulated up to 20 months, unless an International Preliminary Examination has been requested – an option which will soon be closed.

International Preliminary Examination, International Preliminary Examination Authority (IPEA)

An optional part (Chapter II) of the PCT process. The IPEA examines the application for novelty, inventive step, industrial application and sufficiency. It issues at least one written opinion and then an International Preliminary Examination report. The applicant does not have to reply to the report, nor are they bound to accept it, but it can be a useful guide to the chances of succeeding in the national or regional stage.

For EPC contracting states, the IPEA is the European Patent Office. The Patent Offices of Australia, Austria, Canada, China, Finland, Japan, the Republic of Korea, the Russian Federation, Sweden, the United States of America, and the European Patent Office act as International Preliminary Examining Authorities.

Opting for Chapter II and requesting an IPEA was formerly the only way to secure a 30-month time limit before the application would enter the national (or regional) phase. Now the International Phase is nearly always 30 months: only a handful of countries still apply the 20-month limit, and they are parties to regional arrangements that enable applicants to secure a 30-month international phase anyway. The demand for IPEAs has therefore diminished dramatically over the last decade.

International Preliminary Report on Patentability

A report on the patentability of a PCT application, prepared by the International Searching Authority.

International Registration

The term used for what an applicant obtains under the Madrid Agreement or Protocol. The International Registration of itself is of little value – it is only when it leads to registration of international trade marks in the designated states party to the Madrid Agreement and Contracting States to the Protocol that it becomes truly useful.

International Search Report, International Searching Authority

A report on prior art in a PCT application, and the authority that carries out the search. The authority is a national (or regional) patent office appointed under the PCT to carry out the task: they are the Patent Offices of Australia, Austria, Canada, China, Finland, Japan, the Republic of Korea, the Russian Federation, Spain, Sweden, the United States of America, and the European Patent Office.

Invalidity

A patent, registered trade mark or registered design will be considered to be invalid if it has defects that should have prevented it from being registered. Cf. **revocation**, which is a consequence of supervening matters – such as non-use in the case of a trade mark.

Invalidity Opinion (or Validity Opinion)

A legal opinion on how a court might rule on the validity of an issued patent. Often sought before patent litigation, where validity might be challenged.

Invalidity Search

A search to identify patent and non-patent documents which may have a bearing on the claims of a patent. This can help establish the soundness of a patent portfolio, which may be useful for licensing or in an acquisition. Also called an opposition search.

Invent, First to

See **first to invent**.

Invention

The subject-matter of patent protection, not defined in either the UK Patents Act 1977 or the European Patent Convention. However, most patent laws do state at some length what may not be patented – computer programs, business methods, discoveries, and so on. The Soviet Union had a definition in Article 21 of the Principles of Civil Law:

> An invention is a new technical solution of a problem in any field of the national economy, social and cultural construction, or national defence which possesses essential distinctive features and yields a positive effect.

The characterisation of an invention as a technical solution to a problem is widespread in modern patent systems, although the list of fields in this definition reflect the priorities of a socialist society rather than the conventional concerns of patent law. 'Distinctive features' are not usually the stuff of patents, either, and the implications of the requirement for a positive effect are mind-boggling.

In US law, anyone who 'invents or discovers *any* new and useful process, machine, manufacture or composition of matter, or any new and useful improvement' (emphasis added) may qualify for a patent: 35 USC §101. The invention must have utility (§101), be novel (§102) and be non-obvious (§103). The legislation contains no exclusions save for one narrow one concerned with nuclear weapons, but it is inherent in the wording of the statute that many novel creations, not being a process, machine, manufacture or composition of matter, will not be patentable. The Supreme Court acknowledged in *Diamond v Chakrabarty* 447 US 303, 309 (1980) that Congress intended by its wide language (including the repeated use of the word 'any') that §101 should extend to 'anything under the sun that is made by man'.

See also **manner of manufacture**.

Invention Promotion Firm

A business that provides services to inventors to help them develop or market their inventions.

Inventive Concept

An expression that in one sense means little, if anything, different from the simple word 'invention', although it might serve a purpose by making it plain that the reference is to the invention in the abstract rather than in the form of a specific embodiment. A patent application may only cover one inventive concept. See **unity of invention**.

Inventive Height

See **Erfindungshöhe**.

Inventive Step

A necessary feature of an invention, if a patent is to be granted over it. The European system talks about inventiveness, while in the US the expression used is 'non-obviousness'.

Section 3 of the UK Patents Act 1977 provides that it must not be obvious to an unimaginative person skilled in the art, compared to what is already known. All matter forming part of the state of the art is to be taken into account, except matters included in patent applications with earlier priority dates published after the invention's priority date. The steps that a judge must work through in applying the inventive step test are set out in the *Windsurfing* case, as adapted by the Court of Appeal in *Pozzoli v BDMO* [2007] EWCA Civ 588; [2007] FSR 37. This involves the following steps:

1. a. Identify the notional 'person skilled in the art'.
   b. Identify the relevant common general knowledge of that person.
2. Identify the inventive concept of the claim in question or, if that cannot readily be done, construe it.
3. Identify what, if any, differences exist between the matter cited as forming part of the 'state of the art' and the inventive concept of the claim or the claim as construed.
4. Ask whether, when viewed without any knowledge of the alleged invention as claimed: do those differences constitute steps which would have been obvious to the person skilled in the art or do they require any degree of invention?

In *Conor v Angiotech* [2007] UKHL 49; [2008] RPC 28 at [42] Lord Hoffmann approved the following statement by Kitchin J in *Generics (UK) Ltd v H Lundbeck A/S* [2007] RPC 32 at [72]:

> The question of obviousness must be considered on the facts of each case. The court must consider the weight to be attached to any particular factor in the light of all the relevant circumstances. These may include such matters as the motive to find a solution to the problem the patent addresses, the number and extent of the possible avenues of research, the effort involved in pursuing them and the expectation of success.

It is sometimes enough to show commercial success amounting to a secondary indication of inventive step. The cases in which this might happen are fairly rare, and it will only apply if the facts are clear. The reasoning behind this approach was explained in characteristically lucid terms by Laddie J in *Haberman and V & A Marketing Limited v. Jackel International Limited* [1999] EWHC Patents 269, [1999] FSR 683 at 699 to 701.

See also **obviousness**.

Inventiveness

See **inventive step**.

Inventor

The actual deviser of an invention, according to the Patents Act 1977 (section 7(3)). That cannot be considered to be an especially helpful definition, especially given that there is no definition of 'invention'. The European Patent Convention contains no definition at all of 'inventor'. US patent law is similarly unforthcoming, though the USPTO's online glossary refers to 'one who contributes to the conception of an invention', opening the possibility of joint inventors. In the US system, the inventor or inventors alone can file the application for a patent.

Inventor's Certificate, Certificate of Invention

A document issued in the Soviet Union and other communist countries as an alternative to a patent. In the Soviet system, it was up to the inventor whether they wished to have a certificate or a patent. If they opted for the former, the state was entitled to work the invention and the inventor would be remunerated according to the savings and other benefits produced by the invention, and receive other privileges. Patents were more commonly awarded for foreign inventions.

IP

This could stand for **intellectual property** or Internet Protocol (a set of rules for transmitting data across a packet switched network, which *inter alia* defines addressing methods, hence IP addresses). The context will usually make it clear but it can still sometimes give pause for thought. In each case, the abbreviation is probably used more often than the expression for which it stands – not surprisingly, given the number of syllables that can be saved.

IPC

See **International Patent Classification**.

IPKat

The doyenne of intellectual property **blawgs**. See also **Pedrick Patent**.

IPREG

See **Intellectual Property Regulation Board**.

Italian Torpedo

See **Belgian Torpedo**. The ability to sink a patent infringement claim using an Italian action claiming a declaration of non-infringement has had doubt cast on it by the decision of the Italian Supreme Court in *BL Macchine Automatiche v Windmoeller und Hoelscher* (2004), which is based on the fact that in a declaration action the claimant denies that a tort has been committed, thus depriving the Italian court of jurisdiction unless the defendant happens to be domiciled there.

In the English courts, invalidity is a defence to a claim for infringement so if validity is in issue it cannot be decided upon separately. The courts will not take jurisdiction over declarations of non-infringement of non-UK patents if validity is also in issue.

ITC

International Trade Commission, a US government agency that performs a judicial function and (according to The Art of IP War blog) provides a rich man's loophole in intellectual property litigation.

ITU

Intent to use. See **allegation of use**.

J

Jacob, Lord Justice (Sir Robin Jacob) (1941–)

Graduated in physics from Cambridge University and in law from the London School of Economics. Called to the Bar in 1967.

Junior Counsel to the Treasury in Patent matters from 1976 to 1981, when he was appointed Queen's Counsel. Appointed to the Bench in 1991, holding the office of Senior Judge of the Patents Court from 1995 to 1997. Supervising Judge for Chancery matters in Birmingham, Bristol and Cardiff from October 1997 to September 2001 then was the Judge in Charge of the Patents List again until he was promoted to the Court of Appeal in 2003. He lists 'Arsenal FC' among his recreations in *Who's Who*.

JEB

The Joint Examination Board set up in 1990 by the Chartered Institute of Patent Agents and the Institute of Trade Mark Agents. It handles examinations for entry onto the Institutes' respective registers.

Jellinek

1. *Re Jellinek's Application* [1946] RPC 59, in which the concept of 'goods of the same description' was considered by the judge. The three-part test laid down in his judgment (nature and composition of the goods, purpose for which the goods are used, channels of distribution through which goods reach consumers) is applied even now in cases where it is necessary to identify similar goods or services, following the judgment of Jacob J in *British Sugar v James Robertson and Sons Ltd.*
2. Mercedes Jellinek was the daughter of an Austrian motor dealer and entrepreneur, who, as a condition of handling Daimler cars, insisted that they should be named after his daughter. The rest is trade mark history.

Jepson Claim (US)

A characterising patent claim, named after *Ex parte Jepson*, 1917 C.D. 62, 243 O.G. 525 (Ass't Comm'r Pat. 1917), where the invention is an improvement on a previous invention. Jepson claims are similar to the 'two-part form' of claim in European practice prescribed by the European Patent Convention (Rule 43(1)), with a preamble in which the state of the art is described followed by a form of words like 'wherein the improvement comprises . . .' or 'wherein the combination with . . .' (US practice) or 'characterised in that . . .'(European practice), and then the elements or steps that are new or improved over the prior art. The point of **novelty** is the limitations distinguishable over at least the contents of the preamble. A Jepson claim may read, for instance (emphasis added):

> In a *staple cartridge* insertable within a surgical stapler and containing staples and comprising an elongated body including one or more longitudinal slots for slidably receiving one or more longitudinal pusher bars comprising a firing mechanism of said surgical stapler, and a plurality of drivers engageable by said pusher bars for ejecting the staples from the cartridge, said staple cartridge releasably fastened to a said surgical stapler,
> *the improvement comprising* a lockout mechanism *connected to* said longitudinal slots for preventing said pusher bars from passing more than one time through said longitudinal slots.

See *Ethicon v United States Surgical Corporation*, where that claim was alleged to have been infringed.

The applicant can use a Jepson claim to draw the examiner's attention to a point of novelty while avoiding having to present arguments and possibly amendments to communicate it to the examiner, which might be damaging in future litigation, as in *Festo*.

On the other hand, a Jepson claim admits that that subject matter described in the preamble is prior art, facilitating the argument that the improvement is obvious in light of the admitted prior art. Prosecutors and applicants are reluctant to admit anything as prior art for this reason, and so this claim style is seldom used in modern practice in the US.

Jif

The brand name of the product in suit in *Reckitt & Colman v Borden*, being lemon juice sold in a plastic container shaped to resemble a lemon.

Joint Authors

The collaborating creators of a single copyright work whose separate contributions to it are merged. Joint ownership of copyright in the work follows, unless some other arrangement has been agreed. See **joint ownership**.

Joint Ownership

A generally undesirable state of affairs in all areas of intellectual property law. In patents, either of joint owners may work the invention without reference to the other (though they cannot assign or licence their rights). In copyright, where the producer and principal director of a film are constituted joint authors and therefore joint owners of copyright, a similar rule applies. They are tenants in common rather than joint tenants. In trade mark law, joint ownership should simply be anathema – it is fundamentally at odds with the basic distinguishing function of a trade mark.

Joint Venture

Any arrangement between two businesses to conduct some sort of venture together. Participation is not usually the main activity of either party, which explains why a joint venture (or JV) may differ from a partnership. The venture may be carried out by a company formed for the purpose, in which the joint venturers hold shares and which is usually subject to a shareholders' agreement, but it may be based simply on an agreement between them. It is a common form of vehicle for cooperation between intellectual property owners, and the contracts that govern the arrangement are likely to contain complicated provisions about the ownership of new intellectual property created by the JV as well as the IP brought to the venture by the parties. See **background intellectual property, foreground intellectual property**.

JPTOS

Journal of the Patent and Trademark Office Society, a monthly journal published by the eponymous (American) society.

K

Kind Codes

Codes, including a letter and in many cases a number, which distinguish the kind of patent document (for example publication of an application for a utility patent – patent application publication; patent; plant patent application publication; plant patent; or design patent) and the level of publication (for example first publication, second publication or corrected publication). For example DE-A1 is the German *Offenlegungsschrift* (application laid open for public inspection) while a DE-C1 is the German *Patentschrift* (first publication of the granted patent). Prescribed in WIPO Standard ST. 16. See **publication codes**.

Kirin-Amgen

A Californian pharmaceutical company and the claimant in *Kirin-Amgen Inc v Hoechst Marion Roussel Limited* [2004] UKHL 46, a judgment of the House of Lords (now the UK Supreme Court) which is for the time being the last word on the interpretation of patent claims. Their Lordships agreed that, while a purposive approach is appropriate, the *Improver* questions are no longer the right way to go about it. It is simply a matter of applying the **Protocol on Interpretation of Article 69**. There is no doctrine of equivalents in European patent law, so what is not claimed in a patent is disclaimed, with a saving for future developments if drafted in such a way that a person skilled in the art would understand the description in a general enough way to include it.

Kleine Munze

German 'small change': an expression that has come to be applied to certain mundane matters that copyright law protects, which are admitted to the copyright system (which, of course, in German is an author's rights – *urherrberrecht* – system) only because so little in the way of creativity is demanded.

Knock-Out Search

A search of pre-existing intellectual property rights designed to discover whether there are any that would make a proposed new application a complete non-starter. See **screening search**.

Know-How

According to a resolution of **AIPPI** (Yearbook 1974/1, pp. 104–6), know-how is: 'knowledge and experience of a technical, commercial, administrative, financial or other nature, which is practically applicable in the operation of an enterprise or the practice of a profession'.

HM Revenue and Customs adopt a more restrictive definition, beginning with a contentious statement:

> Know-how is a type of intellectual property. It is industrial information or techniques likely to assist in:
> ● the manufacture or processing of goods or materials; or
> ● the working of a source of mineral deposits; or
> ● the carrying out of any agricultural, forestry or fishing operations.

Limiting it to information relevant to industrial or technical processes is extremely narrow, but consistent with the context. The European Commission, with a different purpose, defines know-how as 'specific knowledge held by an individual or company on a product or production process, often obtained through extensive and costly research and development'. It then goes on the say:

> Under the Community competition rules know-how is normally deemed to be a body of technical information that is secret, substantial and identified. Secret means that the know-how package as a body or in the precise configuration and assembly of its components is not generally known or easily accessible. Substantial means that the know-how includes information which must be useful. Identified means that the know-how is described or recorded in such a manner as to make it possible to verify that it satisfies the criteria of secrecy and substantiality (Article 1(i) of Commission Regulation (EC) No 772/2004 of 27 April 2004 on the application of Article 81(3) of the Treaty to categories of technology transfer agreements.)

It is still confined to technical information, though, unlike the wider AIPPI definition.

See also **trade secret**.

Kokai

An unexamined Japanese patent application.

Kokoku

An examined and allowed Japanese patent application.

Kort geding

Dutch, meaning 'short procedure'. A variety of preliminary relief proceedings enabling the owner of intellectual property to secure an injunction within a few months by way of provisional measure. The proceedings, which are brought before the district court of The Hague, are *inter partes*. A decision is given within a couple of weeks after the hearing. If the judge grants an injunction, this will be accompanied by a penalty sum (*astreinte*) per violation or per day for which the defendant will be liable to the claimant. The sums involved are commonly very substantial. Combined with the Dutch courts' former alacrity in granting cross-border injunctions, the *kort geding* procedure made The Netherlands a most attractive venue for intellectual property litigation.

KSR International Co v Teleflex, Inc.

A US Supreme Court case (550 US 398 (2007)) on obviousness, which reverts to the standard set down in ***Graham v John Deere*** (**Graham factors**) and closes the door on a movement towards requiring an indication in the art in the direction of the alleged invention.

L

Laches

A delay in bringing an action after knowledge of the circumstances giving rise to a claim, which is sufficient to prevent a person from obtaining an equitable remedy. A substantial lapse of time, coupled with circumstances (such as loss of evidence or agreement to abandon a claim) which make it inequitable to grant relief, will bar claims for remedies such as specific performance, injunction, rescission and rectification.

Derived from the equitable maxim, *Vigilantibus non dormientibus æquitas subvenit* (equity aids the vigilant, not those who sleep on their rights). In *Fisher v Brooker* – the case involving the authorship of 'A Whiter Shade of Pale', and in particular the Hammond organ part (which was derived, ironically, from J.S. Bach's cantata, *Wachet auf, ruft uns die Stimme*, BWV 140, known in English as *Sleepers, Awake*) – Matthew Fisher's 40-year delay in bringing his claim to co-authorship was not defeated by laches or acquiescence, partly because Gary Brooker had benefited from sole ownership of the copyright for all that time.

In the US, an inventor wrongly omitted from a patent application has six years to take action from when he becomes aware of the fact, after which a rebuttable presumption of laches arises. See also **limitation of actions**.

Lack of Unity

A ground for refusing a patent application. Usually leads to the filing of **divisional** applications. See **unity of invention**.

Laddie, Mr Justice (Prof. Sir Hugh Laddie) (1946–2008)

One of the leading English intellectual property lawyers of his time as a member of the Patent bar, QC, and High Court Judge (1995–2005). At the Bar, he was responsible for devising what became known as the Anton Piller order, the eventual scope of which he regretted. As a judge, he decided many important IP cases including *Arsenal v Reed, BHB v William Hill, Amgen v TKT, Wagamama v City Centre Restaurants, Coflexip* and *Eddie Irvine v TalkSport.*

He left the bench in 2005, saying the work was 'unstimulating' and being uncomfortable with the general Chancery Division workload he also had to undertake, becoming a consultant to Willoughby & Partners (now Rouse Legal) and a professor at University College London where he founded the Institute of Brand and Innovation Law.

Lambert Agreements, Lambert Toolkit

A set of five Model Research Collaboration (one-to-one) Agreements and four Consortium (multiparty) Agreements for universities and companies that wish to undertake collaborative research projects with each other, promulgated by the UK Department for Business, Innovation and Skills.

Landscaping

The process of evaluating the existing patents in a particular field, the better to understand where a new development or product stands in relation to the competition.

Lanham Act (US)

The main piece of Federal trade mark legislation in the United States. Dating from 1946, it is based not on the **intellectual property clause** of the US Constitution but on the **commerce clause**.

Lapse

The fate of an IP right following a failure to pay renewal or maintenance fees. It may often be reinstated within a limited period if the owner can show good reason for the failure to pay.

Learned Society Publication Exception

In the old British patent law, there was a grace period of six months for matter disclosed in a paper delivered to a learned society or published in its journal. It still exists in some places, but not Britain.

Legal Professional Privilege

The principle, found in all the common-law jurisdictions, that all communications between a professional legal adviser and his or her clients are protected from disclosure except with the consent of the client. Note that the privilege is the client's, not the lawyer's. It is an essential safeguard, assuring the client that they can take legal advice based on a full disclosure of their case to their advisers without running the risk that this might compromise their claim, as it would were the disclosure to become available to the other side.

The Proceeds of Crime Act 2002 requires solicitors who suspect their clients of tax evasion, money laundering and other offences to report them to the authorities without telling the clients they have done so, subject to a maximum punishment of 14 years in jail. This is a significant derogation from the principle of legal professional privilege.

In the European Union, which is at least as important a jurisdiction in the field of competition law as the Member States individually, the concept is very different. In particular, it caused problems with advice from inhouse counsel: in *Case 155/79, AM & S v Commission* 1982 E.C.R. 1575 the CJEC held that principles of confidentiality apply only to communications made for the purpose of and in the interests of the client's defence, by an independent lawyer – which, despite professional rules in common law countries, meant a lawyer not employed by the client. In Joined Cases T-125/03 and T-253/03, *Akzo Nobel Chemicals Ltd. and Akcros Chemicals Ltd., v. Commission* the Court of First Instance elaborated on the independence of an attorney by holding that the supervision or regulation by a legal professional body does not render an in-house counsel independent.

There are whole books devoted to the principle, and in England it is clear from the cases that the scope of the principle is far from certain. See also **attorney–client privilege**, the term used in the United States.

LES

The Licensing Executives Society, an international organisation for people with an interest in technology transfer or intellectual property licensing.

Lessig, Lawrence

American academic and political activist, a director of the Edmond J. Safra Foundation Center for Ethics at Harvard University and a professor of law at Harvard Law School. Formerly professor of law at Stanford Law School and founder of its Center for Internet and Society, founding board member of Creative Commons, a board member of the Software Freedom Law Center and a former board member of the Electronic Frontier Foundation.

Letters Patent

Literally, an 'open letter' from the sovereign notifying the grant of some privilege, including a monopoly for a new invention. Sometimes used in reference to a bound formal copy of a patent provided to the inventor when a patent is issued.

Licence (n), License (vt) (or vice versa in some non-British versions of English)

'Permission', according to Stanley Berwin, 'to carry out some act given by a person who otherwise would have power to prevent it.' It has a wide meaning in the regulatory field as well as signifying permission to use a piece of property, including **intellectual property**.

A licence might be exclusive, sole or non-exclusive: if it contains the sort of restrictions that are inherent in an exclusive relationship it is likely to have to comply with competition laws. Section 30(4) of the Patents Act 1977 permits licences to be granted over patents or applications, and deals also with sub-licences, which may be assigned or mortgaged in their own right. It states that a licence or sub-licence shall vest by operation of law in the same way as other personal property. An exclusive licensee of a patent has the same rights to bring infringement proceedings as the proprietor of the patent. The licence must be registered at the Patent Office.

Licences of copyright are dealt with in section 90(4) of the 1988 Act, which provides that a licence is binding on every successor to the licensor's title except a purchaser in good faith for valuable consideration and without notice, actual or constructive, of the licence, or a person deriving title from such a purchaser. Exclusive licences must be in writing, and the exclusive licensee has the same rights and remedies except against the copyright owner as if the licence had been an assignment. The same rules apply to registered designs.

An exclusive licence of a trade mark must be written and an exclusive licensee has the same rights to sue for infringement as if the trade mark had been assigned. A non-exclusive licensee has the right (which may be displaced by contract) to require the owner of the trade mark to take action if an infringement affects his interests, and if the proprietor does not heed the call to do so the licensee may do so himself.

Berwin adds that: 'A licence under **letters patent** or copyright is preferable to an outright assignment because the rights will automatically revert to the licensor on termination arising from breach or insolvency [of the licensee].'

In addition to contractual licences, the law also provides for **compulsory licences** and **licences of right**.

Licence of Right, Licensing of Right

A licence available, subject only to settlement of the royalty payable and possibly other terms, to all comers. If a (UK) patent owner agrees to having the patent endorsed 'licence of right', renewal fees are halved.

The Patents Act 1977 provided for the duration of all 'new existing patents' to be extended from the old 16-year term to 20 years, subject to their being endorsed 'Licence of Right' during the four-year extension. During this period, the patentee must grant a licence to anyone requesting one on terms that, if not agreed, are to be settled by the Comptroller-General of Patents.

Licensing Executives Society

See **LES**.

Life Cycle Management

A technique to extend the effective life of patent protection, usually of pharmaceuticals, generally involving patenting variations (different isomer, inclusion of another ingredient, different dosing) of the same product of a patent and releasing them onto the market at intervals. See also **evergreening**.

Likelihood of Association

See **association, likelihood of**.

Likelihood of Confusion

1. A term used in trade mark law. In the US, the statutory basis (Trademark Act Section 2(d), 15 USC. Section 1052(d) for refusing registration of a trademark or service mark because it is likely to conflict with a mark or marks already registered or pending before the USPTO. In the European Union, if a likelihood of confusion (including a likelihood of association) is present because of similarities between mark and sign, there are relative grounds for refusal of registration and (as the case may be) an infringement.
2. The title of Ron Coleman's **blawg**.

Limitation

The exclusive rights given by registration of a trade mark may be limited by a statement attached to the registration. In particular, this might cover geographical issues: formerly, a limitation could be used to overcome a geographical objection, by ensuring that the exclusive rights did not apply in that location. Now that goods travel so freely, of restricted value. See also **disclaimer.**

Limitation of Actions

Doctrines, both statutory and equitable, that ensure stale claims are not litigated. In the United Kingdom, they are now mostly found in the Limitation Act 1980, which extinguished the right to bring an action outside specified time limits commencing from the date a cause of action accrues, subject to the amendments wrought by the 'clumsy draftsmanship' (an assessement quoted without attribution by Berwin) of the Latent Damage Act 1986. Fraud, concealment and mistake misleading the claimant may prevent time running. A cause of action accrues when the breach is committed in the case of torts that do not require proof of damage to be actionable. There is no limitation period applicable to a claim for infringement of copyright: see *Brooker v Fisher* [2009] UKHL 41. See also **laches**.

Limited Title Guarantee

With one exception, the same implied covenants in transfers of property as those implied by **full title guarantee** under the Law of Property (Miscellaneous Provisions) Act 1994.

The difference lies in the last of the implied covenants. The seller covenants that the transferor has neither encumbered the property nor granted third-party rights, and is not aware that anyone else has done so since the last disposal for value. There is no covenant relating to the transferor's predecessors in title.

Link (EU)

A necessary element for a finding of trade mark infringement under Article 5(2) of the Directive (the anti-dilution provision). In a conventional trade mark infringement action, the requisite connection would be made by reference to the existence of a likelihood of confusion, but confusion is not an issue in Article 5(2).

If there is a link in the mind of the relevant public between the claimant's trade mark and the conflicting sign, and it is clear that the third party is seeking to ride on the coat-tails of the registered mark, the advantage being taken of the repute of that mark will be considered unfair.

Lisbon Agreement for the Protection of Appellations of Origin and their International Registration

Concluded 31 October 1958, revised in Stockholm in 1967 and amended in 1979.

Literal Infringement

1. Patent: an infringing article or process that contains every integer of a claim.
2. Copyright: an infringing copy that reproduces the earlier work, or a substantial part of it, in all respects. A copyright law that gave protection against only literal infringements would be almost completely ineffective as the slightest alteration would avoid infringement. See **non-literal infringement**.

Literary Work

A type of work that may be protected by the law of copyright, though only (under the Copyright, Designs and Patents Act 1988 and much other legislation around the world) if it is original. The 1988 Act states that a literary work is any work that is written, spoken or sung other than a dramatic or musical work, and goes on to say – stretching credibility just a little – that 'accordingly' [*sic*] this includes a compilation or table, a computer program, preparatory design material for a computer program, or a database (which for these purposes must be assumed somehow to differ from a compilation or table, which stretches credibility further still).

Local Novelty

The principle that a patent can be invalidated by prior publication only if the publication was in the country granting the patent. This was the test applied in the pre-EPC patent law of the UK, the Patents Act 1949, and it is still extant in some countries whose patent laws were influenced by that legislation (for example New Zealand). A local novelty test permits patents of **importation**.

Locarno Agreement Establishing an International Classification for Industrial Designs

The international agreement that created the eponymous international classification for industrial designs. Concluded in 1968, amended in 1979. Fifty-one contracting parties.

Locarno Classification

International Classification for Industrial Designs.

Logo

An abbreviation of the word logotype, logogram or logograph. A logotype is a piece of type containing a word or two or more letters – convenient for setting diphthongs, for example. A logograph or logogram is a character or combination of characters representing a word. It has come to mean an emblem used by an organisation to identify itself, so a form of trade mark in the widest sense: in trade mark law, more usually referred to as a **device**, **design** or **figurative trade mark**.

London Agreement

An international agreement, under the EPC. Intended to reduce the costs of European patents by making post-grant translation requirements less onerous. See **Community Patent.**

Long-Felt Need or Want

A secondary indication of inventiveness which can prove important if an invention appears to be obvious. A known problem in a technical area, which has remained unsolved over an extended period. If the solution were obvious to those skilled in the art, they would have solved the problem. In a Canadian case, *Pope Appliance v Spanish River*, the combination of features in a paper machine, supposed to avoid workers' fingers being crushed, was alleged to be considered obvious. However, workers were still suffering crushed fingers long after the combination was alleged to have become obvious, so clearly it hadn't.

Look and Feel

The non-literal elements of a computer program (or other type of copyright work) that may be protected in an infringement action, originating in *Whelan v Jaslow*.

Lookalike Product

An expression with no precise legal meaning, used to denote products made for and sold by retailers incorporating what the retailers would argue are features common to the get-up of similar products, but which the manufacturers of the equivalent branded products would argue are distinctive features of their get-up such that the retailers (usually supermarket chains) are competing unfairly. It is alleged that consumers purchase lookalike products because they are confused by the similarities, such as the shade of red used by The Coca-Cola Company on its cans and bottles. There is also widespread belief among consumers that supermarkets' own brand products are manufactured by the same people who make the branded ones, a belief that Kellogs for one works hard to dispel.

Loss of Rights

The consequence of a failure to comply with a time limit in the European patent system. It is an administrative step, and does not involve a decision on the refusal of the European patent application or the grant, revocation or maintenance of the European patent, or the taking of evidence.

M

Macg CC

Macgillivray's Copyright Cases, a series of law reports covering the period 1901–49 edited by Evan James Macgillivray, also author of *A Treatise up on the Law of Copyright: In the United Kingdom and the Dominions of the crown, and in the United States of America*, London, 1902.

Machine-or-Transformation Test

Before the Supreme Court's opinion in *Bilski*, the touchstone for patentability of business methods and computer software in United States law: indeed, said to be the exclusive test for it in the **CAFC**'s judgment in that case. Now must be considered a clue to patentability rather than a test, let alone the exclusive test.

In fact, it long predates computer technology and has much broader application to process claims. According to the theory, a claim to a process qualifies as patentable only if: (1) it is implemented with a particular machine, that is, one specifically devised and adapted to carry out the process in a way that is not concededly conventional and is not trivial; or (2) it transforms an article from one thing or state to another.

Madrid Agreement Concerning the International Registration of Marks

A special arrangement under the Paris Convention dealing with international registration of trade marks. Made in 1891, it came into operation in 1893, but because of the time limits it imposed on national offices and the fee structure provided for it was only attractive to registries that operated along the lines of the French registry: no substantive search before registration. Revised at Brussels (1900), Washington (1911), The Hague (1925), London (1934), Nice (1957) and Stockholm (1967), and amended in 1979.

The UK, conscious of the need for a cheap and speedy way to obtain trade mark registrations in foreign countries, lobbied for many years to secure modifications to the Madrid Agreement which eventually emerged as the **Madrid protocol**.

Madrid Agreement for the Repression of False or Deceptive Indications of Source on Goods

Covers all goods bearing a false or deceptive indication of source which directly or indirectly shows one of the contracting states or a place in a contracting state as being the country or place of origin. Such goods must be seized on importation, or their importation must be prohibited, or other actions and sanctions must be applied.

The Agreement was concluded in 1891, and revised at Washington in 1911, at The Hague in 1925, at London in 1934, at Lisbon in 1958, and at Stockholm in 1967. It has 35 contracting states.

Madrid Protocol

The 1989 international agreement (not to be confused with the 1991 Protocol to the Antarctic Treaty) which takes the system for international trade marks set up by the Madrid Agreement and changes those parts of it that some countries, including the UK, found unpalatable. An application (not a registration) in one's home country is the starting point, and the consequence of a successful **central attack** is the opportunity to transform the lost international trade marks into national (or, as the case may be, regional) applications rather than losing the whole lot completely. The UK joined promptly, as it was morally obliged to do having spent decades lobbying for it, and the Protocol came into operation three months after when, to widespread surprise, the People's Republic of China ratified it, the fourth country to do so.

Madrid Union

The body that brings together the states that are parties to the Madrid Agreement and Protocol.

Magill

A key judgment of the CJEC on the application of the European Community rules on competition (in particular, Article 86 as it was, 82 as it became and 102 as it is now) to the exercise of intellectual property rights. Joined cases C-241/91 P and C-242/91 P *Radio Telefis Eireann (RTE) and Independent Television Publications Ltd (ITP) v Commission of the European Communities* [1995] ECR I-00743 (6 April 1995) decided that, (although '[s]o far as dominant position is concerned, it is to be remembered at the outset that mere ownership of an intellectual property right cannot confer such a position'):

> the exercise of an exclusive right by a proprietor may, in exceptional circumstances, involve abusive conduct. Such will be the case when broadcasting companies rely on copyright conferred by national legislation to prevent another undertaking from publishing on a weekly basis information (channel, day, time and title of programmes) together with commentaries and pictures obtained independently of those companies, where, in the first place, that conduct prevents the appearance of a new product, a comprehensive weekly guide to television programmes, which the companies concerned do not offer and for which there is a potential consumer demand, conduct which constitutes an abuse under heading (b) of the second paragraph of Article 86 of the Treaty; where, second, there is no justification for that refusal either in the activity of television broadcasting or in that of publishing television magazines; and where, third, the companies concerned, by their conduct, reserve to themselves the secondary market of weekly television guides by excluding all competition from the market through denial of access to the basic information which is the raw material indispensable for the compilation of such a guide.

Maintenance

The act of keeping something, or someone, in good shape: in the IP world, keeping the grant valid, primarily by paying the required fee to the office where it is registered.

Making Available

The exclusive right that copyright owners should enjoy, courtesy of Article 6 of the WIPO Copyright Treaty. An important component in the adaptation of copyright laws to meet the challenges of the Internet, reflected in many national copyright laws around the world.

Malicious Falsehood

A tort, comprising the uttering of a falsehood *male fide*. The person making the statement must know it will cause damage or that it was wrong. Wider than the law on defamation (although defamation actions such as trade libel, slander of goods, and slander of title fall under this rubric). The false statement may lack the essential characteristics of a libel or slander: for example, falsely stating that a lawyer has retired is unlikely to be defamatory, but even so it is likely to cause damage to her practice. If the requirements of the Defamation Act 1996 are made out, it is not necessary to show special damage, otherwise the claimant must prove actual financial loss.

A malicious falsehood claim may look like an attractive supplement to a trade mark infringement or passing-off claim, but if it adds nothing it is likely to be treated with suspicion by the judge – as happened in *BA v Ryanair* [2001] FSR 32.

Man Who Broke the Bank at Monte Carlo, The

Francis, Day & Hunter Ltd. v. Twentieth Century Fox Corp. [1939] 4 D.L.R. 353 is a Privy Council case involving a song published by the plaintiffs and a film of the same title made by the defendants.

Lord Wright held that a name alone cannot possess copyright unless it is sufficiently original and distinctive. '"To break the bank" is a hackneyed expression, and Monte Carlo is or was the most obvious place at which that achievement or accident might take place.'

Manchester Manifesto

A document published in November 2009 by the University of Manchester Institute of Science Ethics and Innovation entitled 'Who Owns Science?' (http://www.isei.manchester.ac.uk). Perceived by the patent community as an attack on the patent system, and – they think – a misguided one. The Manifesto questions the value of intellectual property in general, but is concerned mostly, perhaps exclusively, with patents. The problem, put briefly, is that we treat innovations as a form of private property, through the medium of the patent system. Is this an appropriate model for dealing with innovation? This is not the place to try to provide an answer.

Manchester Palace of Varieties

Manchester Corporation v Manchester Palace of Varieties Ltd [1955] 1 All ER 387) was the most recent case in which the **High Court of Chivalry** was convened – the first time it had sat since 1732. It involved the theatre's unauthorised use of the coat of arms of Manchester Corporation (see **heraldry**). The sole judge of the Court of Chivalry is the hereditary Earl

Marshall, the Duke of Norfolk, though he normally appoints a lawyer as his surrogate. In the Manchester case it was the Lord Chief Justice, Lord Goddard, who devoted the first part of his judgment to answering the question whether the court still existed and much of the rest of it to deterring would-be plaintiffs from moving the court again without very good reason. In this he proved to be very successful: although it seems that there have been some suitable cases, none has been brought before the court since then.

The Council won.

Manner of Manufacture

A classic definition of patentable subject-matter, originally found in Section 6 of the Statute of Monopolies of 1623, which referred to 'letters patent . . . hereafter to be made for the sole working or making of any manner of new manufacture'.

In the **NRDC** case, the Australian High Court adopted a particularly extensive interpretation of the expression. It still features in some patent laws in the Commonwealth, though not in the UK.

Manufacturing Clause (US)

A provision of the International Copyright Act of 1891 which required all copies of books, maps, photographs and lithographs to be produced in the USA. Remained on the statute book (17 USC Sec. 601), preventing the US from joining Berne, until 1986. In March 1984 it had been found to be in violation of the General Agreement on Tariffs and Trade.

Mareva

An order of the English courts preventing a defendant from removing assets from the jurisdiction before trial. Not specifically an IP matter, but may feature in IP litigation.

Market Access Conditions

See **Bristol-Myers, Squibb conditions**.

Marking

The placing of a legend on articles that embody some sort of intellectual property.

A patented product may carry the word 'patent' (or, as the case may be, 'patent pending') along with the patent number on articles made by the patentee or a licensee. Providing the patent number is essential if the legend is to amount to constructive notice. Providing this information enables the patentee to recover damages for infringements without having to show that the infringer had actual notice.

Trade marks are commonly invoked by use of the ® symbol, if registered. In the case of an unregistered trade mark, the letters TM are commonly used in countries where there is any mileage in unregistered trade marks.

The rules applicable to registered designs are much the same as for patents.

Copyright is not a registered right, so a copyright legend is little more than notice to the world that copyright is claimed. The Universal Copyright Convention prescribes a notice in the form © [name of copyright owner] [year of first publication]. The use of such a notice should serve to deny an infringer the possibility of avoiding a claim to damages on the ground that they did not realise that the work was protected.

Markman Hearing

In *Markman v Westview Instruments* the US Supreme Court held that intepreting the scope of claims in a patent infringement action was properly a matter for the court, not the jury. Federal district courts now have a Markman hearing to consider the scope of the claims before the trial of the substantive isues of infringement or validity.

Markush Claim

A form of patent claim to a chemical compound, including as alternatives a group (called a Markush Group) of compounds that are considered to be functionally equivalent (*Ex parte Markush*, 1925 Dec. Comm'r Pat. 126, 128 (1924)). The USPTO says that the proper format for a Markush-type claim is 'selected from the group consisting of A, B and C.' ('Manual of Patent Examination Practice, 803.02', http://www.uspto.gov/web/offices/Pac/mpep/documents/0800_803_02.htm).

A Markush group is an artificial creation in that the compounds that make it up might have nothing else in common. There might be several Markush groups for a single compound, so a patent could cover an enormous number of compounds. Limitations in methods used to index patents mean that that this creates problems for searchers, who have to try to find all Markush structures that might include their chemicals even though the indexes would not include the specific compounds. They also make life difficult for examiners, and in August 2007 the USPTO proposed a number of changes to the use of claims containing alternative language, including Markush-type claims.

MARQUES

An organisation of European trade mark owners, publisher of the Class 46 **blawg**.

Mathys Report

The Mathys Report on British Trade Mark Law and Practice, Cmnd 5601, May 1974, recommended the registration of service marks. This change to the law was implemented in the Trade Marks (Amendment) Act 1984, which came into operation in 1986. Prior to that change (the only significant amendment to the Trade Marks Act 1938 during its entire lifetime) service businesses had obtained what protection they could by registering trade marks in class 16 for printed matter.

Max-Planck-Institut, Max Planck Institute

A collection of 80 German academic institutes under the auspices of the Max-Planck Gesselschaft, named after the great physicist. In intellectual property circles, a generic reference to the Max Planck Institute will invariably mean the Max Planck Institute for Intellectual Property, Competition and Tax Law, based in Munich, which has contributed enormously to the jurisprudence of intellectual property. At the time of writing (May 2010), it is conducting a survey on the Community trade mark system for the European Commission. The Institute edits **GRUR** and produces the *International Review of Intellectual Property and Competition Law* (IIC).

McKesson Reference (US)

A reference in an **Information Disclosure Statement** to a communication (such as an office action response, or notice of allowance) with a patenting authority in a related patent application. In *McKesson Info. Solutions, Inc. v. Bridge Med., Inc.*, 487 F.3d 897, 908, 926 (Fed. Cir. 2007) **inequitable conduct** was found where the applicant failed to notify the USPTO of such references.

Means-Plus-Function Claim (US)

A patent claim that includes a technical feature expressed in functional terms, thus extending the claim to cover equivalents. For example, 'means for converting a digital electric signal into an analogue electric signal', or 'fixing means for uniting A and B' instead of the more limiting 'screw' or 'nail'. A 'step-plus-function' claim is a variant on this theme, used to describe the steps in a method invention ('step for converting . . . step for storing . . .').

35 USC. 112, paragraph 6, provides:

> An element in a claim for a combination may be expressed as a means or step for performing a specified function without the recital of structure, material, or acts in support thereof, and such claim shall be construed to cover the corresponding structure, material, or acts described in the specification and equivalents thereof.

Interpreting this seemingly simple statement has proved to be a surprisingly difficult task:

- Claims are usually intended to be a succinct summary of the invention that stands alone and is interpreted largely on its own merits. The means-plus-function claim tacitly imports and relies on the entire specification for interpretation, which is implausible. This is also the reason for disallowing **'omnibus'** patent claims.
- The courts, as well as the USPTO, have not been entirely consistent in specifying rules for when the 'means-plus-function' interpretation is triggered. A claim reciting 'means for [a specific function]' probably triggers the rule. The courts have construed variations like 'means of', 'means by', or even 'component for [a specific function]', with inconsistent results.
- Both the courts and the USPTO have also proposed, modified, and deprecated several tests for determining the scope of 'equivalents' of

a means-plus-function element. This problem is exacerbated by the use of the term 'equivalents', which is apparently similar to but not identical with the use of the same term in the 'doctrine of **equivalents**' test of patent infringement.

Extensive analysis has been done on interpretation of the scope and requirements of the means- and step-plus-function claim style. Despite the complexity of this area of law, which includes many ambiguous and logically contradictory opinions and tests, many practitioners and patent applicants still use this claim style in an independent claim if the specification supports such means-plus-function language. See Armstrong, James, *Essentials of Drafting US Patent Specifications and Claims*, 2nd edition, Tokyo: Katsumei Kyokai, 2002, pp. 47–51, and Landis, John, *Mechanics of Patent Claim Drafting*, p. 41.

Mechanical Rights

The rights which must be obtained from the owner of copyright in a musical work to make a recording and then to manufacture copies of it. In the UK these rights are represented by the Mechanical Copyright Protection Society (MCPS), while the closely related rights that govern the same activities for on-line distribution are the preserve of the joint MCPS-PRS (Performing Rights Society) venture, PRS For Music.

Medical Treatment

An area of science from which most countries exclude the possibility of obtaining a patent, on ethical grounds. However, like most things in the patents world, there is still scope for obtaining a patent of some sort even though the invention looks like a method of treatment. Veterinary treatment is often dealt with in the same way.

Member States

Used with capital initials as in the European Community and other treaties to indicate countries which are members of the European Community and therefore of the European Union. The initial members of the original three Communities (the European Coal and Steel Community, the European Atomic Energy Community and the European Economic Community) were France, Germany, Belgium, The Netherlands, Luxembourg and Italy ('the Six'). The United Kingdom, Ireland and Denmark joined in 1973; Greece in 1981; Spain and Portugal in 1986; Sweden, Finland and Austria in 1995; Poland, Latvia, Lithuania, Estonia, Hungary, Malta, Cyprus, the Czech Republic, Slovakia and Slovenia in 2004; and Bulgaria and Romania in 2007.

MERCOSUR

Mercado Común del Sur, a free trade organisation comprising the six southernmost countries of South America which envisages a regional patent organisation using the Brazilian office as its central office.

Mere Descriptiveness (US)

Under the Trademark Act Section 2(e)(1), 15 USC. Section 1052(e)(1), registration of trademarks and service marks must be refused where the proposed mark merely describes an ingredient, quality, characteristic, function, feature, purpose or use of the specified goods or services. This is very similar to the equivalent test in European Union trade mark law.

The degree of descriptiveness depends on the specific goods or services. There is a spectrum of descriptiveness ranging from the completely arbitrary or fanciful through suggestive, merely descriptive, and finally, generic terms for the goods or services.

Merely Ornamental (US)

A US trade mark will not be allowed if its use is merely ornamental: this is known as an ornamentality refusal. *In re Big American Man*, Serial No. 76200528 (January 18, 2005) [not citable] (see the TTA Blog's comment) suggests that ornamentality may turn in part on the size of the sign, and if presented 'in an extremely large fashion' (perhaps substantially filling the front of a T-shirt) it would amount to ornamentation whereas a small logo on the breast (as in that case) would more likely be regarded as a trade mark.

Metadata

Structured data about data. Metadata help describe and identify a document and facilitate its retrieval, whether the document is a printed one or in electronic form on the Internet or an intranet.

Mickey Mouse Protection Act

See **Bono, Sonny**.

Misuse

An emerging concept in both copyright and patent laws, primarily in the US, but also in Canada. A broad concept, embracing unclean hands, abuse of process and tortious interference to deal with issues that in other jurisdictions such as the EU will probably be dealt with by competition law.

Mobil

The case – Enlarged Board of Appeal decision G2/88 – which created the concept of the **second medical use** (or **Swiss**-style) claim.

Monopoly

1. An economic concept, where a single undertaking has sufficient market power to dictate the terms on which customers will have access to the goods or services it offers. In its practical application in competition law, it is recognised that a monopolist does not actually need to control 100 per cent of the market. Ownership of intellectual property, especially a patent, can create such market power, depending on the substitutablity of non-patented alternatives.
2. The mischief dealt with in the Statute of Monopolies (21 Jac. 1, c.3) was a legislative reaction to the abuse of the Royal prerogative to grant monopolies by letters patent over known substances such as salt, and limit the grant to the 'true and first inventor' of a 'new manufacture'. It is variously dated 1623 and 1624: see **Statute of Anne** for an explanation.

3. A well-known board game, which merits a mention here because of the US trade mark action brought by its makers against the maker of another board game called Anti-Monopoly, in which the board is monopolised at the start of the game and the object is to work back to a state of free competition. The case was eventually (in 1992, after nine years) decided by the Court of Appeals for the Ninth Circuit in favour of Anti-Monopoly.

Monopoly Prices

A price greater than that which would prevail in a competitive market, where supply and demand are in balance and consumer welfare is maximised. If another unit were made, the producer would have to sell it at a loss. A monopolist will be inclined to limit production to the level at which the marginal cost and marginal revenue are equal, so consumers will not have access to as many of the goods as they want and will pay more for them. The monopolist will reap monopoly profits.

Moral Damages

In Brazil, usually linked to the recovery of damages for moral rights (as opposed to economic rights in copyright) and damages to personal rights such as to the image of a person. The concept has also been used to refer to damage caused to the reputation of mark in a case by the Superior Court of Justice involving the counterfeiting of luxury goods. The reasoning is that the widespread use of a similar luxury handbag would hurt the image of the mark as an exclusive object.

Moral Rights

A category of author's rights protected under the Paris Act (1972) of the Berne Convention, and therefore (though very reluctantly) in the Copyright, Designs and Patents Act 1988. Lord Denning, in the debate on the matter in House of Lords when the bill that became that Act was under consideration, described moral rights as 'a contradiction in terms'. They certainly fit uncomfortably in a common-law copyright statute.

Berne required the protection of the right of paternity and the right of integrity. To them the UK law added a right to privacy in certain films and photographs (needed to redress the balance after the law had changed to award copyright in photographs to the photographer) and a pre-existing right to prevent false attribution of authorship, a right which is engaged only in the most unusual (and therefore amusing) circumstances: see, for example, *Clark v Associated Newspapers Ltd* [1998] RPC 261 and *false attribution, right against*.

French law on moral rights is rather more extensive. It includes the *droit de **divulgation** and the droit de **repentir**.* However, it is widely considered that even French law gives little of benefit to authors: one of the few instances of a successful claim being mounted involved, ironically, a 'colourised' version of an American work, John Huston's movie, *The Ashphalt Jungle*. The case was brought by the director's daughter, Angelica Houston, in 1991: see Alan Riding, 'Film Makers Are Victors in a Lawsuit on Coloring' *New York Times*, 25 August 1991.

Morality

A concept with an increasingly tenuous connection to the law, but public policy and morality still have a part to play in determining the limits of intellectual property protection. See **public policy**.

Moron in a Hurry

A regrettable expression in this day and age, first used by Foster J in *Morning Star Cooperative Society v Express Newspapers Limited* [1979] FSR 113 (a different day and age, perhaps). The publishers of the Communist Party newspaper sought an injunction to prevent Express Newspapers from launching a new tabloid newspaper under the name *The Daily Star*, which was light on politics (especially of the left-wing variety) and heavy on the sort of photographic works not seen, for ideological as well as aesthetic reasons, in the *Morning Star*.

The judge asked whether the plaintiffs could 'show a misrepresentation express or implied that the newspaper to be published by the defendants is connected with the plaintiffs' business and that as a consequence damage is likely to result to the plaintiffs', and stated that: 'if one puts the two papers side by side I for myself would find that the two papers are so different in every way that only a moron in a hurry would be misled'.

See also *Newsweek Inc. v. British Broadcasting Corp.* [1979] R.P.C. 441 (CA Civ), per Lord Denning MR, and the Canadian trade mark case *C.M.S. Industries Ltd. v. UAP Inc.*, 2002 SKQB 303, where the court ruled that UAP had infringed the plaintiff's trademark. It also came up in the

Apple litigation, with Apple, Inc.'s lawyers contending that iTunes cannot be confused with Apple Corps. That case concerns the breach of a previous trade mark settlement agreement.

Mosaicing

Assembling a number of elements of prior art that have not been put together in the prior art, in order to show that an invention lacks inventiveness. Mosaicing is permitted in the context of obviousness, provided the mosaic is one that can be put together by an unimaginative man with no inventive capacity (see Lord Reid in *Technograph v Mills & Rockley*). It cannot be used in novelty examinations, though in Europe and some other jurisdictions a reference in a prior art document to another document allows the combination of documents to be taken into account for a novelty objection.

MPEP

The *Manual of Patent Examining Procedure* of the USPTO. Most other offices have similar manuals (for example the *EPO Guidelines*, the *UK IPO Manual of Patent Practice*). These works are available to the public, and can be consulted online.

Multiple Design

Multiple design applications may be encountered in several national and regional design systems, including the EU (and Member States) and China. Under the Geneva Act of the Hague Agreement the number of designs that can be included in an application is limited to 100. Some systems restrict multiple designs by requiring that all the articles concerned fall into the same class of the **International Classification for Industrial Designs**. Others simply allow many quite unrelated designs to be filed for in one batch.

Multiple Priorities

A problem for a coalition government, perhaps, but also a variant on the ordinary approach to claiming priority which is permitted under Article 4F of the Paris Convention.

Musical Work

In what must be the least helpful piece of language on the statute book anywhere, the UK Copyright, Designs and Patents Act 1988 defines a musical work as a work consisting of music.

It expressly does not include any words or action intended to be sung, spoken or performed with the music. These are left to fend for themselves as literary or dramatic works. Annotations or directions written on a score, as in *Stimmung* by Karlheinz Stockhausen, where the score includes instructions to the singers such as 'Echo more or less the sounds that were made by the person who was speaking in front of you', are nevertheless part of the musical work.

A musical work is something different from the notes on the stave – more than just 'the dots'. It is a work that is intended to appeal to the sense of hearing, not to be appreciated in its written form. In *Sawkins v Hyperion Records Ltd* [2004] EWHC 1530 (Ch) (1 July 2004) the High Court held that a musicologist who had recreated works by a long-dead composer was the owner of copyright in a musical work, a controversial decision that nevertheless seems consistent with the authorities.

Perhaps the extreme case is John Cage's famous work for prepared piano, *4'33"* (1952), a three-movement work in which the pianist refrains from playing the instrument for the period that gives the work its title. Cage demonstrates that there is no such thing as pure silence, at least not on earth: the work is in fact more an absence of piano-playing than true silence, and the audience will hear the sounds that add up to an indeterminate composition – a species of modern music of which there are many examples, including *Stimmung*. In September 2002 the songwriter and producer Mike Batt settled out-of-court an action for infringement brought by Cage's publishers over a piece entitled *One Minute Silence*, attributed to Batt/Cage. It would have been interesting to see whether a claim for **false attribution** of authorship would have stood up.

Must-Fit

In the designs **New Deal**, the government was determined to deny car manufacturers (and perhaps other manufacturers of complex products) the opportunity to monopolise the spare parts market because of the rights they owned in the designs of the complex products. This is in many ways the paradigm case of intellectual property rights overreaching, extending protection into areas where they are not supposed to give any. The first step was to exclude copyright from the industrial designs field; the second was to fill the resulting gap – insofar as it was going to be filled with anything – by creating unregistered design right; and the third was to make as many holes as seemed desirable in what was already a fair-weather umbrella.

Must-fit was the first of these holes. It recognises the fact that designers have no freedom to design certain aspects of their work. A mechanical part has to engage with certain interfaces offered, perhaps, by the designers of other components – flanges, apertures, bolt holes, studs, and so on. As far as the designer is concerned, these are mandatory. Put another way, if the designer of the article into which the component has to fit has the right to prevent copying of those elements of the design, they are able to prevent anyone from making replacement spare parts – which, historically, have been rather more profitable than fully assembled cars. To deal with this problem, unregistered design right acquired what immediately became known as a 'must-fit' exception.

The words do not appear in the statute, nor do they appear in the EC Directive or Community designs regulation – but the language used to create the exception in the 1988 Act is followed in the Community legislation, which therefore has its own 'must-match' exception. And in the Community legislation, it extends to registered designs which, back in 1988, it did not need to, as registration required eye-appeal and features dictated by function were excluded from protection.

Must-Match

The 'must-fit' exception dealt with the problem of elements of a design that had to be copied in order to enable a replacement part to do its job. But what about those replacement parts – or those elements of parts – of which aspects of the design were mandatory because the part in question had to look exactly like the one it was replacing (before, as the case may be, the shape of the original part was modified in a collision, or by chemical reaction with road salt or some other corrosive compound)? The concerns of makers of mechanical parts had been dealt with in the 'must-fit' exception, but another group of car parts makers was waiting to pick up the baton from them.

The 'must-match' exception excludes from protection features which are dependent upon the appearance of another article of which the article is intended by the designer to form an integral part. In the EC legislation, the idea of a similar exception proved highly contentious because only the UK had such a provision in its design law. Other member States did not see the same need for provision to be made – they had no such problem. The result was an unattractive deal known as the **'freeze-plus compromise'**.

Mutatis mutandis

Latin, 'by changing those things which need to be changed' or more simply 'the necessary changes having been made'. For example, Art. 14(6) of the TRIPS agreement says that the provisions of Art. 18 of Berne (which, of course, are concerned with copyright) shall apply *mutatis mutandis* to performers' rights.

N

Nairobi Treaty on the Protection of the Olympic Symbol

All 47 states party to the Treaty, which was concluded in 1981, are obliged to protect the Olympic symbol against use for commercial purposes without the authorisation of the International Olympic Committee.

Naked Licence

The US equivalent to a **bare licence**.

National Phase

The part of the PCT procedure in which an international application becomes a series of national (or regional) applications. These proceed as if they had been filed as ordinary national applications, and the International Application which spawned them ceases to exist. Applications enter the national or regional phase 30 (but in some places 31) months at the latest from the priority date. Note that in some EPC countries there can be no national phase, as the only way to secure a patent is to file for a European designating that country.

National Security

A reason for stopping, or at least delaying, a patent application, and also for requiring at least some applications to be presented first to the applicant's home patent or office or designs registry. Foreign applications may usually be filed if permission is obtained.

In the UK, an application that contains information the publication of which might be prejudicial to the defence of the realm or the safety of the public may be made subject to a security notice, preventing or restricting its publication or communication (and therefore stopping the application proceeding to grant, and also blocking foreign applications except in North Atlantic Treaty Organisation (NATO) countries where, again, they would not be published and therefore would stall short of grant). The US has a similar requirement: China requires first filing in China if the inventor is Chinese or the applicant a Chinese corporation. Some countries (including Switzerland and Australia) have no national security provisions in their patent laws.

National Treatment

The fundamental principle of international intellectual property law, found in the Paris, Berne, Rome, Universal Copyright and other conventions, that parties must treat nationals of other parties in the same way that they treat their own nationals for the purposes of IP protection. A French national therefore enjoys the same protection under UK copyright law as a British citizen, and a British inventor can file an application for a US patent.

The application of this principle to copyright is modified by the **comparison of terms rule**, which in the European Union is itself subject to the general prohibition of discrimination against nationals of other Member States in the Treaties: on this point, see **Collins, Phil**.

NDA

Non-disclosure agreement.

Neem

Azadirachta indica, a tree in the mahogany family Meliaceae native to the Indian subcontinent, the products of which have many traditional medicinal uses. In 1995 a European patent was granted to the US Department of Agriculture and multinational W. R. Grace & Company, covering an anti-fungal product derived from neem. The Indian government claimed in opposition proceedings that the process for which the patent had been granted had actually been in use in India for over 2000 years. The opposition succeeded but Grace appealed, claiming that prior art about the product had never been published in a scientific journal. That appeal was unsuccessful and the patent was revoked in 2005.

Neighbouring Field

In inventiveness cases under the EPC, the person skilled in the art is supposed to know something about fields of expertise neighbouring his own, and of areas in which the technical problem solved by the invention might be encountered.

Neighbouring Rights

Collective term for the rights, most of which are called copyright in common law copyright systems, that are not authors' rights – rights in phonograms (sound recordings) and broadcasts, and the rights of a producer of a film – together with performers' rights and perhaps a few other minor rights too. There is some authority for including the rights of the creator of a database and rights in semiconductor topographies.

Often called related rights, but that is not the literal translation of the French original, *droits voisins*.

New

What an invention must be for a patent to be granted over it (it also has to involve an inventive step and be capable of industrial application), and what a design must be to be registered (and also to have the protection of Community unregistered design right). In the case of a patent, an invention is considered new if it does not already form part of the state of the art. The designs legislation uses a similar approach, albeit couched in the negative terms that the drafter of the EC legislation appears to like so much: a design is new if 'no identical design or no design whose features differ only in immaterial details has been made available to the public at the relevant date'.

New Deal

A shorthand way to refer to one of two events in UK intellectual property law (though originally coined to describe the Keynesian programme of public works initiated by President Roosevelt to counter the Great Depression in the 1930s):

1.   The radical changes to the patent system brought about by the European Patent Convention and the Patents Act 1977; and
2.   The reforms of design law that took place in 1989, when the Copyright, Designs and Patents Act came into force. Copyright was largely excluded from the area, to most people's relief, and a new unregistered

design right was created to fill some of the resulting vacuum (the rest of the vacuum being deliberately left). At the same time the Registered Designs Act 1949 was amended substantially, losing the requirement that a design be original as well as novel (which had been thought for a long time not to add anything) and having the eye-appeal test modified. The maximum period of protection for a registered design was increased from 15 to 25 years, too.

Nice Agreement

The most common classification system for goods and services. It divides the universe of goods into 34 classes and that of services into 11. Everything is in one class, nothing should be in more than one (but deciding which is the appropriate class is not always a simple matter). The Agreement, concluded in 1957, was revised at Stockholm in 1967 and at Geneva in 1977, and it was amended in 1979. Eighty-three contracting parties, but 147 trade mark offices use the classification.

Niche Fame

A problem for the application of the law on dilution of trade marks which has exercised the Ninth Circuit in the US and is emerging as an issue in the EU. The Federal Trademark Dilution Act gives protection to marks that are 'famous'. What if the mark is only famous in a particular market? In the EU this has arisen where a Community Trade Mark has a reputation in only one Member State; in the US, the problem is that the market is one with which only a relatively small number of consumers are familiar. The Court of Appeals for the Ninth Circuit clarified what is needed to show niche fame in *Thane International v. Trek Bicycle Corporation*, 305 F.3d 894, 2002 U.S. App. LEXIS 18344 (9th Cir. Sept. 6, 2002), warning that in general protection is limited to household-name trade marks but acknowledging that in *Avery Dennison Corp. v. Sumpton*, 999 F. Supp. 1337, 46 U.S.P.Q.2d (BNA) 1852 (C.D. Cal. 1998), rev'd, 189 F.3d 868 (9th Cir. 1999) it had held that niche fame in a geographic or product market might suffice. To keep matters in proportion to the degree of fame generally needed, niche fame must be concentrated in a highly specialised market segment with an identifiable customer base. Consumers within that niche must be likely to make associations between marks that would not be made by the general public.

Nicholson, Sir Robin

Chief scientific adviser to the Cabinet who in the mid-1980s was commissioned to carry out a review of the intellectual property system in the UK. See also **Gowers**. His report, published as a green paper (at a time when such publications really did have green covers) under the title Intellectual Property Rights and Innovation (Cmnd 9117), which contained much that was interesting (along with much that contradicted Whitford, and a great deal that attracted criticism from the IP professions, such as a recommendation of petty patents), sank pretty much without trace and had little influence on the subsequent White Paper, Intellectual Property and Innovation (Cmnd 9712) – the significance of the missing word in the title is a mystery.

No-Challenge Clause, No-Contest Clause

A clause in a licence agreement that prohibits the licensee from challenging the validity of the intellectual property licensed to it: generally a restriction on competition which will not be tolerated, and contrary to public policy by most standards.

No-Fume Ltd v Frank Pitchford

A classic British patent decision, which forms the basis for permitting claim by result if no other method is possible, (1935) 52 RPC 231, (Romer LJ).

Nominative Use, Nominative Fair Use

The use of a trade mark to denote the goods or services of the trade mark owner, a doctrine of US trade mark law that provides an affirmative defence to an infringement action. The nominative use test essentially states that one party may use or refer to the trademark of another if:

1. The product or service cannot be readily identified without using the trademark (for example the trademark is descriptive of a person, place, or product attribute).
2. The user only uses so much of the mark as is necessary for the identification (for example the words but not the font or symbol).

3. The user does nothing to suggest sponsorship or endorsement by the trademark holder.

European readers will recognise this as a close relative of Article 6(1) of the trade marks Directive.

Non-Con Filing

A foreign filing of a patent application which does not claim Convention priority. This might happen if the filing is made outside the 12-month priority period, and does not create any difficulty if it is done before early publication anywhere (but after that, novelty will be lost). The filing date of the non-con foreign filing will be the date of the foreign filing rather than the priority date.

Non-Disclosure Agreement (NDA)

See **confidentiality agreement**.

Non-Literal Infringement

Of a copyright infringement, not taking the claimant's work word-for-word if it is a literary work: the sense is extended to other types of copyright work. Most infringements are to some extent non-literal, although there are often parts that are literal copies. See **look and feel**.

Non-obviousness

Another way of looking at the need for inventiveness or an inventive step for a patent to be validly granted.

Non-pecuniary Remedy

A remedy other than one consisting of an award of money – damages or an account of profits. Includes injunctions, declarations, orders for delivery up, destruction and seizure, and so on.

Non-Practicing Entity (NPE)

A relatively neutral expression coined by Patent Troll Tracker to describe the subjects of its tracking activities. See **troll**.

Non-prejudicial Disclosure

Under Article 55 EPC the disclosure of an invention prior to the filing of a European application is not considered prejudicial to the novelty or inventive step of the invention claimed where the disclosure is at an officially recognized international exhibition, or arises from a breach of confidence. The concession only applies if the disclosure occurred no more than six months before the European patent application was filed.

Non-traditional Trade Marks

A trade mark consisting of something other than the usual words, numbers, letters and logos. Includes such exotica as sounds, colour, olfactory signs, gestures, shapes and even the vertical opening motion of a Lamborghini car door.

Non-use

A potentially fatal condition for a trade mark. If a trade mark is not used, it eventually stops distinguishing one undertaking's goods or services from those of others and the justification for the grant to that undertaking of exclusive rights (which might restrict the use of an ordinary word) evaporates. It is no longer doing the important and socially useful job of minimising consumer search costs. In such circumstances, it can be removed from the register – though usually only on the application of someone who (presumably) wants to use something very like it themselves. Legislation sets an arbitrary period of non-use after which applications for revocation may be entertained: five years is common.

Some trade mark systems require periodic confirmation, by affidavit, that a trade mark is in use. Failure to file such an affidavit can also lead to revocation. The USA and Canada have such requirements.

Norwich Pharmacal

In *Norwich Pharmacal Co. v Customs and Excise Commissioners* [1974] AC 133, a patent owner knew that infringing goods were entering the UK, but was unable to identify them. In the course of performing their duties, the Commissioners had information that would identify them, and had unwittingly played a part in facilitating the importation of infringing goods. The House of Lords held that, where a third party had become involved in unlawful conduct, they were under a duty to assist the person suffering damage by giving them full information and disclosing the identity of wrongdoers. If the third party incurs expense in assisting compliance with an order, the person seeking assistance must reimburse those expenses, which would be reflected in an award of damages against the ultimate tortfeasors.

The court has jurisdiction to order persons who have information that may lead to the identification of the defendant to disclose that the information. A Norwich Pharmacal order, granted on an *ex parte* application, is a last resort: other means of identifying the wrongdoer have to be exhausted first. Only if the alternative is that the claimant is left unable to commence proceedings against a named defendant will the court grant an application for such an order, and the prospective claimant must have a genuine intention of commencing proceedings.

Notice of Allowance

A written notification from the USPTO that an application has been allowed: in the case of a trademark, that it has survived the opposition period following publication in the *Official Gazette*. The issue of a notice of allowance is merely a step on the way to registration, in the case of a trade mark establishing the due date for filing a **statement of use** (for which a basic period of six months is allowed). Notices of allowance are only issued for applications that have been filed based on an intent to use basis.

Novelty

1.   A requirement of the patent system: an invention, to be patentable under the European Patent Convention (or the Patents Act 1977, or other national law complying with it) must be new. Since the Patents Act 1902, the Patent Office in the UK has carried out a search to determine whether a claimed invention is indeed novel – but with finite time

and resources at its disposal, no patent office can perform a perfect search and determine novelty questions definitively. An invention is considered novel in the European system if it does not form part of the **state of the art**. See **absolute novelty**, **relative novelty**, **local novelty**.
2. A requirement of many registered design laws: in the UK and the European Union, to be capable of registration, a design must be new. The definition (in the Registered Designs Act 1949 as amended, the Directive and the Community Designs Regulation) is no identical design, or design whose details differ only in immaterial details has been made available to the public before the application or priority date.

Novelty Search

A search carried out to identify patents and non-patent literature which may affect the patentability of an invention. Prudently performed before writing and filing the patent specification, so may be called a pre-application search. Synonymous with **patentability search**, narrower than a **state of the art** search.

NRDC

1. A long-forgotten British organisation, the National Research Development Corporation, set up by the government in 1948 to finance technology businesses and commercialise publicly funded research and development. It is credited with facilitating the development of carbon fibre, asbestos plastic composites and semiconductor technology, as well as the hovercraft for which it is probably most famous. Privatised in 1992 as the British Technology Group (now, inevitably, BTG plc).
2. A decision of the High Court of Australia (*NRDC v The Commissioner of Patents* (1959) 102 CLR 252), broadening the scope of the concept of a manner of manufacture as a definition of an invention. Followed in all the Commonwealth countries that still used the definition.

Nunc Pro Tunc

The Latin phrase (described by Wikipedia as being 'in common legal use in the English language', which will come as a surprise to many English lawyers and especially Lord Woolf) means 'now for then'. It applies to situations in which something is permitted to be done after the time limit has expired: a court ruling *nunc pro tunc* can retroactively correct an earlier ruling. A *nunc pro tunc* assignment similarly has retroactive effect to transfer property that should have been transferred by an earlier instrument.

Nungesser

1. Charles Eugène Jules Marie Nungesser was a First World War French flying ace, who disappeared in 1927 while trying to fly the Atlantic non-stop for the first time, from east to west. Two weeks later Charles Lindbergh made the first such flight (solo, at that), in the opposite direction.
2. Case 258/78, *Nungesser v Commission (Maize Seed)* [1982] ECR 2015, marked the first application of EC competition law to intellectual property licensing. There, the Court held that the application of Article 81 depended on the nature of the territorial protection granted to the licensee, and drew a distinction between open exclusive licences (which were not prohibited, the 'open' part referring to the fact that they permitted parallel imports) and absolute territorial protection.

O

OAMI

See **OHIM**.

OAPI

Organisation Africaine de la Propriété Intellectuelle, which unites a number of Francophone African countries. It grants unitary patents and trade marks, so individual countries cannot be designated. A PCT application may designate OAPI.

Observations (UK)

Both the Patents Act 1977 and the Trade Marks Act 1994 provide for those who feel so inclined to make observations to the examiner dealing with a published application. The person making the observations does not become a party to any formal proceedings, but may be able to show the examiner good reason why the right requested should not be granted, at all or without some amendment. Not generally favoured by patent practitioners.

'Obvious To Try'

Where the difference between an invention and the prior art is small, it would be obvious to the person skilled in the art to try what is claimed – so the invention will lack inventiveness. Such an objection can best be refuted with evidence of the superiority of the invention.

Obviousness

A patent will only be granted for an invention (in the UK and European systems, at least) if it involves an inventive step, and it will not be considered to do so if the invention is obvious to a person skilled in the art, having regard to what is already in the state of the art. This does not however include unpublished patent applications, as the skilled person would not have access to them. The application of the rule by the English courts is assisted by the **Windsurfing International** test.

OCILLA

The Online Copyright Infringement Act, a US statute that creates conditional **safe harbor** for internet service providers and others. They will not be liable for their own infringing acts or for the infringing acts of users of their services, provided of course that the conditions are met. Part of the **DMCA**.

Octrooi

Dutch, patent – or more generally an official document conferring a privilege, so it corresponds quite closely to the English 'patent' and French *brevet*.

Odol

A German brand of mouthwash, the owner of which successfully obtained cancellation of an identical trade mark for steel products: 25 Juristiche Wochenschrift 502 (1924). This is seen as an early example of a remedy being granted against dilution of a trade mark. Ironically, the manufacturer recommends that the product be considerably diluted by the user.

Offenlegungsschrift

A published unexamined German patent document (see **Auslegeschrift**).

Offensive Patenting

The strategy of surrounding a competitor's patent with applications sufficient to swamp or dominate it. Expensive, and virtually pointless.

Official Action, Office Action

A term of art in patent and trade mark circles, meaning a communication from the examiner, often but not always raising objections to an application. After receiving an adverse office action, the applicant must respond within the set time limits, and professional representatives often work to a tariff setting out fixed fees for receiving and responding to office actions.

Official Mark

A type of trade mark known in Canadian law, and often an obstacle to registration of similar trade marks. The Trade-marks Act, Section 9(1), provides that:

> No person shall adopt in connection with a business, as a trade-mark or otherwise, any mark consisting of, or so nearly resembling as to be likely to be mistaken for,
> . . .
> (n): any badge, crest, emblem or mark
> (i) adopted or used by any of Her Majesty's Forces as defined in the National Defence Act,
> (ii) of any university, or
> (iii) adopted and used by any public authority, in Canada as an official mark for wares or services,
> in respect of which the Registrar has, at the request of Her Majesty or of the university or public authority, as the case may be, given public notice of its adoption and use

This formidable protection is therefore available on request by a wide range of public bodies, and is not limited to particular goods or services. If it were limited to the names and other indicia of such bodies, it would be more understandable, but it allows such bodies easily to create supertrade marks. It might however be preferable to the tsunami of trade mark applications now filed by public bodies in the UK, including the renamed UK Intellectual Property Office which has thus surrendered much of the 'official mark'-type protection given by section 112 of the Patents Act 1977. (See **Patent Office, Gowers.**)

OHIM

The Office for Harmonization in the Internal Market, the mysteriously named institution of the European Union that administers the

Community trade mark and design systems. A strong lobby pressed the UK government to secure this institution for London, but in a classic piece of EC horse-trading the UK settled for the Medicines Evaluation Agency, and the Community Trade Marks Office (as it was generally known until it was given its official title) went to Spain. It is situated in Alicante, which is probably more agreeable than Harrow in many ways, though (not being on the Bakerloo line) rather less accessible.

Olcott International

The world's first patent annuity (and now trade mark renewal) firm. Founded in 1961 by the late Bernard Olcott, patent attorney, electrical engineer and inventor, out of a need to deal with his own patents. He saw a novel application for computer technology, and used a proprietary program and database to organise and pay annuities. The firm continues to provide that service, especially to corporate IP owners, covering over 100 countries.

Old Piano Roll Blues, The (US)

A figure of speech derived from the title of a ragtime piece by Cy Coben. It denotes the argument (also familiar to patent lawyers elsewhere who use less idiomatic language than US lawyers to describe legal principles) that a general-purpose digital computer running a new program is itself a new machine and might therefore be the subject of a patent, or the counter argument that this cannot be enough to amount to an invention. In the Supreme Court case of *Gottschalk v Benson* 409 U.S. 63 (1972) the argument was raised in Benson's brief, and the US government responded that this amounted to asserting that inserting a new piano roll into an existing player piano converted the old player piano into a new player piano. Trashed by Chief Justice Archer in his dissenting opinion in *In Re Alappat* (see *Alappat, In re*):

> Yet a player piano playing Chopin's scales does not become a 'new machine' when it spins a roll to play Brahms' lullaby. The distinction between the piano before and after different rolls are inserted resides not in the piano's changing quality as a 'machine' but only in the changing melodies being played by the one machine. The only invention by the creator of a roll that is new because of its music is the new music.

Olfactory Trade Mark

A clever name for a smell trade mark, which following the CJEC decision in *Sieckman* is a category of sign that is unlikely to be capable of graphical representation and therefore incapable of falling within the statutory definition of a trade mark.

Olympic

Various indicia associated with the Olympic Games (a four-yearly commercial festival with associated sporting competitions) receive strong protection under trade marks (and other) legislation as a result of the **Nairobi Treaty**. The word 'Olympic' and the device of five interlocking rings cannot be registered as trade marks, or used in commerce, in many countries. When a country has the misfortune to be awarded the Games, even stronger protection is put in place, of which the London Olympic Games and Paralympic Games Act 2006 is an example.

The restrictions apply to the Summer and Winter Games alike, and to the Paralympic Games.

Omnibus

Latin, 'for all'. An omnibus patent claim is one that includes a reference to the description or the drawings but not to any specific technical feature of the invention: 'Trundlene as described in the description', 'A trundle-humper according to figure X'. Acceptable under the EPC provided they are absolutely necessary (Decision T 150/82, Guidelines for Examination in the EPO c.iii.4.17), more often accepted in the UK (Manual of Patent Practice 14.124), not allowed at all in US utility patents (but mandatory in US design and plant patents which are permitted to have only one claim, which must therefore by definition be an omnibus one).

OMPI

French acronym for *Organisation Mondial pour la Proprieté Intellectuelle*. To the author's mind, it has a more satisfying resonance than WIPO (however one pronounces the first syllable – 'why' or 'wee', or even with a short 'i').

On-Sale Bar (US)

A patent may not be granted if the invention that is the subject of the application was on sale more than one year prior to the priority date. See also **period of grace**.

One-Click (or 1-Click)

The familiar name for a US patent, or the invention protected by it, granted to Amazon.com Inc. to protect a business method (US patent 5960411). Claim 1 was for:

> A method of placing an order for an item comprising:
>
> under control of a client system, displaying information identifying the item; and
>
> in response to only a single action being performed, sending a request to order the item along with an identifier of a purchaser of the item to a server system;
>
> under control of a single-action ordering component of the server system, receiving the request;
>
> retrieving additional information previously stored for the purchaser identified by the identifier in the received request; and
>
> generating an order to purchase the requested item for the purchaser identified by the identifier in the received request using the retrieved additional information; and
>
> fulfilling the generated order to complete purchase of the item
>
> whereby the item is ordered without using a shopping cart ordering model.

Claims 1 to 5 (and 11 to 26) were subsequently rejected on re-examination of the patent, but Amazon.com has responded by restricting the broadest claims (1 to 11) to a shopping cart model.

Open-Source

A technique of licensing computer software (and an adjectival phrase applied to such software) where the distribution includes or comprises the source code version of the program, which in the classic software licensing transaction is kept a closely guarded secret. The terms of an open-source licence use **copyleft** techniques to perpetuate the freedoms granted by the copyright holder. Use of the expression is controlled by the Open Source Foundation, which approves the terms of such licences.

Opposition, Opponent

An action in the appropriate office by a third party to prevent registration of an intellectual property right, or (in the case of post-grant opposition regimes such as the EPO) to have it cancelled, and the person who brings it:

1. Patents. Any person may give notice to the EPO of opposition to a European patent within nine months of the publication of the mention of the grant of a European patent in the European Patent Bulletin. Oppositions are dealt with by the opposition divisions of the EPO. EPC Contracting States are not obliged to provide for oppositions: UK patent law does not, so apart from making **observations** the only thing to do is to attack the validity of the patent once granted.

   Patent oppositions were abolished in Japan from 1 January 2005.

   There is no formal opposition period in US patent law, but any person may provide evidence adverse to a patent application or granted patent. This can be during pendency of an application prior to publication, or after publication if accompanied by the written consent of the applicant (a protest) or during the period of enforceability of a granted patent (a re-examination).

2. Trade marks. In the US, an opposition is a proceeding before the Trademark Trial and Appeal Board (**TTAB**) in which the plaintiff seeks to prevent the issuance of a registration of a mark. Similar to a proceeding in a federal court. Any person who believes that he or she will be damaged by the registration of a mark may file an opposition.

   In the European Union trade mark system, a period of three months is allowed after advertisement of the application for opposition to be filed. In the UK, this period has been reduced to two months with a further month granted on request. Extensions may be granted if the parties agree.

Orange Book (US)

A compilation in which drug manufacturers list patents relevant to their drugs, as a mechanism to delay generic competition. The equivalent in Canada is called, confusingly, the Patent Register.

Ordre publique

A ground for refusal of an application for an intellectual property right, equivalent to **public policy**.

Original

1. Copyright: the threshold qualification for copyright protection for a literary, dramatic, musical or artistic work. In the UK, it means little more than not copied, whether from another's work or the same person's own earlier work, except in the case of databases and computer programs. In those cases, it means that the work is its author's own intellectual creation. This wording appears on the face of the Copyright, Designs and Patents Act 1988 only in connection with databases: for computer programs, it is necessary to consult the EC Directive on legal protection of computer software, which appears to have been inadequately implemented in the amendments to the 1988 Act. The 'author's intellectual creation' standard is commonly found in the copyright laws of other countries, especially those that subscribe to the 'author's rights' approach.
2. UK unregistered design right: the same as in copyright (see the **Pig Fenders** case).
3. Registered Designs Act 1949: version 1 of this Act (which was in force until 1989) provided that a design could be protected by registration if it were novel and original. It is hard to conceive of a design that would satisfy the first leg of this test without exceeding the requirement of the second leg by some considerable margin. As it therefore added nothing to the law except confusion, it was deleted in the **New Deal**.

Orphan Work

A work, the holder of the copyright in which cannot be found. Adopted by the Gowers Review, which proposed a twofold legislative solution to the problem: an exception to copyright protection, and a register of orphan works. The first part of this is similar to the approach taken in the United States. Legislation was included in the Digital Economy Bill but dropped before it became law in 2010, during the 'wash-up' preceding the dissolution of Parliament. See **extended collective licence**.

Overall Impression

An important concept in European Union designs law. In addition to being novel, a design must have **individual character**, which is defined in terms of the overall impression it makes on informed observers.

Overreaching

The tendency of intellectual property rights to interfere with matters that should, from perspectives other than the narrow legal one, be beyond their compass.

Overstickering

The practice of placing labels over the packaging of parallel imports so as to replace the trade identity of the manufacturer (usually a pharmaceutical company) with that of the parallel importer. See **Paranova conditions**.

P

PACE

The EPO's Programme for Accelerated Patent Application Processing. See **accelerated procedure, accelerated processing, accelerated examination**.

Paediatric Extension

A form of **Supplementary Protection Certificate** designed to give an incentive to pharmaceutical companies to develop and obtain marketing approval for paediatric medicines. The market for such products is often too small to be of much interest to the pharmas. Regulation (EC) no 1901/2006, which made the necessary amendments, came into force on 26 January 2007.

PAIR

Patent Application Information Retrieval, a system operated by the USPTO that allows secure online access to documents relating to US patent applications. Equivalent to the European EPOLine. See http://portal.uspto.gov/external/portal/pair.

Palming Off (US)

A tort known to the law of the United States which is very similar to **passing off**.

Paragraph IV Certification (US)

A declaration that a patent listed in the **Orange Book** is invalid, or will not be infringed by the generic drug in an **ANDA**.

Parallel Imports

Goods legitimately bought in one country, then imported into another country outside – in parallel to – the trade mark owner's own distribution network. The parallel trade is fuelled by differences in prices between different national markets, even within the European Union. See also **exhaustion**.

Paralympic

See **Olympic**.

Paranova Conditions

See **Bristol-Myers Squibb Conditions**.

Paris Convention for the Protection of Industrial Property

An international treaty dealing with patents, trade marks, designs and unfair competition. It establishes the basic principle of **national treatment**, sets down minimum standards of protection for **industrial property** rights, creates the **priority** system for international applications, and requires members to legislate against **unfair competition**. The UK has always taken the (convenient, self-serving) view that a combination of the law of **passing off** and trade descriptions legislation met the latter requirement. Concluded in Paris on 20 March 1893, revised at Brussels on 14 December 1900, at Washington on 2 June 1911, at The Hague on 6 November 1925, at London on 2 June 1934, at Lisbon on 31 October 1958, and at Stockholm on 14 July 1967, and amended on 28 September 1979. There are 169 members (April 2010); the most significant non-member is Taiwan.

Parker v. Flook

A decision of the US Supreme Court, 437 U.S. 584 (1978), the second in the so-called **patent eligibility trilogy**. The Court ruled that an invention that departs from the prior art only in its use of a mathematical algorithm may be patented only if the implementation is novel and non-obvious. The algorithm itself must be considered as if it were part of the prior art.

Parody

'Parody', derived from the Greek word for a burlesque poem or song, means 'a composition in which the characteristic turns of thought and phrase of an author are mimicked and made to appear ridiculous, especially by applying them to ludicrously inappropriate subjects. Also applied to a burlesque of a musical work' (*Shorter Oxford English Dictionary*). By a process of transference, it has also come to mean 'a poor or feeble imitation, a travesty' (Ibid.). The meaning of the verb form follows from these definitions, but perhaps it is one of those irregular verbs: 'I parody, you copy, he pirates'. Note that it covers references to both the style and the work, a distinction not explored by the consultation paper or **Gowers**, but a crucial line that helps to demarcate the application of copyright. See **caricature**, **pastiche**.

Passing Off, Passing-Off

To hyphenate or not to hyphenate? According to *A Dictionary of Modern Legal Usage* by Bryan A. Garner (New York: Oxford University Press, 2001), as a noun phrase it should be two words. He notes that some authors have hyphenated it, and points to Suman Naresh, 'Passing-Off, Goodwill, and False Advertising' (*Cambridge Law Journal*, 45, p. 97, 1986) (to which I would add Christopher Wadlow's magisterial work, *The Law of Passing-Off: Unfair Competition by Misrepresentation*, 3rd edition, London: Sweet & Maxwell, 2005); but observes that: 'this rendering of the phrase is recommended only when it acts as a phrasal adjective'.

Passing off is a tort, a common law action that a trader can use to prevent another trader (usually, but by no means always, a competitor) from taking advantage of the first trader's reputation. In the classic situation this involves a straightforward representation that B's goods are, or are identical to, A's, or even that B is or is associated with A. Being a creation of the common law, the passing-off action has proved highly adaptable, especially by comparison with statutory trade mark law which can only be changed very slowly (consider the interval between the Trade Marks Acts of 1938 and 1994, during which time the only modification of any significance was the introduction of registration for service marks in 1986).

The modern law of passing-off was formulated in the **Advocaat** case, but a more helpful definition is found in the **Jif** lemon case, where Lord Oliver summarised the law in what has become known as the Classical trinity, under which heading it is described in detail.

Outside the United Kingdom (principally in the United States), the expression may have a wider meaning, extending to the substitution of one brand of goods when another brand is ordered; trademark infringement where the infringer intentionally meant to mislead or deceive purchasers; and trademark infringement where there is no proof of intent to deceive but likelihood of confusion is proven.

Pastiche

'Pastiche' comes from the Italian *pasticcio*, meaning pasty or pie, which is of little assistance, but it has come to mean 'a medley; a hotchpotch, farrago, jumble; [specifically] . . . a musical composition made up of different pieces from different sources, a pot-pourri; . . . a picture or design made up of fragments pieced together, or in professed imitation of the style of another artist' (*Shorter Oxford English Dictionary*). See **parody**.

Patent

Short 'a' (as in Stackridge), or long 'a' (as in Ayers): either appears to be acceptable in British English, according to the *Oxford English Dictionary* – it was the subject of lengthy correspondence in the *CIPA Journal* some years ago – though in American English the OED gives only the short 'a' version.

Noun: an exclusive right, of 20 years' duration in most of the world, granted over an invention that is new, involves an inventive step and is capable of industrial application, unless it is excluded from protection. In the words of Abraham Lincoln, patents 'add the fuel of interest to the fire of genius'. The legislation excludes from the scope of protection certain matter (**excluded matter**) that might look like an invention but specifically is not. Importantly, this includes a program for a computer (see **software patent**) and a method of doing business (see **business method** patent), though these are only excluded from being considered inventions (and therefore being patentable) as such. The door is therefore left open to inventions that involve for example a computer program, which is just as well as otherwise a large number of inventions would be excluded.

Adjective: (1) open, referring to the document which in days gone by evidenced the grant of a exclusive right (not necessarily to an invention) to which the Royal seal was attached at the end such that it could be opened and read without the need to break the seal (see **letters patent**); (2) the product of some inventive process (patent medicine) or an inventive product (patent leather, definitely with a long 'a'), though the past participle of the verb to patent is more often used in this sense.

Verb: to secure a patent for an invention (cf. to trademark or to copyright, expressions which often, especially outside the USA, serve to highlight the ignorance of intellectual property law of the speaker or writer), hence 'patented'.

Patent Agent

1. In countries where an attorney must be qualified in law, a practitioner who has a qualification in patent law but not in general law. They cannot represent their clients in court.
2. A member of the Chartered Institute of Patent Agents who acts for their clients in all matters relating to the technical aspects of patents. Patent agents usually have a technical degree and must pass a complex hybrid examination on procedure and drafting. A patent agent also has the right of audience in the Patents Court in appeals from the Patent Office; a patent agent holding a Litigator Certificate has right of audience in any case before the Patents Court and in the Court of Appeal in appeals from the Patents Court.

Patent agents are also permitted to use the appellation 'patent attorney', which in the United States is used to denote a fully qualified lawyer practising patent law. The title 'European Patent Attorney' may be used by those who have passed the **European Qualifying Examinations**, which include a test of the candidate's ability to work in French and German as well as English.

Patent Application

An ambiguous expression which might mean either:

1. The legal state of affairs that is constituted when a person requests the competent authority to grant him a patent and that request is still outstanding.
2. The content of the document or documents which that person filed with a view to initiating the above; most pertinently, a description of the invention together with at least one claim purporting to define it.

See *Oxonica Energy Ltd v Neuftec Ltd* (2008) EWHC 2127 (Pat) (Peter Prescott QC). The first of these meanings is an institutional fact, and is temporal by its very nature. It ceases to exist as soon as an application is withdrawn, refused or granted. The second is a historical fact that exists for ever, no matter what the Patent Office or anyone else does. When even a patent professional speaks of an application, it is not always apparent which meaning is intended. The same could be true of applications for other registered intellectual property rights.

Patent Attorney

A legal practitioner working in the patents field and who is entitled to represent clients before a local patent office. Some jurisdictions restrict the use of the title 'attorney' to qualified lawyers (for example, the US and South Africa). In the UK, where the title 'attorney' was historically used by the counterparts in the common law courts of solicitors, the designation 'patent attorney' is restricted to those with a patent qualification. See **European patent attorney** and **patent agent**.

Patent Clearance

An assurance that a proposed new product or process does not infringe any valid third-party patents. This is established (insofar as it can be established at all) by a search of existing patents and a careful analysis of the results.

Patent Co-operation Treaty (PCT)

The Patent Co-operation Treaty established a mechanism to simplify and reduce the cost of obtaining patent protection throughout large parts of the world – which otherwise could be phenomenally expensive. The International Bureau of WIPO carries out many of the formalities, which avoids the need to repeat the steps in many countries where a patent is sought.

This is a simplified filing procedure, which in some countries also deals with the search required for patentability to be established. A single application, in one language, is all it takes to get protection in the countries that are party to the PCT, which is most of the countries of the world that are likely to be of interest – 142 of them (May 2010). The most important non-member is Taiwan, and there are further gaps in South America and the Islamic world. Since 2000, the priority of patent applications originating in WTO members that are not parties to the PCT have been recognised under the PCT.

There is an international phase where a preliminary search is carried out by one of the International Searching Authorities, after which the International Bureau of WIPO publishes the application and coordinates the preliminary examination by one of the International Preliminary Examination Authorities. The application then enters the national phase in which the countries in which protection is sought apply their own rules. The main advantage is that the PCT defers much of the expense (including translation costs) of a filing programme, although it is not a fast process. The PCT system also offers the possibility of dealing with some formalities like naming inventors and applicants and filing certified copies of priority documents once with the International Bureau rather than several times.

Patent Eligibility Trilogy

The collective name for three key US cases on patentability of computer software: *Gottschalk v Benson*, *Parker v Flook* and *Diamond v Diehr*. Presumably now *Bilski* has been decided it has become a tetralogy.

Patent Examination Highway, Patent Prosecution Highway (PPH)

An arrangement between a number of patent offices whereby patent applicants who have received an examination report from one of the relevant national intellectual property offices may request accelerated examination of a corresponding patent application filed in another relevant country. The first opened in 2007 between Japan and the Republic of Korea, and several others have followed since although many remain tentative and experimental. The two expressions appear to be in use interchangeably, though PPH is the more commonly encountered.

Patent Family

'[A] set of patents taken in various countries to protect a single invention (when a first application in a country – the priority – is then extended to other offices)' (OECD, Economic Analysis and Statistics Division, *OECD Science, Technology and Industry Scoreboard: Towards a Knowledge-Based Economy*, Paris: OECD Publishing, 2001). Or, in the words of the

USPTO's online Glossary: 'the same invention disclosed by a common inventor(s) and patented in more than one country'.

An artificial construct, in that the grouping is created by a search agency or database operator such as Derwent or INPADOC for the convenience of researchers.

Patent families may be closely related or extended. Members of the former have a common priority application number and date. The latter typically results from complex relationships but with members sharing at least one common priority application from different countries, or relationships resulting from divisions, continuations or continuations-in-part.

There are a couple of special types of patent family. A trilateral patent family is part of a filtered subset of patent families for which there is evidence of patenting activity in all trilateral blocs (that is, the US, Japan, and at least one EPC Contracting State). Triadic patents are a series of corresponding patents filed at the European Patent Office (EPO), the United States Patent and Trademark Office (USPTO) and the Japan Patent Office (JPO), for the same invention, by the same applicant or inventor. (OECD, *Main Science and Technology Indicators*, Vol. 1, Paris, 2005.)

Patent Flooding

Patenting every possible way of doing something.

Patent Law Treaty (PLT)

The international convention that sets out formal procedures regarding national and regional patent applications and patents. Includes mostly maximum standards, so contracting states may choose to be more generous to applicants (the exception being filing date requirements, which are absolute). Entered into force on 28 April 2005; 25 contracting parties.

Patent of Addition

See **addition, patent of**.

Patent of Importation

See **importation, patent of**.

Patent Office (UK)

An institution established by the Patent Law Amendment Act 1852 to rationalise the grant of patents (which under that Act were for the first time granted for the whole United Kingdom rather than the separate countries) and ensure that Charles Dickens's *A Poor Man's Tale of a Patent* (http://www.readbookonline.net/readOnLine/2530/; Dickens's work can also be read in an edition edited by Jeremy Phillips: *Charles Dickens and the Poor Man's Tale of a Pantent*, Oxford: ESC, 1984) remained in the realm of fiction – which is where it clearly belonged: prior to 1852, it was necessary to apply to seven separate offices before a patent would be granted, but Dickens took full advantage of artistic licence and boosted this to a total of 34.

The name Patent Office is protected by section 112 of the Patents Act 1977, which makes it an absolute offence punishable on summary conviction by a fine on level 4 (up to £2500) to use the name. The Gowers Review recommended that the institution rename itself UK Intellectual Property Office (now shortened to Intellectual Property Office, or just IPO, which fails to distinguish it from any other country's intellectual property office). The new name is an operating name of the Patent Office, which remains the real name of the institution – which incorporates the Trade Marks Registry and the Designs Registry, names that do not enjoy the same statutory protection.

The adoption of Gowers's recommendation, and the effective surrender of the protection of section 112, necessitated a number of rather circular trade mark applications, and the subsequent dropping of the 'UK' part another round of applications.

Patent pending

An indication that a patent has been applied for to protect an alleged invention. The words are often applied to products that embody the invention, alerting third parties to the existence of the application and enabling them to take a view about whether they might be about to do something that might in due course be an infringement. This may also set the date from which damages may be claimed.

Different jurisdictions have different rules governing the use of the designation. Section 111 of the UK Patents Act 1977 makes it an offence to claim that a patent has been applied for where this is not the case (or where the application has been withdrawn or refused). Note that section 62(1) provides that an award of damages or an account of profits might not be awarded if the infringer had no reason to believe that there was a patent to infringe, and that merely because goods bear the legend 'patent' or 'patented' or something else conveying that meaning the defendant will not be assumed to have reason so to believe, unless the patent number is also shown (see **marking**). Of course, this does not apply to patent applications, because no infringement action can be brought anyway, but it does mean that it is prudent to quote application numbers too.

Patent Pool

An arrangement under which a plurality of patent owners bundle together their proprietary technology by means of cross-licensing, either to facilitate cooperation between themselves or with a view to granting licences for the bundle rather than for individual patents – a form of one-stop shopping. Not automatically permitted under the EC patent licensing block exemption or the later technology transfer block exemptions.

It may also refer to the pooling of technology for more benign purposes, in particular making available certain pharmaceutical products that might be helpful in the treatment of AIDS – but this is a highly controversial area, given that the patent system appears to enable rich pharmaceutical companies to charge high prices and limit supply to countries, particularly in sub-Saharan Africa, where there is an urgent need for such treatments.

Patent Prosecution Highway (PPH)

See **Patent Examination Highway**.

Patent–Registration Linkage

The practice of linking drug marketing approval to the patent status of the originator's product and not allowing the grant of marketing approval to any third party before the end of the patent term unless by consent of the patent owner. A significant issue in trade agreements, especially between the US and developing countries.

Patentability Search

A search of patent and other literature designed to establish whether what is thought to be an invention will be capable of becoming patented.

Patentable Subject Matter

In broad terms, the subject-matter of patents is inventions, but this simple proposition masks a great deal of complexity. There is no universally accepted definition of what is patentable, though it is generally required that an invention be relevant to practical affairs. The European system requires a technical effect, which makes software patents and business methods patents difficult (though not impossible) to obtain. The United States patent system has generally been more generous to such inventions. See **unpatentable subject matter**.

Patent Term Extension

See **extension of patent term**.

Patent-to-Patent Citation

Patent citation analysis can reveal useful information about what is happening in various sectors of technology. The flow of technology can be traced, through time, from one patent to another and from one technical area to another. Patent-to-patent citations reveal whether different sectors of technology are building upon each other.

Patentanwalt, Patentassessor

German patent attorney in private practice and in industry, respectively. Both undergo the same process to qualify, including a period working in the Bundespatentamt, the Bundespatentgericht and private practice, as well as sitting examinations.

Patentee

The person who has been granted a patent, or (as the case may be) the holder of a patent.

Patents Act 1977

The governing legislation in the United Kingdom, representing a dramatic change to an internationalist approach based on the European Patent Convention. Section 130(7) makes the (probably) unprecedented statement:

> Whereas by a resolution made on the signature of the Community Patent Convention the governments of the member states of the European Economic Community resolved to adjust their laws relating to patents so as (among other things) to bring those laws into conformity with the corresponding provisions of the European Patent Convention, the Community Patent Convention and the Patent Co-operation Treaty, it is hereby declared that the following provisions of this Act, that is to say, sections 1(1) to (4), 2 to 6, 14(3), (5) and (6), 37(5), 54, 60, 69, 72(1) and (2), 74(4), 82, 83, 100 and 125, are so framed as to have, as nearly as practicable, the same effects in the United Kingdom as the corresponding provisions of the European Patent Convention, the Community Patent Convention and the Patent Co-operation Treaty have in the territories to which those Conventions apply.

Patents County Court (PCC)

Set up in 1990 under the Copyright, Designs and Patents Act 1988 (section 287(1) of which empowered the Secretary of State to make an order to give the court jurisdiction) as an alternative venue to the **Patents Court** for certain disputes concerning patents, registered designs and, latterly, trade marks. Its jurisdiction extends to Community trade marks and designs where the courts of England and Wales are competent, as well as other intellectual property cases where an ordinary County Court may be competent. This jurisdiction covers many copyright matters.

The idea was to create a forum where simpler cases could be dealt with under a procedure that would be cheaper and more streamlined than that in the High Court. In practice, however, the Woolf Reforms of 1998 made much the same streamlined procedure available in all courts. The effectiveness of the new court was also compromised by the way that some practitioners appeared to be doing their best to recreate the complexity of High Court proceedings.

One still significant difference between the PCC and the High Court is that cases at the PCC can be argued by solicitors or **patent agents**, rather than having to be presented by counsel.

The PCC has the status of a County Court, but there is no restriction on the complexity of cases it can hear, or on the levels of damages it can award. Caps on costs were introduced in September 2010. Cases can be transferred from the PCC list to be heard by the High Court at the discretion of the PCC, and the High Court also routinely transfers cases from its list to the PCC. As with the High Court, appeals from PCC decisions (if leave to appeal is granted) are heard by the Court of Appeal.

The PCC was originally, and rather inconveniently, situated at the Edmonton court complex, in north London. It was later relocated to the Central London County Court. The PCC's judge was from 1990 to 2000 Judge Peter Ford: in Spring 2001 Judge Michael Fysh QC succeeded him and Colin Birss QC took the position in September 2010. Cases are heard by the judge or an appointed deputy judge.

Patents Court

A court of the Chancery Division of the High Court, to which all patent cases are automatically allocated (unless they are commenced in the Patents County Court, from whence they may however be transferred).

Patentschrift

German, a granted patent application.

Paternity Right

The right, given by section 77 of the Copyright, Designs and Patents Act 1988, to be identified as the author or (in the case of a film) director of one's work in certain circumstances. The Act requires that the right be asserted in accordance with section 78, otherwise no infringement can take place. Section 78 requires the assertion to be in writing, and frequently has the effect of depriving the author of the protection of the right. It was the government's intention to introduce the most limited right it could get away with, and it relied on the fact that the Berne Convention only requires members to give authors the right to claim to be the author, which was thought to excuse the requirement for assertion.

Patrimoine National

Literally, 'national heritage'. In French patent law, no priority application may be filed outside France for an invention deemed to form part of the *patrimoine national.* The concept serves a similar purpose to the national security provisions in many patent laws. There is no hard-and-fast definition of the expression, and in practice what the Defence Ministry decides can be reversed by the courts.

Patry, William

An American copyright lawyer, copyright counsel to the US House of Representatives in the early 1990s, Professor of Law at the Benjamin N. Cardozo School of Law, author of a seven-volume treatise on US copyright law entitled *Patry on Copyright,* and of *Moral Panics and the Copyright Wars* (Oxford: Oxford University Press, 2009), and Senior Copyright Counsel at Google, Inc.

PCT

See **Patent Co-operation Treaty**.

Pecuniary Remedy

See **damages**.

Pecuniary Rights

See **Economic Rights**.

Pedrick Patent

Arthur Paul Pedrick was an examiner at the UK Patent Office and later (after his retirement) a prolific inventor, with 162 patent applications to his name between 1962 and 1976. Many addressed problems associated with his cat, Ginger, perhaps the prototypical **IPKat**, and in at least one case the cat from next door, Blackie (his chromatically selective cat flap being designed to distinguish between the two). Although his inventions were virtually devoid of practical application, and it seems that none of his applications ever proceeded to grant, his activities amounted to a useful critique of the patent system and in Ian Brindley BL O/137/10, 6 May

2010 the examiner rejected a later application as obvious against Pedrick's patent application for using passing vehicles to generate electricity.

Peer-to-Patent

See **community patent review**.

Pendency

In an application process, typically for patents, the time taken to achieve one action (usually an **office action** (see **official action**)), measured from a reference date to the date of completion of the action.

Performance

An act over which the copyright owner has exclusive rights. May include reciting, rendering, playing, dancing, or acting, and may further include broadcasting by radio or television of a performance and the reception of such a broadcast.

Performer's Protection

Under the Performer's Protection Act 1963, it was an offence knowingly to make a record or film directly or indirectly from the performance of a musical or dramatic work without the consent, in writing, of the performers; or to sell or let such a work on hire or to use it for public performance. The court was also empowered to restrain the commission of such acts.

In *RCA v Pollard* [1982] 3 All ER 771, [1983] FSR 9 and *Sellars v Universal Artists* [1987] FSR 362 the courts contrived to build a right to claim damages and other civil remedies on the foundations of these offences. In 1988 performer's protection gave way to **rights in performances**.

Performers' Property Rights

The second set of rights in performances. Once the recording has been made, these come into play. The performer's permission is needed to make copies of that recording, and a performer may be entitled to remuneration for broadcasting, other types of communication to the public by electronic transmission, public performance and rental of those copies.

Performers' Rights, Performers' Non-property Rights

One of the two sets of rights in performances, to control the broadcasting or recording of a live performance. Performers' rights initially belong to the performer and subsist, independently of any copyright in the work performed, in the performance. Where the performer is under exclusive contract to another (for example, a record company) that other generally enjoys the rights in the performance.

Performing Rights Tribunal

The forerunner in the UK to the **Copyright Tribunal**, with rather narrower jurisdiction.

Period of Grace

A period during which something can be done without the usual consequences following. In European Union designs legislation, nothing done in the year preceding the filing of an application for registration will compromise the novelty of the design. In the US patent applications also enjoy a 12-month period of grace, as they do in other countries including Australia, Canada and Mexico. Japan has a six-month period of grace, but only in respect of certain publications. Many laws give a sort of grace period where there has been an unauthorised disclosure of the invention or design, protecting the applicant from the consequences of that wrongful act.

The expression might also refer to a period after a deadline within which the action can be completed, usually on payment of an additional fee. Renewals in all Paris Convention countries benefit from a period of grace.

Perpetual Motion Machine

The paradigm case of an invention that is considered to be incapable of industrial application, and therefore also of being patented.

Person Skilled in the Art

See **skilled man**, **PHOSITA**.

Personality Rights

See right of **publicity**.

Petition for Review

The formal request for a review of a decision by the supreme court for the jurisdiction, including the **Enlarged Board of Appeal** of the EPO for European patent matters.

Petition To Make Special

A formal request to the **USPTO**, seeking to have a patent application examined before others in the same technological art. There are several reasons that might support such a petition, including the fact that an infringement is taking place, that the invention relates to certain important matters (including treatment of cancer or HIV/AIDS), and that the inventor is approaching his or her sixty-fifth birthday).

Petty Patent

See **utility model**.

Phantom Mark (US)

A trade mark containing variable elements. An application for a phantom mark will be rejected on the grounds that it includes more than one mark in a single application. Elsewhere, the phantom marks could form a **series**.

Phonogram

According to the **Phonograms Convention** and the **Rome Convention**, an exclusively aural fixation (so it does not include, for example, the sound tracks of films or videocassettes), whatever its form. Protection may be provided as a matter of copyright law, *sui generis* law, unfair competition law or criminal law.

Phonograms Convention

The Convention for the Protection of Producers of Phonograms against Unauthorized Duplication of their Phonograms, also known as the Geneva Phonograms Convention, is a 1971 international agreement relating to copyright protection for sound recordings. It applies the principle of national treatment, requiring members to protect a producer of phonograms who is a national of another contracting state against the making of duplicates without the consent of the producer, the importation of such duplicates where the making or importation is for the purposes of distribution to the public, and the distribution of such duplicates to the public. Protection must last for at least 20 years from the first fixation or the first publication of the phonogram, although national laws frequently provide for a 50-year term of protection as is required in the European Union under the directive. See also **Rome Convention**.

Phonorecords, Phonograms

The material objects that store or fix sounds. Include tapes, compact discs, vinyl records and memory sticks. Film soundtracks receive special treatment in some countries' copyright laws.

PHOSITA

Person Having Ordinary Skill in the Art – the counterpart in US patent law of the hypothetical skilled addressee of a UK (or European) patent.

Photograph

1. A type of artistic work, protected (subject to qualification and origi-
    nality) under the Copyright, Designs and Patents Act 1988 irrespective
    of artistic quality. It is defined as a recording of light or other radia-
    tion on any medium on which an image is produced or from which
    an image may by any means be reproduced, and which is not part of
    a film. Under the 1911 Act, films were protected as multiple photo-
    graphs. The definition strives to be technologically neutral, embracing
    all means of recording radiation – X-rays and digital cameras as well
    as strips of celluloid.
2. A medium in which it is generally permissible to provide illustrations
    to form part of a patent application, provided they are monochrome.
    Some patent offices will permit colour photos, but they are rarely
    necessary.

Piano Roll

A recording medium for music, used to control a **player piano**. A
perforated roll of paper.

Pig Fenders

The article the subject of the design in the first case on infringement of
UK unregistered design right, *C & H Engineering v F Klucznik & Sons Ltd*
[1992] FSR 427. A form of barrier, three sides of a rectangle, that can be
placed around the open end of the shelter provided for the animals, of a
suitable size and configuration to allow grown animals to come and go at
will while containing their offspring.

PIL

Parallel import licence.

Piracy

The unauthorised duplication of goods protected by intellectual property
laws – usually, material protected by copyright, such as sound recordings,

films or computer software. Exact copying on a commercial scale is the hallmark of piracy. Piracy can be distinguished – up to a point – from counterfeiting in that trade marks are not necessarily applied to the copies to complete the deception, but that is no hard and fast distinction.

'Pistache'

A **musical work** by Mike Westbrook, featured on the album *Citadel/Room 315* (1975). See **pastiche**.

Pith and Marrow

The essential features of an invention which courts have tried to identify by various means: one approach to claims construction adopted by the English courts was called the 'pith and marrow' approach.

PIUG

Patent Information Users Group Inc.

Planck, Max (1858–1947)

German physicist, founder of quantum physics, winner of the Nobel Prize in Physics 1918.

Plant Breeders' Right

The right given to breeders by the **International Convention for the Protection of New Varieties of Plants**. Implemented in the UK in the Plant Varieties Act 1997 which gives new, distinct, uniform and stable varieties of certain species of plants monopoly protection for 25 to 30 years. The UK law usually requires a new variety name. The monopoly right extends to such acts as marketing seeds, tubers and cuttings intended for reproduction of the variety. Licences may be granted by the owner.

Plant Patent

A type of patent known in the USA which covers asexually produced plant varieties. See also **plant breeders' rights** which are different.

Player Piano

A pianoforte that, controlled by a piano roll, plays music without further human intervention. Also known as an autopiano and as a pianola, though Pianola was the registered trade mark of the Aeolian Company, the first manufacturer of player pianos (see **generic**, **genericide**).

Poor Man's Copyright

The practice of posting a copy of one's own work to oneself, to establish (with the assistance of the postal authorities) a date by which the work must have been created.

Portfolio

All the rights owned by an intellectual property rights holder. Often specifically a patent portfolio, trade mark portfolio and so on.

Preamble

An introductory statement in a document, explaining its purpose: in US patent practice, the formal introductory clause of a patent claim.

Precautionary Designation

Designation of a Contracting State in an international application filed under the Patent Cooperation Treaty which must be confirmed prior to 15 months from the priority date.

Preferred Embodiment

Part of the description of an invention in which the author of the patent documents may set out a description of how the invention can be worked. There might be several embodiments described, of which one will be described as the preferred embodiment. See also **best method, best mode**.

Preliminary Examination

The examination to which patent applications (and perhaps applications for other forms of intellectual property) are subject when they are first submitted, directed to matters such as compliance with formalities. See **substantive examination**.

Prior Art

Previously used or published material, including technology, that might destroy the novelty or inventiveness of a invention or at least set the context in which the invention has to be assessed. Includes everything known and used in the technical field of a patent application, at the date of the application or the priority date if it has one. Written material (including patent specifications, textbooks, journals and so on) is the main constituent of prior art, but it also includes oral disclosures and use in public. The prior art must generally be described in patent applications, but the EPO requires only the closest art. A prior art search is a common, and easy, precaution to take before filing an application. See **state of the art**.

Prior Right, National

In the European Patents system, a prior right derived from a national patent in one of the member countries.

Prior use

In most patent systems, a form of anticipation or disclosure: in the US, a defence. If an alleged infringer has been using an invention before a patent is applied for, they can rely on that prior use as a defence to an infringement action. It requires a first-to-invent approach.

Priority

The concept, fundamental to the Paris Convention, that an applicant for a piece of intellectual property should be allowed a period of time in which to file applications to protect the same subject-matter in other countries that are party to the Convention, protected against the possibility that another might step in first with an application of their own. Thus the applicant for a patent has a priority period of 12 months during which to file overseas applications (including applications under the Patent Co-operation Treaty) during which time no later-filed application can take precedence to his. An applicant to register a trade mark or design has a six-month priority period. See also **internal priority**.

Note that the **first-to-invent** rule in the US patent system overrides the priority rules of the Paris Convention.

Privacy, Right to

1. A right given by the Copyright, Designs and Patents Act 1988 to protect a person who commissions, for private and domestic purposes, a photograph or film against certain uses of the work that would intrude upon their privacy. Thus the commissioner of wedding photographs has a remedy should the photographer display copies of the photographs in public in the course of promoting their business. Under the previous (1956) Copyright Act, copyright in a commissioned photograph (or portrait) vested in the commissioner (the author of a photograph was the person who owned the roll of film – or photographic plate – when it was exposed), but the general ownership rule was applied to photographs in the 1988 Act and this right was added to ensure that one consequence of this did not create problems for commissioners.
2. A right unknown in English law, though that has not prevented lawyers acting for a motley assortment of so-called celebrities trying to create one using the law on breach of confidence, the Human Rights Act and the Data Protection Act.

PRO

Performance Rights Organisation, a copyright collecting society that deals in the rights that control performances of certain copyright works.

Problem–solution approach (EPC)

An approach to determine questions of inventiveness, used in the European Patent Office. First, identify the problem which the invention seeks to solve; second, identify the nearest piece of prior art (containing the largest number of features of the patent or application under consideration); third, identify the features of the patent or application that are lacking in this prior art; and fourth, consider whether these features are disclosed in the prior art such that it would be obvious to add them to the prior art.

Process Claim

A patent claim may be to a product or a process, and generally product claims give the stronger protection especially as infringement of process claims can be difficult to prove (given that the process is unlikely to be worked in public).

Product

1. The law on design protection in the EU (at Union and national, including Benelux, level) is concerned with designs for what are referred to as 'products'. The word is defined to mean any industrial or handicraft item other than a computer program, and expressly includes packaging, get-up, graphic symbols, typographic typefaces and parts intended to be assembled into a complex product.
2. In patent law, a product may be the subject of a patent itself, or it may be the product of a patented process. See **product claim**, **product-by-process claim**.

Product Claim

One of the two main types of patent claim and usually the stronger of the two. A product claim is infringed regardless of how the product is made – even if the infringer has devised a much more efficient way to make the product. It may also cover an entirely different use of the product.

Product-by-Process Claim

A patent claim that defines the product by reference to the process by which it is manufactured – 'Trundlene obtained by the process of claim X'. Of particular utility in the chemical and pharmaceutical industries. Allowed in the European system only if the product itself is patentable and cannot be adequately described (by reference to composition, structure or other testable parameters). US practice generally holds otherwise.

The product defined in a product-by-process claim in the UK must itself be novel and inventive. This brings UK law into line with that of the European Patent Office.

Professional Representative

A general term with a more specific meaning in the context of the Community trade mark and designs systems, for the purposes of which professional representatives are registered – although other practitioners have rights to deal with applications before **OHIM**.

Program

A series of coded instructions and definitions which when fed into a computer automatically directs its operation in performing a particular task. The spelling (in British English) has been controversial: the *Oxford English Dictionary* tells us:

> The more common earlier (and predominantly Scottish) form program was retained by Scott, Carlyle, Hamilton, and others, even after the borrowing of senses directly from French in the late 18th cent. and early 19th cent.; it conforms to the usual English representation of Greek γραμμα, in e.g. ANAGRAM n., CRYPTOGRAM n., DIAGRAM n., TELEGRAM n., etc. The influence of French programme led to the predominance of this spelling in the 19th cent. The forms programme and program have since become established as the standard British and US spellings respectively, with the exception that program is usual everywhere in senses relating to computing.

Programmed Computer Claim

A form of indirect patent claim to a computer program or other non-patentable (US: patent-ineligible) subject-matter. It rests on 'the legal doctrine that a new program makes an old general purpose digital computer into a new and different machine' (*In re Johnston*, 502 F.2d 765, 773 (CCPA 1974), from the dissenting opinion). The novelty resides in what the machine is doing, of course, but the claim directs attention to the programmed computer.

The argument against the validity of such claims, deployed in *Gottschalk v Benson*, is expressed in one of those wonderful phrases that lawyers in the USA apply to such graphic effect: the **Old Piano Roll Blues**, derived from the title of a 1940s song by Cy Coben, performed by Al Jolson. It states that putting a new piano roll into an old player piano does not convert the latter into a new machine, and contains a further allusion to the decision of the Supreme Court in *White-Smith v. Apollo*, concerning copyright protection for piano rolls.

Prosecution

The process of pursuing an application for a patent, trade mark, registered design or other registered intellectual property right through the stages required by the applicable law.

Prosecution History Estoppel

See **file wrapper estoppel**.

Protected Designation of Origin (PDO)

The name of an area, a specific place or, sometimes, the name of a country, used as a designation for an agricultural product or a foodstuff which comes exclusively from there, or whose quality or properties are significantly or exclusively determined by the geographical environment (which might include natural and human factors), or which is produced, processed or prepared exclusively in that geographical area. Wine and olive oil are prime examples of products that enjoy such protection.

Protected Geographical Indication (PGI)

Similar to a Protected Designation of Origin, but indicating a less-than-exclusive connection with the geographical location. It might be partially produced, processed or prepared there. Newcastle Brown Ale was a PGI, but when the brewer decided to move production across the River Tyne to Gateshead it had to apply to cancel the registration (done by Commission regulation 952/2007).

Protected Geographical Status

An omnibus term covering Protected Geographical Indications, Protected Designation of Origin, and Traditional Speciality Guaranteed, different forms of protection for the names of regional foods, known to European Community law since 1992. Derived from the Stresa Convention of 1951, the first international agreement on cheeses. Expanding in scope as a result of bilateral arrangements made by the EC Commission with other countries, and the Commission is seeking to have the subject brought within the scope of the **WTO**.

Protected Marks (New Zealand)

Signs the use of which is restricted under a variety of statutes, including the New Zealand Trade Marks Act 1953. The list includes official emblems and hallmarks of states and intergovernmental organisations, New Zealand flag and ensigns, flags or emblems of other countries, geographical names registered in respect of certain goods, international non-proprietary pharmaceutical names, common names of any (chemical) element or compound, generic names for pesticides and agricultural chemicals, and plant varieties. Similar to **official marks** in Canada.

Protected Signs, 6 ter Protected Signs

A range of signs, including state emblems, official hallmarks and emblems of intergovernmental organisations, which may not be registered or used by virtue of Article 6 ter of the Paris Convention. See **protected marks**, **official marks**, **protected words**.

Protected Words

A class of words that cannot be registered as or form part of trade marks under the Trade Marks Act 1994. Not an expression used in the Act, but it does feature in the Manual of Trade Mark Registry Practice.

Protocol on Interpretation of Article 69 EPC

Article 69 is the provision in the European Patent Convention that deals with infringement. The Protocol sets out how courts should go about interpreting patent claims to see if an infringement has been committed. It seeks to ensure that the interpretation of patent claims in the European system tends neither towards a purely literal approach (sometimes referred to as a British approach, though the English courts long ago decided that a purely literal approach was not appropriate) nor towards treating the claims as mere guidelines (referred to as the German approach). It says:

Article 1

General principles

Article 69 should not be interpreted as meaning that the extent of the protection conferred by a European patent is to be understood as that defined by the strict, literal meaning of the wording used in the claims, the description and drawings being employed only for the purpose of resolving an ambiguity found in the claims. Nor should it be taken to mean that the claims serve only as a guideline and that the actual protection conferred may extend to what, from a consideration of the description and drawings by a person skilled in the art, the patent proprietor has contemplated. On the contrary, it is to be interpreted as defining a position between these extremes which combines a fair protection for the patent proprietor with a reasonable degree of legal certainty for third parties.

Article 2

Equivalents

For the purpose of determining the extent of protection conferred by a European patent, due account shall be taken of any element which is equivalent to an element specified in the claims.

Following the judgment of the House of Lords in **Kirin-Amgen**, the Protocol is the definitive statement of how patent claims should be interpreted: neither literally, nor using them only as guidelines. The provision about equivalents was added by **EPC 2000**. The lack of a definition of 'equivalent' is thought to make it ineffective.

Protocol on Recognition (EPC)

The Protocol on Jurisdiction and the Recognition of Decisions in Respect of the Right to the Grant of a European Patent deals with proceedings in national courts and tribunals relating to European patents.

Protocol Questions

A series of questions that are used by the courts to facilitate the application of the Protocol on Interpretation of Article 69. They bear an uncanny resemblance to the **Improver** questions.

Provisional Patent Application, 'Provisional'

Some countries permit an initial, relatively cheap, patent application to be filed, which enables the applicant to get a priority date. The main feature omitted in a provisional is the claims, which account for a large part of the cost and complexity of a regular application. The description may be very basic, perhaps nothing more than pages from a laboratory notebook A substantive application can then be filed within the prescribed period – usually a year. Provisonals are a feature of the old British system and survive in some Commonwealth countries. The USA has had a system of provisional applications since 1995.

No enforceable rights are acquired through the filing of a provisional application.

Provisional Protection

Publication of a patent application is often said to give provisional protection for the invention, in that someone doing something that is within the scope of the claims is placed on notice that they might infringe the patent when it is granted. The infringement action will claim back to the date on which the infringer was placed on notice. Best practice is to send the other party a copy of the application. Under the EPC, if the claims have not been translated into the language of the Contracting State concerned and provided to the alleged infringer or to the national patent office, provisional protection might not apply.

Publication

1.   The making public of a patent or patent application by a patent office. There is usually what is called early publication of the unexamined application at 18 months after the application or priority date. There might also be publication on acceptance for the purposes of pre-grant opposition, and there is also publication on grant.

2. The characteristic of prior art that may be used against a patent or application. The precise requirements differ between countries, and there is a considerable body of case-law on the subject, but in general if a reference is available to a single member of the public free of any secrecy obligations (whether express or implied) it is considered to have been published. See **novelty**.

3. The disclosure of an invention to the public such that its novelty is destroyed and no patent can be granted for it. This is why the application should ideally be filed before any disclosure is made to anyone. However, there are usually exceptions to this general rule: exhibition at a certified international exhibition, unauthorised disclosure by a third party in contravention of an obligation of confidence, presentation of a paper before a learned society, or publication in a learned society journal (old British law, now rare), or use in public for the purposes of a reasonable trial (also old British law, now rare).

Publication Codes

Alphanumeric codes indicating the status of a patent publication. Unfortunately, practice varies between patent offices which tends to reduce the value of the exercise. However, 'A' always represents first publication and 'B' second publication, which is helpful as far as it goes until one encounters a country that publishes before examination and another that publishes only on grant – both such publications will be designated 'A'. In the EPO, the following codes are used:

- A1 – pre-examination publication with search report.
- A2 – pre-examination publication without search report.
- A3 – publication of search report only.
- B1 – publication on grant.
- B2 – publication on grant, post-opposition.

In some EPC Contracting States, European Patents validated in those countries have special designations (for example E in Austria, T in Germany and Spain). See also **kind codes**.

Publication Right

A copyright-like right enjoyed by publishers of previously unpublished literary, dramatic, musical or artistic work. It lasts for 25 years. See the Copyright and Related Rights Regulations 1996 (SI No 2967).

Public Domain

Originally, land owned on some basis that allowed members of the public to make use of it. Now extends to describe the status of creative works, products, processes and (though less frequently) commercial signs that are not protected under any intellectual property law. *West's Encyclopedia of American Law* (Farnington Hills, MI: Thomson Gale, 2nd revised edition, 2004) says: 'literary or creative works over which the creator no longer has an exclusive right to restrict, or receive a royalty for, their reproduction or use but which can be freely copied by the public'.

Items in the public domain are available for free copying and use by anyone. The copying of items that are in the public domain is not only tolerated but encouraged as a vital part of the competitive process. See **Boyle, James**.

Public Lending Right

A programme to compensate authors for the use of their works by lending through public libraries – which is assumed to deprive them of some sales. Twenty-eight countries have such programmes at present. The existence of such a right is important in the context of the rental and lending right in EU copyright law, because Member States are not obliged to give copyright owners exclusive rights in these areas if there is already a mechanism in place to give them equitable remuneration.

Public Policy

A ground for refusing grant or registration of intellectual property rights, often linked with morality. An invention may be contrary to public policy (as contraceptives once were); so too may a trade mark or a registered design. There is no express exception in UK copyright law, but *Glynn v Weston Feature Films* [1916] 1 Ch 261 1721 provides an example – albeit a rather old one – of a copyright work being denied protection from infringement on morality grounds.

Public Prior Use

Generally, prior use would be anticipatory of an invention, but in a first-to-invent system such as that in the USA it can provide a defence to an infringement action. However, in the US public prior use can still amount to an anticipation under 35 USC § 102(b).

Publicity, Right of

The inherent right of a human being to control the commercial use of his or her identity, known in some jurisdictions (for example Illinois) but not in English law. Sometimes known as personality rights, though this is often a common or colloquial expression.

Pullman Bonds

David Pullman is a financial entrepreneur who devised the form of financial security that bears his name (and is a registered trade mark). The bond involves the 'securitisation' of a royalty stream, creating an asset that can then be used as security to raise funds – commonly, selling shares or bonds in a special-purpose vehicle (a company set up for that purpose). The great thing for the copyright owner is that they can retain ownership –much better than selling the copyright outright. In the sub-prime mortgage sector, a similar technique has created problems. See also **Bowie Bonds**.

Purposive Construction

An approach to interpreting patent claims that looks less at the precise words used and more at the purpose behind them. Its classic formulation is in the opinion of Lord Diplock in *Catnic Components v Hill & Smith Ltd* [1981] FSR 60, [1982] RPC 183 (HL). The case concerned steel lintels. The plaintiff had a patent for lintels with the 'second rigid support member extending vertically from or near the rear edge of the first horizontal plane or part adjacent its rear edge'. The defendant's lintel had the rear support member inclined at an angle of some 6 to 8 degrees to the vertical, and the case hinged on whether when the patent said 'vertical' it meant it exactly.

Looking at what the applicant had in mind rather than the precise words used, in the specification, their Lordships held that the verticality of the support member plaintiff's lintel was inessential as the invention worked just as well with a slight incline (as in the defendants' product). The defendants had argued that the verticality was essential and therefore there was no infringement of the pith and marrow of the patent. Because the inclination made no significant difference to the performance of the lintel, the House of Lords took the view that the pith and marrow of the patent had not been infringed.

The approach to construing patent specifications adopted in that case is described as 'purposive'. Lord Diplock said that 'the kind of meticulous verbal analysis in which lawyers are too often tempted by their training to indulge' was inappropriate in construing a patent specification: the real issue was whether practical persons, skilled in the art, would understand that the patentee intended strict compliance with a particular word or phrase to be an essential requirement of the invention. However, para-doxically, he stressed that there was no separate question of 'non-textual infringement': the only thing that could be infringed was the patent as it stood, the only uncertainty lying in what the text meant. His Lordship said that the important thing was the understanding of 'persons with practical knowledge and experience of the kind of work in which the invention was intended to be used'. The key question was whether such a person would read the language of the patent as demanding strict compliance, excluding any variant even though it might have no material effect on the way the invention worked. To a builder, the defendant's lintel was as good as the patentee's: he or she would treat the rear support member as vertical for his or her purposes: and it was to the builder (or the builder's merchant) that the specification was addressed.

You might think, as I did, that had the word 'substantially' been included so as to qualify 'vertically', much trouble could have been avoided. The claim does contain that word, but it qualifies the word 'horizontally' which describes another part of the lintel. The draftsman of the patent apparently believed that the concept of 'extending vertically' simply meant that the top of the face had a more elevated position than the bottom, not that it had to be directly above, so the word 'substantially' would have been redundant.

Q

Quater

Latin ordinal number, fourth: encountered particularly in international conventions, for example Article 4 quater of the Paris Convention.

Quia Timet

Latin, 'because he fears'. A type of injunction granted to restrain a wrongful act that is threatened or imminent but has not yet taken place. Important in intellectual property actions, especially passing-off actions. The basic principles for the grant of such an injunction were set down by Pearson J in *Fletcher v. Bealey* (1884) 28 Ch.D. 688 at p. 698: proof of imminent danger; proof that the threatened injury will be practically irreparable; and proof that whenever the injurious circumstances ensue, it will be impossible to protect the plaintiff's interests, if relief is denied.

Quiet Possession

In English law, there is an implied warranty in all contracts for the sale or supply of goods that the buyer will enjoy quiet possession of his purchases. If someone has the right to stop him doing what he would normally expect to be able to do with those goods, the term is breached unless the purchaser had notice of the other party's claim, or where it is clear that the seller is only transferring such title as he has. The implied warranty cannot be excluded by a term of the contract.

The owner of intellectual property rights could disrupt the purchaser's quiet possession of the goods. In *Niblett Ltd v Confectioners' Materials Co Ltd* [1921] 3KB 387 the goods were labelled in such a way that they could not be sold without infringing a third party's trade mark. The Court of Appeal held that there was a breach of warranty.

There will also be a breach of warranty where quiet possession is disturbed by a patentee even though the patent was only granted after the goods were sold.

Quinquies

Latin ordinal number, fifth: encountered particularly in international conventions, for example Article 5 quinquies of the Paris Convention.

R

Re-establishment of Rights

See *restitutio in integrum,* **restitution**.

Re-examination

A procedure available in some patent systems – in particular, the US – for examining a patent again, in the light of newly discovered prior art. Equivalent to revocation.

Re-filing

See **abandonment**. This can be done in the course of prosecuting a patent, under the US system. The application is refiled either as a **request for continued examination** (RCP) or **a continuation in part** (C-I-P) application. Priority is preserved, except for the new matter in a C-I-P.

Reach-Through Claim

A type of **free beer claim** in which the actual subject of the application is a method (perhaps a research tool or screening assay) but which attempts to cover substances that could be discovered or identified by using the invention. Generally not allowed: *In Re Petrus A.C.M. Nuijten*, CAFC, 2006-1371 (Serial No. 09/211,928), EPO Board of Appeal decision T-1063/06.

Reach-Through Royalty

A royalty for the use of an invention calculated not on the value of the screening assay or research tool the subject of the patent but on the value of the active compounds discovered by the assay.

'Reads On'

A patent claim is said to read on something if every element of the claim is present in the document with which it is being compared. A claim that reads on prior art is invalid, and for infringement to occur the alleged infringing matter must read on the claim. Mainly US usage.

Reasonable and Non-Discriminatory Licensing

See **FRAN**.

Receiving Office

The office that receives an international application in the PCT or Madrid systems. In the PCT it is responsible for checking the applications for formalities.

Reduction to Practise

Actually making whatever it may be that a patent protects. Filing a patent application containing a sufficient disclosure of the invention is constructive reduction to practice. One of the criteria used when deciding who has the right to an invention under a 'first-to-invent' rule (meaning, in effect, in the US). It is not enough just to devise the invention: the inventor must make a working model or draw up a patent application.

Refusal

The fate of a patent, trade mark, registered design or other application which does not comply with the requirements of the law within any applicable time limit.

Regenerating Priority

Article 4C(4) of the Paris Convention enables a patent application filed after the first one, for the same subject matter, to give rise to a priority right – but only if certain specific conditions have been met. The specific conditions are that:

1. the later application was filed in or for the same country as the first application, and
2. at the date of filing of the later application, the first application had been unconditionally withdrawn, or abandoned or refused, had not been published, and did not leave any rights outstanding, and
3. at the date of filing of the later application, the first application had not been used for priority purposes for any other application.

If these conditions are met the later application can then give rise to a priority right. Its filing date is taken as the starting point of the 12-month priority period. The first application may be entirely disregarded. This is useful for applicants who wish to reset the clock in cases where the subject matter has not been disclosed at the date of filing of the later application.

Regional Phase

The second phase of an international patent application (that is, an application made under the **Patent Co-operation Treaty**) following the international phase, 30 months after the international filing date or earliest priority date. The application will go through a national phase where national patents are sought, but if the international application designates a European Patent or other regional patent, the second phase will not be called 'national' but 'regional'.

Registered Design

The appearance of an article or product, or features of it, for which the law gives protection if certain conditions are satisfied. There is considerable diversity around the world in this area of intellectual property protection, but in the European Union the laws of the Member States (including the Registered Designs Act 1949 in the UK) are harmonised and their substantive law is the same as that applying to Community designs. A design for a product will be protected if it is new and has individual character, irrespective of whether it has eye-appeal. There are exceptions to what may be registered intended to preserve competition particularly in the car spares market: see **repair clause**. Protection is given for five years, renewable four times (so 25 years in total).

The **Hague Agreement** facilitates international registrations of designs.

Registered Designs Act 1949

The short title of three different pieces of UK legislation: the original Act was heavily amended in 1988 and then again in 2001. More than one version might be relevant to a single case (though not, thankfully, all three).

Registered Invention

The name used in the Nicholson Report to denote a lesser form of patent protection, also called **utility model** or **petty patent**.

Registered User

Under the Trade Marks Act 1938, a licence of a trade mark was a problem. On the face of it, the trade mark would not be used by the owner and in the fullness of time might be challenged and revoked on the grounds of non-use. Use by a simple licensee would not save it – but use by a registered user would. So a licence had to be in a particular form and it had to be registered with the Trade Marks Registry. This provision did not survive into the 1994 Act, but it did live on in some UK-inspired trade mark laws elsewhere in the world.

Registration

1. Of a trade mark, means the entering on the register of particulars of the trade mark, which event is also marked by the issue of a certificate. Although the rights granted by registration are commonly backdated to the date of the application, the owner cannot usually take action against infringers until registration has taken place. Registration will usually be taken as *prima facie* evidence of distinctiveness. Traditionally, trade marks have been items of property whose existence was recorded on a register, but modern practice in the European Union (and in various other countries that have adopted laws based on the EU model) makes registration the event that brings the right into existence.

2. Of a design, the entry of particulars on the register, as with a trade mark. However, in most design registration systems (including the EU) there is no substantive examination, and the system has the characteristics of a deposit system rather than a true registration system.
3. Of a patent, which (unlike a trade mark or a design) is a creation of the law (the underlying entity being an invention), the entry of the particulars on the register is a formal step: the key event is the grant of the patent.
4. May also refer to the validation in a dependent state or territory of an intellectual property right granted in the main jurisdiction – for example, a Chinese patent in Hong Kong, a British trade mark in Jersey.

Regulation

In the European Union, a legislative instrument that has direct effect on Member States without the need for it to be transposed into national law.

Reissue (US)

Where an issued patent is defective, the patent owner can surrender it and refile the original application to correct the defect. This would be the case, for example, where the issued patent fails to claim the full scope of the invention, or close prior art is found after grant. This procedure permits an inventor to submit the patent application again with broader claims and try to get the full coverage to which he is entitled. New features may not be added to the invention. There is a time limit of two years from the date of grant of the original patent, after which a reissue application with broader claims than the original one may not be filed.

Related Rights

See **neighbouring rights**.

Relative Grounds

Given that there are absolute grounds for refusal of registration of a trade mark (in the European Union, its Member States' national trade mark systems and the Benelux trade mark system) it is logical to assume the existence of relative grounds, too. Absolute grounds are concerned with defects inherent in the sign for which the applicant hopes to secure registration: relative grounds are concerned with conflicts between the applicant's sign and others' earlier rights, including not only registered trade marks that are valid in the jurisdiction concerned but also copyright, rights in designs and common law rights.

Calling these relative grounds for refusal is, however, in many ways a misnomer. OHIM never refused registration on relative grounds: the Community Trade Mark (CTM) system has always relied on oppositions, not *ex officio* refusals, to keep the register clean. The UK, one of the last bastions in Europe of *ex officio* refusals on relative grounds, was transformed into an opposition system on 1 October 2007, placing a significant burden on trade mark owners who must oppose applications that conflict with their rights, and perhaps pay for a watching service to alert them to such applications.

Relative Novelty

A novelty standard especially in patent law under which printed publication anywhere destroys novelty, but use or oral description does so only if it takes place in the country concerned. This is the test used in US patent law.

Remedies

The various pecuniary and non-pecuniary solutions (or partial solutions) to a rights-owner's problems that the courts might be able to deliver.

Renewal

Those intellectual property rights for which one has to pay – the registered ones – need to be renewed periodically. Trade marks usually last for ten years between renewals, and the renewal fee in most countries is roughly the same as the initial application fee (with class fees to pay, too). Some countries require a declaration of use of the trade mark to be filed when it is renewed: others assume that a rational trade mark owner would not pay them money for something they were no longer using and which would turn out to be useless if they ever had to try to enforce it.

Registered designs generally require renewal at shorter intervals – five years in the European Union. Patents usually attract an annual renewal fee, or annuity (hence the existence of a number of patent annuity firms which computerise the process of keeping patents up to date for their clients). Some countries require payment of annuities even while a patent is still pending.

It is usually possible to pay renewal fees late (commonly up to six months) with a penalty.

Repackaging

An activity engaged in by parallel importers of pharmaceutical products within the European Union. Because of different prescribing protocols and practices, the packs of drugs on sale in one Member State (where they are relatively cheap) might not be suitable for supply in the (more expensive) market of another Member State. The packages must therefore be opened up and the contents (usually secure in blister packs) packed in different quantities. The parallel importer's trade mark will be applied to the packaging – indeed, the parallel importer is obliged to identify itself – and the search for the limits of what is acceptable has generated a substantial body of case law. See **Bristol-Myers Squibb conditions**.

Repair

A problem when the article one wishes to repair is the subject of a patent. Generally repairing the article will not infringe the patent, but it is not always very clear when one has crossed the border from repair into the territory of reconstruction.

Repair Clause

The provision in the Directive on legal protection of designs that seeks to secure the freedom of spare parts manufacturers to produce the parts necessary for the repair of a complex article, such as a motor car. See **must-match**.

Repentir, Droit au

The moral right in French law for an author of a copyright work, without having to give a reason, to withdraw it from the public. The author will have to indemnify publishers and others who suffer prejudice as a result.

Repercussive Effect

In patent claims, a dependent claim might have a repercussive effect on the claim on which it depends, such that the matter introduced in the dependent claim clarifies a point of interpretation of the independent claim. In *Warheit v Olympia Tools* [2003] FSR 6 which involved a patent for self-adjusting pliers, there was nothing in claim 1 that required the fastener to pivot. Dependent claim 2 referred to the fastening means having a fastener stationarily secured to the second member, so the repercussive effect of this on claim 1 was to make clear that the fastener did not have to pivot.

Reproduction

An act restricted by copyright, dealt with in Article 8 of the Berne Convention which does not clarify the meaning of the word save to say that any manner or form is covered.

Reproduction Rights Organisation (RRO)

A **collecting society** set up to administer the right to reproduce copyright works. In the UK, the Copyright Licensing Agency is the main RRO.

Request for Continued Examination (US)

A request by an inventor for continued prosecution after the patent office has issued a 'final' rejection. The inventor pays an additional filing fee and continues to argue his case with the same patent examiner. Equivalent to the old continuing prosecution application.

Research Disclosure

A commercial defensive publication service whose function is voluntarily to make technology part of the state of the art, thus ensuring that no one will be able to patent it.

Research Exemption

See **Bolar exception**.

Reserved Words

See **protected words**.

Restitutio in Integrum, **Restitution**, **Restoration**

See **restoration, re-establishment of rights**.

Restoration

Patents or applications that have been allowed to lapse can be restored but only after the applicant surmounts some formidable hurdles. The lapse must not have been intended – it cannot just be a matter of the applicant having changed their mind. It must also have resulted from an inadvertent error in an otherwise well-functioning docketing system. Restoration, where it is available, will only remain possible for a limited period after lapse.

Restraint of Trade

A contract that is excessively restrictive of a party's freedom to trade will be void and unenforceable at common law. The court will only uphold it if the restrictions contained in a contract are in the interests of the parties and the public. Where there is an obvious inequality of bargaining power between the parties, particularly where covenants restrict competition between employee and employer or the future activities of a seller of a business, or where the contract regulates the conduct of members of a trade association, or retailers are select or excluded from a network, the restraint might be considered unreasonable. Statutory competition rules will also apply.

The reasonableness of a restraint or restrictive covenant is a question of fact in each case. It will depend largely on the term of the restriction and the geographical area covered. If the obligation be severable from the rest of the contract the court will be inclined to 'blue pencil' it so as to keep the rest of the contract in force – but it will not insert new words or adopt a meaning that the parties did not originally intend.

Restricted Act

The term that is used in Part I of the Copyright, Designs and Patents Act 1988 to describe the acts that are the exclusive right of the copyright owner.

Restriction Requirement, Requirement for Restriction (US)

In the course of prosecuting a patent application, the Examiner may require that the claims be restricted to a single 'independent and distinct' invention. See **unity of invention**.

Retrait, Droit au

See *droit au* **répentir**.

Revalidation

A patent already granted in one country may be revalidated in another country, though the number of countries permitting this sort of extension of protection is now small. It happens in some Latin American countries, in the Gulf Cooperation Council (GCC) countries and in Saudi Arabia.

Reverse Confusion

In trade mark law, where the junior user eclipses the senior user, perhaps simply because the junior user is a bigger entity and spends more on advertising and promotion.

Reverse Engineering

The process of understanding how a product is made by disassembling it, making measurements and analysing it. In this way it is possible to create a copy of the product. In the classic reverse engineering case, *BL v Armstrong Patents Ltd*, the defendants plotted the so-called x, y and z coordinates which determined the configuration of the exhaust pipe in suit and used a vector bending machine to replicate the component. Cf. **decompilation**.

Reverse Passing Off

Classical passing off involves a misrepresentation that the defendant's goods or services are the claimant's. In a reverse passing off, the defendant claims that the claimant's goods or services are his: *Bristol Conservatories Ltd. v Conservatories Custom Built* [1989] RPC 455.

Revocation

The procedure for removing a flawed patent, trade mark, registered design or other registered IP right from the register (for example because a patented invention lacks novelty or because formalities have not been complied with). In systems with no pre-grant opposition procedure (for example UK patents) revocation amounts to a post-grant opposition though with more generous time limits (or none at all). Also available to a defendant in an infringement action, in the UK as a counterclaim. In the USPTO any patent claims that are determined to be unpatentable in re-examination proceedings are cancelled. See also **cancellation**.

Right of Prior Use

The right to carry on doing what one was doing before the priority date of a patent that on the face of it gives the patentee the right to stop one doing it.

Rights in Performances

Rights given to performers or to those to whom performers are under exclusive recording contracts. Governed in the UK by Part II of the

Copyright, Designs and Patents Act 1988. Rights in performances are similar to but distinct from copyright, and may be grouped together with other neighbouring or related rights. Governed internationally by the **Rome Convention**, but by no means all countries recognise them – a major exception being the United States, hence the **Phil Collins** case. Rights in performances are also the subject of certain EC directives and the WIPO Phonograms and Performances Treaty (see **WIPO Treaties**). See **performers' rights, performers' property rights**.

Rights Management Information

In the **WIPO Treaties**, 'information which identifies the work, the author of the work, the owner of any right in the work, or information about the terms and conditions of use of the work, and any numbers or codes that represent such information, when any of these items of information is attached to a copy of a work or appears in connection with the communication of a work to the public'.

Rome Convention

There are two Rome Conventions, so be careful. One is on the law applicable to contractual obligations, and it is not dealt with here. The other, dating from 1961, is concerned with the Protection of Performers, Producers of Phonograms and Broadcasting Organisations and is therefore a subject for this work. The Convention is the first international arrangement extending protection from the author of a copyright work to the creators and owners of the physical manifestations of the copyright work or **related rights**, or **neighbouring rights**. It was drawn up in response to the advent of new technologies including tape-recorders, which had made reproducing sounds and images easier and cheaper than ever before. It gave performers protection against certain acts, namely broadcasting and communication to the public of live performances, fixation of live performances, and reproduction of such fixations if the original fixation was made without their consent or if the reproduction is made for purposes different from those for which they gave their consent. It protects producers of phonograms, giving them the right to authorise or prohibit the direct or indirect reproduction of those **phonograms**. Secondary uses of a commercially published phonogram, such as broadcasting or communication to the public in any form, requires the payment of a single equitable remuneration by the user to the performers or to the producers of the phonogram or to both. This rule is, however, optional so a member state may choose whether to apply it or to limit its application.

The Convention also gives broadcasting organisations the right to authorise or prohibit certain acts. These are the rebroadcasting of a broadcast, the fixation of the broadcast, the reproduction of such fixations, and the communication to the public of their television broadcasts if such communication is made in places accessible to the public against payment of an entrance fee.

Exceptions are allowed for private use; the use of short extracts in connection with reporting current events; ephemeral fixation by a broadcasting organisation by means of its own facilities and for its own broadcasts; use solely for the purpose of teaching or scientific research; and in any other cases where national law provides exceptions to copyright in literary and artistic works with the exception of compulsory licences which would be incompatible with the Berne Convention.

The Convention also provides that once a performer has consented to the incorporation of a performance in a visual or audio-visual fixation, the provisions dealing with performers' rights will have no further application.

Open only to states party to Berne or the **Universal Copyright Convention (UCC)**. Seventy-seven contracting parties.

Rospatent

Russian Agency for Patents and Trademarks.

Royalty

1. Usually denotes a sum of money payable for the use of some form of intellectual property, and may be a fixed amount paid in advance or a figure per unit manufactured – or a blend of the two. There is no clearly defined definition of what is meant by this term, which may be encountered in a variety of contexts.

    The right given in consideration of the royalty payment might be that to make goods under another person's patent, design or know-how, to sell goods bearing a trade mark, or to publish or reproduce a copyright work.

    Nor are there any hard and fast rules about how much a royalty should be. Working that out is a valuation exercise so sophisticated as probably to be incomprehensible to mere lawyers.

2.   An association which cannot be made or implied in a UK trade mark, without the appropriate consent.

Royalty Stacking

The problem that once royalties have been paid to all the patent owners whose rights might have a bearing on the ability to make or market a product, it is unprofitable. Anti-stacking provisions in licensing agreements are therefore increasingly common, especially in the life sciences field. See Vicky Clark, 'Pitfalls in drafting royalty provisions in patent licences', Pharmalicensing, 2004, at http://pharmalicensing.com/articles/disp/1087832097_40d7002Id738c.

RRO

Reproduction rights organisation.

Rule of the Shorter Term

See **comparison of terms rule**.

S

Safe Harbor

An American expression (as the spelling makes clear) denoting the provision of the US patent law, 35 USC 271(c)(1), that permits experimental use of patented products including but not limited to pharmaceuticals for the purpose of obtaining marketing authorisation for generic equivalents during the lifetime of the patent. The expression also appears in other contexts, including as a description of block exemption regulations in EU competition law and the artificial constructs that allow personal data to be exported from an EU country to the United States in the face of the Eighth Data Protection Principle of the the data protection Directive.

The safe harbor concept also appears in the Online Copyright Infringement Liability Limitation Act (OCILLA), which insulates Internet service providers from actions for infringements committed by their customers provided they apply a three strikes rule and disconnect them if they fail to respond to notices to stop their unlawful activities.

The expression is also encountered in the context of European Union data protection laws (generally outside the scope of this work): the Eighth Data Protection Principle prohibits transfers of personal data outside the **EEA**, but among many exceptions to this principle is one that allows transfers to organisations in the United States that subscribe to principles agreed between the European Commission and the US Department of Commerce. Because the Principles were primarily the work of the Department of Commerce, and because they are available for use by US organisations, the American spelling is the appropriate one.

Safe Harbour

A refuge delineated by a block exemption regulation in the competition law of the European Union. Agreements meeting the requirements of the regulation (such as, for example, the technology transfer block exemption) will benefit from the safe harbour while agreements with restrictions on competition not expressly permitted by the regulation have to take their chance on the open sea. For the data protection meaning of the expression, see **safe harbor**.

Saisie Contrefaçon

Translates into English as seizure-infringement or (rather less directly) 'inspection of property', and is a collective term for **saisie réelle** and **saisie descriptive**. These orders enable the rights owner to collect evidence of infringement.

Saisie Descriptive

A court order available in France, authorising a bailiff to collect evidence of the alleged infringement at the defendant's premises by (for example) taking photographs of the allegedly infringing products, or buying samples.

Saisie Réelle

One of two types of *saisie contrefaçon* (seizure-infringement) order (best translated into English as 'effective seizure') that may be granted by a French court, available quickly (within a few days of the application) authorising a bailiff to seize all or part of a stock of infringing goods, enabling the rights owner to obtain information about the origin of the goods and the numbers sold. The court with jurisdiction over the place where the seizure is to be carried out is the court to which application must be made.

The making of the order may be subject to the applicant depositing security with the court. The seller of the seized goods, whose business may suffer considerable damage as a result of the order, may claim damages against the rights holder if the suspected goods are found not to infringe. It is open to the judge to order a **saisie descriptive** instead.

Following the seizure, the claimant must file its writ of summons at the court within 15 days (trade marks and patents) or 30 days (copyright) after the seizure. If he fails to do so, the seizure will be declared null and void.

Samizdat

Russian самиздат, a contraction of сам (self) and издательство (publishing house, often rendered дат at the end of the name of a Soviet publishing house): literally, 'self-published', as was the frequent practice among dissidents in the former Soviet Union. Copies were made by a variety of means, including copy-typing or copying in long-hand while making carbon copies, printing after hours and other techniques. Vladimir Bukhovsky described the process in his autobiographical novel, *And the Wind Returns* published in 1978: 'I myself create it, edit it, censor it, publish it, distribute it, and get imprisoned for it.' The effect of such publication on the subsistence of copyright arose in *Bodley Head Limited v Flegon* [1972] 1 WLR 680, [1972] RPC 587, a case concerning A.I. Solzhenitsyn's great novel, *August 1914* (London: Bodley Head, 1972). See Yurke, 'Copyright Issues concerning the Publication of Samizdat Literature in the United States' (*Columbia-VLA Journal of Law and the Arts*, 11, p. 449, 1986–87).

Sandor Obviousness (US)

A rejection for obviousness based on a single reference. Usual practice is to rely on two or more references. In *Ex Parte Sandor Nagy* the examiner relied on only a single reference to reject the claims at issue. Ultimately the case was remanded on appeal back to the examiner.

Scenes à Faire

French, 'scenes to be made' or perhaps 'scenes that must be done'. The doctrine that sets aside as unprotectable by copyright any part of a work that is 'as a practical matter indispensable, or at least standard, in the treatment of a given topic'. *Atari, Inc. v. North Am. Philips Consumer Elecs. Corp.*, 672 F.2d 607, 616 (7th Cir.) (quoting *Alexander v. Haley*, 460 F. Supp. 40, 45 (S.D.N.Y. 1978)), *cert. denied*, 459 U.S. 880 (1982).

Schechter, Frank

Author of 'The Rational Basis of Trademark Protection' (*Harvard Law Review*, 40, p. 813, 1927) and therefore known as the father of dilution theory. Also author of *The Historical Foundations of the Law Relating to Trade-marks* (New York: Columbia University Press, 1925).

Screening Search

A trade mark search designed to find existing trade marks identical to a proposed one under consideration: also known as a 'knock-out' search. If there are identicals already registered for the same or similar goods or services, the would-be applicant knows that the prudent course of action will be to think of a different trade mark, and they have not spent a huge amount of money to find this out. In practice, such searches are often omitted, leading *inter alia* to opposition proceedings, cancelled product launches, rebranding and large legal bills.

Sculpture

Under the Copyright, Designs and Patents Act 1988, a type of artistic work, though artistic quality is not a prerequisite for protection. The Act does not elaborate on the meaning of the expression, but it does say that it includes a cast or model for the purposes of sculpture – which comes close to making the definition circular. It certainly leaves the matter open to interpretation, but there have been few cases on copyright in sculptures for the courts to explore the meaning.

Search

1. Something that is often done before an application for a registered intellectual property right is filed. The status of pre-application searches varies between different countries and different areas of law. In the UK, it is not mandatory to perform a search before applying for a patent or to register a trade mark or registered design.
2. An investigation into the status of existing intellectual property rights or (in the case of rights that depend on novelty) earlier disclosures or matters that anticipate the invention or whatever the person commissioning the search wishes to protect. See **Clearance search, Screening search, patentability search, freedom to operate search** and **validity search**.

Search Order, Search and Seizure Order

See **Anton Piller** order.

Search Report

The report produced by a patent office to which an application has been made, setting out the prior art that has been found and on which the office will rely during the prosecution of the application. It is common nowadays to find that patent offices will want to see the reports produced by other national or regional patent offices.

Second Medical Use Claim

A new medical use for a molecule, product or composition which already has a medical use may be patented. The novelty lies in using it for the new purpose. Also known as further medical use. Sildenafil citrate, for example, was originally patented as a treatment for angina, and it was only later that its more celebrated use became apparent. See **Swiss claim**.

Second Non-medical Use Claim

Another European phenomenon, claiming the use of a material for a new use even if that use were inherent in the first one. It comes from the Enlarged Board of Appeal's decision in G2/88, *Mobil*. In that case a patent for the use of a chemical as a corrosion inhibitor in a car radiator was upheld, despite the fact that the same chemical in the same concentration was already known as a lubricant.

Secondary Indications of Inventiveness

Non-technical factors might swing the inventiveness argument in marginal cases. They include commercial success, fulfilment of a long-felt need, the fact that the prior art is all very old, strong circumstantial evidence pointing away from obviousness, and prejudice in the art against a particular solution.

Secondary Infringement

Dealings with infringing articles – those to make which it would be an infringement of someone's copyright – are actionable in many copyright laws, including the UK's, although they do not constitute primary infringements. These activities include a number of types of commercial dealing, including importing infringing articles and offering or exposing them for sale. The concept also extends to providing facilities for infringing performances and the like. The defendant must know or have reason to believe that a secondary infringement is being committed: if they were in any doubt about the matter the receipt of a demand letter should overcome it.

Secondary Meaning

See **acquired distinctiveness**.

Secondary Source Indicator

A sign identifying not the manufacturer of a derivative product (such as spare parts or model cars), but of the original product (the car which needs the spares, or of which the model is a representation).

See v Scott Paine Order

A form of order made in *See v Scott-Paine* (1933) 50 R.P.C. Colloquially known as an **Earth Closet order** and described under that title above.

Selection Patent

A patent whose claims falls within the scope of an earlier patent, but which discloses that certain embodiments not specifically disclosed in the earlier patent have new and unexpected benefits. The later patent, which effectively selects elements from the earlier one on the basis of superior qualities, is dominated by the earlier one; but the earlier one does not cover the later invention. See also **cross-licensing**.

Septies

Latin ordinal number, seventh. Encountered particularly in international conventions, for example Article 6 septies of the Paris Convention.

Sequence Listing

Part of the description in an application for a patent containing nucleotide or amino acid sequences, furnished to the USPTO on CD, which gives a detailed disclosure of the nucleotide or amino acid sequences and other available information. *Manual of Patent Examination Practice, 2422.03.*

Serial Rights

Serial rights are dealt with in publishing agreements and commonly fall into two categories. First serial rights are the right to publish a work in serial form prior to publication in book form, and second serial rights – which necessarily are less valuable – are for publication in the period after publication in book form.

Series (Trade Marks)

In the UK (and other jurisdictions, but not the Community trade mark system) it is possible to register a series of trade marks. This applies where the marks 'resemble each other as to their material particulars and differ only as to matters of a non-distinctive character not substantially affecting the identity of the trade mark'. In theory this should offer substantial savings (though there is now a supplement of £50 per item after the first two, and a maximum of six items in a series is permitted), but in practice it is difficult to convince the Registry that what appears to be a series is not a set of independent trade marks. The idea is that the marks in a series differ only in non-distinctive respects, so a distinctive word followed by a serial number would probably be acceptable, as would a house mark and product description combination. See also **Phantom mark (US)**.

Service Mark

A trade mark used for services rather than for goods. Hard to believe now, but not capable of being registered in the UK until 1986, following enactment of the Trade Marks (Amendment) Act 1984. The United States still maintains a distinction between the two varieties of what the UK (along with the rest of the EU) now calls trade marks.

Prior to 1986, service providers sought to protect themselves (in addition to taking action, where necessary, for passing off) by registering trade marks for the goods that they did produce – printed matter, in class 16.

Sexies

Latin ordinal number, sixth. Encountered particularly in international conventions, for example Article 6 sexies of the Paris Convention.

Shamanism

See **Boyle, James**, **valuation**.

Shape Trade Mark

The shape of goods or their packaging may be registered as a trade mark under the Trade Marks Act 1994 and the Community trade marks regulation. Formerly, a shape could not be registered in the UK: the House of Lords confirmed in *Re Coca-Cola's Application* [1986] 1 WLR 695 that a bottle shape could not be considered a trade mark under the 1938 Act.

The shape of an article or a product is capable of being protected under the law on designs, whether by registration or otherwise. The laws that grant this protection have been carefully crafted, though arguably only with motor cars in mind. To avoid the possibility of designers thwarting the exceptions so carefully included in design laws, trade mark law makes it clear that the shape of goods or their packaging will not be registrable as a trade mark in certain circumstances. These are if it consists exclusively of:

- the shape which results from the goods themselves;
- the shape of goods which is necessary to obtain a technical result; or
- the shape which gives substantial value to the goods. (Section 3(2))

In *Phillips v Remington*, Jacob J held that the trade mark registered by Phillips was not distinctive, being merely a drawing of the layout of the cutting heads of its Phillishave electric shaver, so a lack of distinctiveness appears to be a potential problem for many shape trade marks too.

Shop Rights (US)

An implied licence to use an invention devised by an employee in the course of their employment, notwithstanding that the employee (in whose name the patent would have been applied for) has not assigned the rights as he should have done. The licence is non-transferable, but also royalty-free.

Sideground

Information and related intellectual property rights that result from a research and development or similar project, but are found alongside the intended or principal results. See **background intellectual property**, **foreground intellectual property**.

Sign

All trade marks are signs, of one sort or another – but by no means all signs are trade marks, though modern practice seems to be limiting the class of non-trade mark signs considerably. The word 'sign' is properly used to denote something that its proponent might like to think is a trade mark but which is not recognised as such by law, or that is used by the defendant in a trade mark infringement action.

Signal Claim (US)

A patent claim for an electronic or electromagnetic signal, which by itself is not particularly interesting but which might be an indirect way to obtain protection for software. The signal might carry information that can be used to achieve a particular result or serve some other useful purpose, for instance controlling a digital computer.

The eligibility of claims of this sort is controversial. 35 USC 101 permits patents to be issued only for 'processes, machines, manufactures, and compositions of matter', and signals fall outside these statutory classes. The law also excludes abstract concepts from patentability, and this includes mathematical formulae and laws of nature which are not inventions (European patent law providing similarly). An abstract arrangement of data on an electromagnetic wave carrier should, it is argued, fall under the same rubric – the carrier is nothing more than a form of energy.

On the other hand it can be argued that the signal is an 'article of manufacture' (forged in a digital transmitter): proponents of signal claims argue that a signal is more than just the energy that carries it. In any event, if $E = mc^2$ it cannot be argued that such claims are 'ephemeral and transitory' subject-matter.

There is a similar lack of agreement about the law in this area. The **USPTO**, in its *Interim Guidelines for Examination of Patent Applications for Patent Subject Matter Eligibility*, instructs examiners categorically to reject any claim that 'recites nothing but the physical characteristics of a form of energy', dismissing such claims as being to 'nonstatutory natural phenomena'. However, in *Ex parte Rice* the **Board of Patent Appeals and Interferences** reversed an objection that recited this same logic and categorically affirmed the patent eligibility of signal claims: but a different conclusion was reached by the Court of Appeals for the Federal Circuit in *In re Nuijten*.

Simkins List

A list of items of prior art. From *Olin Mathieson Chemical Corporation and Others v. Biorex Laboratories Limited and Another* [1970] RPC 157 in which Dr Margaret Simkins, head of the Research Information Department at Smith Kline & French, gave evidence addressing what people were doing to solve the problem of the invention round about or before the priority date. Her evidence – the list of items of prior art – showed that they were following many leads but all missed the point. Against this background it was argued successfully that the invention was not obvious, otherwise it would have been done before.

Simulcast

A contraction of 'simultaneous broadcast', used to refer to programmes or events broadcast at the same time over more than one medium – a concert shown on BBC television and transmitted at the same time on Radio 3, for example. Simulcasts may be presented over the Internet, raising licensing issues if they are not territorially restricted in the same way as the underlying broadcasts.

Singapore Treaty on the Law of Trademarks

Adopted by the Diplomatic Conference for the Adoption of a Revised Trademark Law Treaty, Singapore, from 13 to 28 March 2006. The Treaty is intended to create a modern and dynamic international framework for the harmonisation of administrative trademark registration procedures. It builds on the **Trademark Law Treaty** of 1994, with wider scope and addressing new developments in communications technology. Nineteen contracting parties.

Skilful and Covert Allusion

What an applicant for a trade mark might argue is made by the trade mark: others might be inclined to say it is descriptive.

Skill, Labour and Judgment

What the creator of a copyright work expends on its creation, at least as far as British copyright law (with its low threshold of originality) is concerned.

Skilled Man, Person Skilled in the art

A concept in patent law, important in determining whether an invention is obvious or not. The hypothetical person against whose knowledge is judged the obviousness of an invention for which a patent application has been filed. Articles 56, 83 and 100 of the EPC refer to this hypothetical person. Jacob LJ controversially called the skilled man 'a nerd' in *Rockwater Ltd v Technip France SA*. He shares the 'common stock of knowledge' (per Luxmore J in *British Acoustic Films* 53 R.P.C. 221).

In *Catnic*, where the technology in suit was building materials, the hypothetical skilled person chosen by the court was a builder.

In *Dyson v Hoover* the skilled person was not, as were the expert witnesses in the case, one familiar with cyclonic airflows, which had never previously been applied to the extraction of foreign bodies from carpets: nor was he Mr Dyson, who was more than ordinarily skilled and had rather more than the common stock of knowledge. In the end, Judge Fysh decided that he was a vacuum cleaner technician educated to HND level, so with a scant knowledge of cyclonic airflows insufficient to lead him to use them for the purpose to which they were put by the invention.

See **PHOSITA**. See also the related issue of **informed users** in design law.

Slander of Goods, Slander of Title

See **malicious falsehood**.

Slavish Copying

Copying which is perhaps unnecessarily close and uncritical. In some jurisdictions it might amount to **unfair competition**. At least, it is the antithesis
of **originality**.

Slurry Separator

A device for separating solids from a fluid stream: the subject-matter of
the UK unregistered design case, *Farmers Build v Carier Bulk Materials
Ltd* [1999] RPC 461 (CA), exploring the concept of **commonplace design
features**.

Software

Software is a collection of computer programs, procedures and documentation (but often used as a synonym for computer programs, or
alternatively a collective noun for them) that facilitate the performance of
tasks using a computer or computer system. The expression distinguishes
programs from the physical components of a computer system (hardware)
and certain intermediate programs resident in the hardware ('firmware').

Includes application software (for example word processing programs),
system software such as operating systems, and 'middleware' which con-
trols and coordinates distributed systems or networks. The expression is
also used in a more general sense to describe any electronic content which
embodies expressions of ideas – films, tapes, disks and so on.

Software Directive (Directive 91/250/EEC)

The first excursion by the European Community into copyright law,
intended to prevent Member States from responding in different ways to
demands from computer software producers for protection.

Software Patent

Something that is not available in the European system (though the exclusion only applies to patents for computer programs as such, and a great
deal has turned on those two words). More often obtained in the US. The

subject of very heavy books, so not one to be treated at much length here. See **computer-implemented invention**, **Diamond v Diehr**, **Bilski**.

Sonny Bono Copyright Act

See **Mickey Mouse Protection Act**.

Sosumi

A short musical work and sound recording by Jim Reekes, one of the system sounds in Apple, Inc.'s Macintosh 7 operating system introduced in 1991. The title, which the composer claims was presented to Apple's legal department as a Japanese word with no relevance to music, refers obliquely to the computer company's long-running dispute with Apple Corps. See **Apple**.

Sound Recording

A category of copyright work consisting of recordings of sounds from which the sounds may be reproduced, and (in UK copyright law, at least) a recording of a work (or part of one) from which sounds reproducing it may be produced. The second leg of the definition is required to bring **piano rolls** and musical boxes into the copyright system. Definitions of sound recordings often do not include **film** soundtracks, which often receive protection as part of the film.

Specially Protected Emblems

Certain signs are specified or referred to in section 4 of the Trade Marks Act 1994 as 'specially protected emblems'. They are signs that cannot be registered as trade marks without special permission from the appropriate authorities. See also **protected signs**, and other definitions noted there.

Specific Subject Matter

May refer to the jurisdiction of certain US courts – such as the Court of Appeals for the Federal Circuit, or **CAFC**. More likely to refer to the approach of the CJEC to competition or free movement cases involving intellectual property, where the identification of the specific subject-matter – the core – of the intellectual property rights was an important step towards applying the competition rules in this area.

In the field of patents, the specific subject-matter consists of: 'the exclusive right to use an invention with a view to manufacturing industrial products and putting them into circulation for the first time . . . as well as the right to oppose infringements' (Case 15/74, *Centrafarm v Sterling Drug* [1974] ECR 1147).

As for trade marks, in Case 119/75 *Terrapin* [1976] ECR 1039, the Court decided that 'the basic function of the trade mark [is] to guarantee to consumers that the product has the same origin', a definition later expanded in Case 102/77 *Hoffmann-LaRoche* [1978] ECR 1139, 'by enabling [them] without any possibility of confusion to distinguish that product from products which have another origin'.

As for copyright and designs, the Court has never taken an opportunity to fix the meaning of the expression.

Specification (Patent)

A document in several parts: first, one that describes the invention for which a patent is sought (accompanied by drawings, if appropriate, which it usually is); second, claims; and third, an abstract. Different patent offices will apply different formal requirements for the presentation of this documentation. In *Catnic Components Ltd v Hill and Smith Ltd* [1982] RPC 183 Lord Diplock said that:

> a patent specification is a unilateral statement by the patentee, in words of his own choosing, addressed to those likely to have a practical interest in the subject matter of his invention (i.e. 'skilled in the art'), by which he informs them what he claims to be the essential features of the new product or process for which the letters patent grant him a monopoly. It is those novel features only that he claims to be essential that constitute the so-called 'pith and marrow' of the claim. A patent specification should be given a purposive construction rather than a purely literal one derived from applying to it the kind of meticulous verbal analysis in which lawyers are too often tempted by their training to indulge.

Specification (Trade Mark)

The list of goods and services set out in a trade mark application (and, in the fullness of time, registration) in respect of which the trade mark is to be, or is, registered. Classified according to the Nice Agreement or some other system (except in Canada). It is increasingly common to see trade mark applications based on the class descriptions in the Nice Agreement, which leads to excessively wide specifications, an unwarranted degree of protection, and an increased possibility of opposition or revocation proceedings.

Specimen of Use

A factual example, required in US but not in European trade mark practice, showing how a trade mark is actually being used. An appropriate specimen of use for goods might be a label or tag bearing the mark, or a picture of the goods or packaging for the goods bearing the mark. There are special requirements for using advertising, catalogues or copies of websites as specimens of use for goods (see TMEP Section 904.03). An appropriate specimen of use for **service marks** might be advertising showing use of the mark and making an association with the service. Even though a specimen of use need only show use of the mark in connection with one good or one service per class, the declaration of use itself should refer to all of the goods or services listed in the application. See **allegation of use**.

Springboard, Springboarding

In patents, preparing to launch a product at a time when patents still prevent the launch from taking place. Generally the preparations are also regarded as a form of patent infringement. It is however expressly permitted in some circumstances, for example the work done by generic pharmaceutical manufacturers during the extension (and even during the original term) of the patent.

In *Dyson v Hoover* [2001] RPC 27, the defendants were ordered not to sell their infringing vacuum cleaners for 12 months following expiry of the patent – to negate the 'springboard' advantage they would have obtained over other competitors who had not committed the same infringement. A similar doctrine is encountered in the law on breach of confidence: *Terrapin Ltd. v Builders' Supply Co. (Hayes) Ltd.*, [1960] R.P.C. 128 (C.A.): 'a person who has obtained information in confidence is not allowed to use it as a springboard . . . and a springboard it remains even when all the features have been published or can be ascertained by actual inspection by any member of the public'.

Sprio/Flamco

A Dutch case (Hoge Raad, 9 February 2006) involving the partial nullification of a patent. The partial nullification could only be upheld if the remaining invention would have been within the original patent as read by the skilled person.

Spurious Parts

Spare parts manufactured neither by the capital goods (or complex product) manufacturer nor by the original equipment manufacturers who supply the manufacturer of the complex product. The expression is commonly used – usually without any pejorative implications – in the motor trade.

Squeeze Argument

A defence to an infringement claim where the alleged infringement is close to the prior art. It may be characterised as arguing that the claim means either one thing or another. If it is the first, then the claim is wide enough to include subject matter that is old or (in an 'obviousness squeeze') obvious. If it is the other, then there is no infringement. See also **Gillette defence**.

SSO

See **Structure, sequence and organisation**.

Stallman, Richard

An American computer programmer and 'software freedom activist'. Known as a vociferous opponent of software patents, and the moving force behind the free software movement and the founder of the Free Software Foundation. He is the author of the 'Free Software Song', which sets his words to the Bulgarian folk melody 'Sadi Moma'.

He is also a privacy activist, and is understood to eschew mobile phones, security swipe cards and web browsers because of privacy concerns.

Standard Character Claim (US)

In US trademark registrations, having a 'standard character' claim for a word mark means that the mark is protected regardless of the style or format in which the word mark is actually used.

State of the Art

To be patentable an invention must not be part of the state of the art at the application date. This concept is widely defined in section 2(2) of the Patents Act 1977 (and see also Article 54 EPC):

> The state of the art in the case of an invention shall be taken to comprise all matter (whether a product, a process, information about either, or anything else) which has at any time before the priority date of that invention been made available to the public (whether in the United Kingdom or elsewhere) by written or oral description, by use or in any other way.

It is hard to imagine a more wide-ranging definition of anything, although see also **invention**.

State Street

State Street Bank v Signature Financial Group, 149 F.3d 1368, 47 USPQ.2d 1596 is a key US case on business method patents. State Street had a patent for applying hub-and-spoke technology to mutual funds: the judge held that the exception for business processes, deemed to be outside the statutory classes, was 'an unwarranted encumbrance that should be discarded as error-prone, redundant and obsolete'.

Statement of Use

A form of **allegation of use**.

Statute of Anne

There is disagreement about whether it is correct to date the Act to 1709 or 1710. It came into operation on 10 April 1710, that much is clear, but before Chesterfield's Act, the Calendar (New Style) Act 1750 (c.23), the calendar year started, inconveniently to modern minds, on Lady Day, which as every lawyer knows is 25 March. According to the new calendar, the Act was indeed passed in 1710, but the Chronological Table of the Statutes (London, 1963) lists it as 1709, 8 Ann., c.19 (although Ruffhead numbers it c.21). *Owen Ruffhead, The Statutes at Large: from Magna Carta, to the End of the Last Parliament, 1761*, London: M. Baskett, 1763–65.

Statutory Bar

American legal term for what prevents an otherwise novel invention being patentable, in particular disclosure outside the one-year period of grace allowed by the US law.

Statutory Damages

Measuring the amount of damage caused by a copyright or trade mark infringement can be extremely difficult. The rights owner is likely to have only a vague idea of how many copies or counterfeit articles have been made. Copies of digital material require no physical carrier, so quantifying the damage caused by them is practically impossible. Some copyright systems therefore allow successful rights owners to claim damages on a scale set by law, without proof of actual loss. The amount of such statutory damages might be many times greater than the actual damages that would be awarded.

In the European Union, the Enforcement Directive (Article 13(1)(b)) allows Member States to set damages as a 'lump sum on the basis of elements such as at least the amount of royalties which would have been due if the infringer had requested authorisation to use the intellectual property rights in question'.

In the USA, 17 USC section 504(c) sets statutory damages at between $750 and $30000 for each work in which copyright is infringed – thereby obviating the need to count the number of infringements. If wilful infringement can be proved, the maximum award is raised to $150000, though if the defendant can show that they were not aware and had no reason to believe they were infringing the amount is reduced to a minimum of $200. In certain situations a defendant may escape liability by showing that they believed the act amounted to a fair use. For trade mark cases, the Anti-Counterfeiting Consumer Protection Act 1996 stipulates damages of $500 to $1000 per counterfeit mark, per type of goods or services.

However, statutory damages for copyright infringements are only available in the US courts if the copyright work in question has been registered with the Copyright Office prior to the infringement or within three months after publication. This effectively excludes many foreign works, though a claim for actual damages would still lie.

Other countries set statutory damages at two or three times the going rate for using the right that has been infringed. In the US, the Supreme Court has indicated that: 'few awards exceeding a single-digit ratio between punitive and compensatory damages, to a significant degree. will satisfy due process', *State Farm* v. *Campbell*, 538 U.S. 408 at 425 (2003). In 2007, Jammie Thomas was ordered to pay $222000 for 24 infringements ($9250 per work): a retrial was granted, but statutory damages were increased to $1.92 million. In 2009, Joel Tenenbaum was held to have committed a wilful infringement and the jury awarded $657000 ($22500 per work). The constitutionality of the awards in both cases is being challenged: in the Tenenbaum case the appellant's filing states that the ratio of punitive to compensatory damages is somewhere between 22500:1 and 65000:1 or greater.

Statutory Invention Registration

In the United States, a technique for dedicating an invention to the public, or ensuring that no one would be able to get a patent for it – which amounts to much the same thing. The documents are published (the series of publications being numbered with an H prefix). It remains possible to do this, but early publication in the US has deprived it of most of its purpose.

Stealth Patents

Patents or applications claiming genetic material which has been discovered but of which the function, or functions, remain unknown. Considered to be an enemy of scientific progress, because the applicants tend to sit on the applications (and, in due course, on the patents) and bring research to a halt. The USPTO has issued guidelines designed to prevent stealth patenting, though identifying all the stealth patents already in existence will inevitably be a difficult and lengthy process.

Strasbourg Agreement

Concluded in 1971, amended in 1979. Established the **International Patent Classification** (IPC) which divides technology into eight sections with approximately 70 000 subdivisions. Sixty-one contracting parties.

Strasbourg (Patent) Convention

The Convention on the Unification of Certain Points of Substantive Law on Patents for Invention is a multilateral treaty signed by Member States of the Council of Europe on 27 November 1963 in Strasbourg. It entered into force on 1 August 1980 and led to a significant harmonisation of patent laws among the signatories. It had an influence not only on national patent laws but also on the European Patent Convention, and subsequently on other international treaties in the patent area. Readers interested in learning more might care to read Christopher Wadlow, 'Strasbourg, the Forgotten Patent Convention, and the Origins of the European Patents Jurisdiction', (**IIC**, 2, p. 123, 2010) the title of which speaks volumes about the place of the Convention in modern patent law. Thirteen countries have signed and ratified the Convention, which is not only open (for signature) to all members of the Council of Europe but also (for accession) to all members of the Paris Union. Professor Wadlow's article cannot yet have reached a wide enough audience.

Streaming

A method for delivering **content** in the form of sound recordings, audio-visual works (films), Internet television or other multimedia presentations by telecommunications means, in contradistinction to such media as books, CDs, DVDs, and downloadable computer files. Broadcasts and cable programmes are also a form of streaming media, though in the days before online distribution there was no requirement for an expression to describe them. Streaming media are less vulnerable to unauthorised copying, though stream recorder (or destreamer) software can often be used to record the streaming media.

Structure, Sequence and Organisation

Aspects of a computer program protected by copyright under the approach taken by the court in *Whelan v. Jaslow.*

Subconscious Copying

There is no requirement in copyright law that the infringer have any intention to infringe the copyright owner's rights. Copying can be subconscious in the sense that the copier is unaware that it is happening. It might happen that a composer remembers a snatch of music heard somewhere and, although he is not aware of it, he includes it in a new composition. The same could happen with other forms of copyright work, though music is the most likely candidate for such unconscious recollection.

Submarine Patent

An informal term for a patent that remains unpublished long after its filing date, unseen and undetectable, a menace to later-filed patents whose owners probably believe them to be unsinkable. They are only possible in patent systems which allow for a long delay between filing and publication, and in the European system (including the national systems harmonised with it) applications are published 18 months after filing. This is too short a period to be of much use to submariners, although there remains a related problem of undetectable applications that form part of the state of the art for novelty (though not for inventiveness) purposes.

Before 1995, submarine patents were a significant problem in the United States, but adherence to the TRIPS agreement has brought about changes in US practice. Now US patents run for 20 years from the filing (or earlier priority) date, not from when they are granted (the 'date of issuance') as before. Under the old law, publication could be delayed by filing a series of continuation applications – expensive, but effective, for as long as 40 years in some cases – and secrecy preserved by abandonment and refiling. During the submarine phase, the claims could even be adjusted to reflect new learning in the field, something that was always harder to do in the European system where an amendment cannot introduce new subject-matter. Moreover, the ability to delay the start date for protection also meant that the patent could be placed in a sort of limbo, its effective life being shifted forward (or to the right) into a period in which the relevant technology had become more widely adopted.

In the case of US only applications, the technique can still be a defensive alternative to secret use. The US application can be kept pending while the invention is worked. If anyone tries to patent the same thing, the application can then be allowed to proceed to grant.

The effectiveness of the strategy was to some extent neutralised by the US courts' application of the doctrine of **laches**. Keeping one's patent submerged might be considered to amount to an unreasonable procedural delay, and the applicant could even lose their patent rights.

Submission Company

In the USA, a company (or, presumably, another legal entity) that is not a practitioner entitled to file papers with the US Patent and Trademark Office, but which purports to offer a service submitting such papers on behalf of applicants. Their activities are specifically addressed in rules promulgated by the USPTO. By contrast, LegalZoom, Inc., a company whose charging has attracted criticism (and a class action suit from clients who believe they have been overcharged), appears to be a corporation owned and controlled by lawyers.

Subsist

Verb, meaning to have an existence as a reality or to exist as an entity, applied to intellectual property rights – hence, 'copyright subsists in . . .'.

Substantial Part

UK copyright law provides that an infringement is committed if, without the consent of the copyright owner, one of the restricted acts is performed in relation to the whole or a substantial part of a copyright work. The concept of 'substantiality' is important here, as clearly copyright law would be of no practical effect if an infringer could only be held to account if the whole of a work were taken. The Act does not elaborate on the meaning of the word, though, and quite rightly too: the courts have developed ways to identify what is a substantial part.

In *University of London Press Ltd. v University Tutorial Press Ltd.* Peterson J usefully suggested that 'what is worth copying is *prima facie* worth protecting': in other words, the defendant's selection of an extract is enough to give it the status of a substantial part. Many judgments on the subject begin by quoting this dictum (although the judge only ever offered it as a 'rough practical test'), dismiss it as too simplistic, then quietly apply it. Jacob J (as he then was) said in *Ibcos Computers Ltd v Barclays Mercantile Highland Finance Ltd* [1994] FSR 275 at 289 that the aphorism 'proves too much' because if 'taken literally [it] would mean that all a plaintiff ever had to do was to prove copying' so that 'appropriate subject matter for copyright and a taking of a substantial part would all be proved in one go'.

It is clear that the concept has a qualitative dimension as well as a quantitative one. As Lord Denning said in the debate in the House of Lords on the 1988 Act:

> It has always been said that it is not quantity but quality that is important. If a few key words in a poem are taken, that is a substantial part, even though the poem has 100 stanzas. If you take one key stanza that is a substantial part because of its quality. The courts have always said that they can interpret 'substantial part'.

Substantial Similarity

The name of the test developed by US courts to determine whether a copyright infringement has taken place. Melville Nimmer identifies two different tests for substantial similarity which have been widely adopted and utilised by US courts: 'fragmented literal similarity' and 'comprehensive non-literal similarity'. See also **substantial part**.

Substantive Examination

The stage in the prosecution of a patent application in which the examiner, rather than simply looking at formalities, analyses the application critically, comparing it with the prior art (or state of the art) in order to determine whether it is novel and inventive and therefore whether it may be granted.

Sufficiency

The requirement in most patent laws that a patent application disclose enough about the invention to enable a person skilled in the art to carry it out without having to reinvent it. They might have to perform some experiments, so long as they are reasonably within the skills of that hypothetical individual. US patent law is particularly strict on sufficiency. See **insufficiency**.

Suggestive

In US practice, of a trade mark, requiring imagination, thought or perception to reach a conclusion about the nature of the goods or services on or in connection with which it is used. In the UK it usually carries the meaning of implying something rude or improper, which effectively disqualifies it from being used in this trade mark sense. See **mere descriptiveness**.

Sui generis

Latin, 'of its own kind'. Applied, in the context of intellectual property, to a right designed to address the specific needs of a particular issue, such as the right referred to in UK legislation as 'database right' but called (rather ambiguously) '*sui generis* right' in the EC Directive which created it.

Supplemental Register

A secondary register in the US Patent and Trademarks Office on which trade marks may be entered notwithstanding that they do not meet all the requirements for registration on the Principal Register. This was a necessary device to enable US businesses to secure protection for their trade marks elsewhere in the world using the priority period offered by the Paris Convention. A mark may be registered on the Supplemental Register if it is capable of distinguishing goods and services – there is no need for it actually to do so. The UK, other Member States and the EC trade mark system allow a trade mark to be registered if it is merely capable of distinguishing.

Before the Trade Marks Act 1994, the UK had a similar two-part register, with registration available more readily in Part B.

Supplementary International Search (SIS)

An optional, additional, PCT search performed during the international phase. The applicant's usual International Searching Authority carries out an international search in the normal way: the SIS is intended to improve the chances of finding relevant prior art. Only the Russian and Swedish patent offices, and the Nordic Patent Institute, offer SISs at the time of writing (May 2010).

Supplementary Protection Certificate (SPC)

A certificate giving additional protection, up to five years, functionally equivalent to an extension of the term of a patent which gives certain products – in particular pharmaceutical products – longer protection to compensate for the time-consuming regulatory requirements with which such products have to comply. A creature of European Community law. An SPC will be granted only for the approved drug, not for everything that might be within the claims. See **extension of patent term**.

Suspension

A condition that a government may wish to impose on an intellectual property right, perhaps for primarily political reasons. For example, there have been suggestions that patent protection for anti-retroviral drugs might be suspended in some of the countries that need them most but can least afford them.

Swearing Back, Swearing Behind (US)

A product of the first-to-invent approach to patenting: an inventor can obtain a patent even if their invention has become public before their filing date, by presenting evidence (in the form of a sworn statement) showing an invention date earlier than the publication date of the cited prior art. Requires evidence that is preferably detailed, clear, signed, dated and witnessed.

Sweat of the Brow

The rather graphic name for the originality test applied to determine whether copyright subsisted in a compilation under US law. Originality in a compilation can only be found in the selection and arrangement of the contents, and prior to *Feist* the US courts had applied this simple doctrine. However, in that case the Supreme Court decided that no matter how much work was necessary to create a compilation, a non-selective collection of facts ordered in a non-creative way is not subject to copyright protection.

Swiss Claim

A claim in a patent to a known and therefore in itself unpatentable substance for use in a method of diagnosis or treatment in the form: 'use of [substance] for the manufacture of medicament to treat [disease]'. This approach was first permitted in Opinion G5/83 of the EPO Enlarged Board of Appeal. This gets round the problem that methods of medical treatment or diagnosis were unpatentable because incapable of industrial application, but the **European Patent Convention 2000**, article 53(c), 54(4) and 54(5) removes this disqualification. While making them unpatentable in their own right, it provides that novel substances or compositions for such use ('[substance] for use in the treatment of [disease]') may now be protected. The fact that the substance forms part of the state of the art no longer prevents the invention being new if the use or specific use of the substance is new, so Swiss-type claims are no longer necessary.

Synchronisation Rights

The rights that are engaged when a sound recording is synchronised with a film as part of the soundtrack, or used in a television programme (which is, after all, only a type of film for copyright purposes) or in any other situation where the music appears with images. Commonly taken by the record company in a recording contract.

T

Table

A form of literary work, according to the Copyright, Designs and Patents Act. UK copyright legislation has happily given protection to railway timetables and football pools coupons in the past: being written, they are literary works, and involving a modicum of skill, labour and judgment on the part of the compiler they are considered to be original.

Tarnishment

A form of harm done to trade marks when association arising from the similarity between the defendant's sign and a famous mark (US) or a trade mark with a reputation (EU) harms the reputation of the trade mark, sometimes treated as a variety of dilution. It happens when there is an unauthorised use of the mark which links it to inferior-quality goods or services, or portrays it in an unwholesome or unsavoury or detrimental context.

Teaching–Suggesting–Motivation (TSM) Test (US)

Where an invention consists of combining elements in a novel way, the question of obviousness requires a consideration of whether the prior art contains some suggestion or teaching to combine those elements. Just because all the elements exist does not mean that the invention is obvious. *Winner Int'l Royalty Corp. v. Wang*, 202 F.3d. 1340, 1348 (Fed. Cir., 2000). See also **Graham factors**, **obviousness**.

TEAS

Trademark Electronic Application Service, a facility offered by the US Patent and Trademark Office. Other trade mark registries (including the UK's and OHIM) offer online filing services without feeling it necessary to give them a special name.

Technological or Technical Protection Measures

Measures using computer technology designed to prevent the unauthorised use of copyright material.

Technology Transfer Agreement

An agreement under which technology is transferred from one party to another, usually by means of a licence. So, patent licences and know-how licences (and of course mixed licences of patents and know-how) are types of technology transfer agreements. Since they are frequently exclusive arrangements, their treatment under competition law is important: the EU technology transfer block exemption exempts some agreements in this field from the prohibition of restrictive agreements.

Telle Quelle

French, 'as is'. Under Article 6 quinquies of the Paris Convention every trade mark duly registered in the country of origin shall be accepted for filing and protected as is in the other Union countries. This privilege should be applied for upon the filing of a trade mark application, although a grace period to prove prior registration is available as a rule.

However, they can be denied registration or invalidated in certain circumstances, including where they infringe rights already acquired by third parties in the country where protection is claimed, where they are nondistinctive, descriptive or generic, and where they are contrary to public policy or morality.

TellPat

The name given to the National Intellectual Property Intelligence System, a database operated by the UK Intellectual Property Office to collect the intelligence gathered by industry and enforcement agencies to help combat crime in the intellectual property world.

Ter

Latin ordinal number, third. Encountered particularly in international conventions, for example Article 5 ter of the Paris Convention.

Terminal Disclaimer

When a prior patent of the applicant constitutes prior art against the application, such that it is close enough to look like double patenting, the applicant might have to disclaim the extra term extending beyond the term of the prior patent, so they both expire at the same time. A feature of US patent law.

Tertium Quid

Latin, 'third thing'. In the US Supreme Court case *Wal-Mart Stores, Inc. v. Samara Brothers, Inc.* 529 U.S. 205 (2000) it was used to describe **trade dress** – neither product design nor packaging, but a third thing.

Theft

1. A crime that cannot logically be committed with intellectual property: see *Oxford v. Moss* [1978] 68 Cr App R 183, and *Dowling v. United States,* 473 U.S. 207 (1985):

    > [I]nterference with copyright does not easily equate with theft, conversion, or fraud. . . . The infringer invades a statutorily defined province guaranteed to the copyright holder alone. But he does not assume physical control over the copyright; nor does he wholly deprive its owner of its use. While one may colloquially link infringement with some general notion of wrongful appropriation, infringement plainly implicates a more complex set of property interests than does run-of-the-mill theft, conversion, or fraud.

    A theft takes place (under the Theft Act 1968, at least) when one person takes another person's property with the intention of permanently depriving the owner of that property. Short of forging an instrument of transfer (which did happen in the notorious case, *Kremen v Cohen* 99 F. Supp. 2d 1168 (N.D. Cal. 2000), *aff'd*, 325 F3d 1035, 2002 WL 2017073 (9th Cir. Aug. 30, 2002), and which would usually be actionable under a different rubric rather than theft, *Kremen* being a claim for the tort of conversion), it is impossible permanently to deprive the owner of intellectual property of that property. Any commentator who speaks, or writes, about intellectual property theft (or copyright theft, the main variety of this sin) is therefore doing nothing more than grinding an axe, using a rhetorical device.

2. An invention may be expropriated – perhaps the documents in which it is described are stolen – and a patent application filed by the thief. The true owner can have the patent (or the application) assigned to it. Even if the thief has allowed the patent to lapse, it can be assigned in this way, and in any event publication of the stolen material will not be considered to destroy the novelty of the invention.

Thicket of Patents

Carl Shapiro (of the University of California at Berkeley) described in 'Navigating the Patent Thicket: Cross Licenses, Patent Pools, and Standard-Setting,' in Jaffe, Adam B. et al. (eds), *Innovation Policy and the Economy* (Vol. I), Cambridge, MA: MIT Press, pp. 119–50, 2001, how '[i]n several key industries . . . our patent system is creating a patent thicket; an overlapping set of patent rights requiring that those seeking to commercialise new technology obtain licenses from multiple patentees'.

In '*Patents and Pharmaceuticals*', a paper given on 29 November 2008 at the Presentation of the Directorate-General of Competition's Preliminary Report of the Pharma-sector inquiry, Sir Robin **Jacob** said:

> Every patentee of a major invention is likely to come up with improvements and alleged improvements to his invention. By the time his main patent has expired there will be a thicket of patents intended to extend his monopoly. Some will be good, others bad. It is in the nature of the patent system itself that this should happen and it has always happened.

They are also referred to by other names: 'multiplicity of patents, referred to as "patent thickets" and "patent floods"' in Mattias Ganslandt, 'Intellectual Property Rights and Competition Policy', IFN Working Paper No. 726, 2008, p. 12; and 'One commonly applied strategy is filing numerous patents for the same medicine (forming so called "patent clusters" or "patent thickets")', in European Commission, 'Pharmaceutical Sector Inquiry, Preliminary Report (DG Competition Staff Working Paper)', 28 November 2008, p. 9. The expression 'minefield' might also be encountered.

Third-Party Observations

In many countries, third parties are permitted to draw prior art to the attention of the examiner dealing with someone else's application (usually, but not necessarily, a competitor). The third party does not become party to the proceedings, which remain between the applicant and the office, but equally has no say in how, or even if, the examiner uses the information.

Thornhill Claim (UK)

A claim with exactly the same scope as a specific priority document.

Three-Step Test

1. In relation to permitted acts under the law of copyright. Copyright is not an absolute right. Certain acts are permitted in relation to copyright works in all copyright laws. The Berne Convention allowed for this, but ensured that member countries did not drive a coach and horses through basic principles of copyright protection by imposing what has become known as the three-step test. Exceptions to copyright may be created:
    a. in certain special cases;
    b. that do not conflict with the normal exploitation of the work; and
    c. that do not unreasonably prejudice the legitimate interests of the author/right-holder.
    Nowadays, the three-step test appears not only in the Berne Convention (Article 9 (2)) but also in the Agreement on Trade-Related Aspects of Intellectual Property Rights (TRIPS) (Article 13), the WIPO Copyright Treaty (WCT) (Article 10) and the WIPO Performances and Phonograms Treaty (WPPT) (Article 16). Several European Community Directives also contain the test.
2. A test – '**abstraction, filtration, comparison**' – devised in *Computer Associates v Altai* to determine whether there was an infringement of copyright in a computer program.
    This approach has been influential outside the United States, for example in *John Flanders Computers v Chemtec* where Rimer J tried with limited success to apply it to an English case.

Three Strikes

A colloquial phrase for the graduated response to copyright infringements in the form of online filesharing. Infringers will be given two warnings before having their Internet connections terminated. The name derives from baseball, a game the rules of which are incomprehensible to almost all Europeans, in which the batter is given two attempts to hit the ball after which, if he misses it again, he is out. The expression was adopted in criminal law, as in the 1990s state legislatures mandated a custodial sentence for third-time offenders.

In the context of online filesharing, the concept begins with rightsholders monitoring peer-to-peer filesharing traffic and informing internet service providers (ISPs) when they find infringers using the ISP's service, the ISP giving warnings and eventually (not necessarily, but in the classic case, on the third occasion) disconnecting them. In the UK, the Digital Economy Act 2010 paves the way for detailed legislation on the subject; in France, the *loi* **HADOPI** purports to impose a three-strikes rule but the Conseil constitutionel has ruled this to be contrary to the rights of the individual (Internet access being increasingly viewed as a fundamental right); in the US, the Online Copyright Infringement Liability Limitation Act (OCILLA) makes the **safe harbor** that it provides for ISPs conditional on them acting against users of their services who engage in filesharing according to a 'three-strikes' protocol.

TK

Traditional knowledge.

Top-Level Domain

The domain name system is organised into national top-level domains (or 'cc TLDs', the 'cc' part being a reference to the International Organization for Standardization's two-letter country codes, set out in ISO 3166) and generic top-level domains (gTLDs). In the ccTLD system are domains such as .tv, .tm, .fr and .us; the ISO 3166 code GB (for the United Kingdom of Great Britain and Northern Ireland) was not however adopted by the creators of the gTLD system, who used .uk instead. Some ccTLDs have sub-domains (for example co.uk).

The generic system is not country-specific: the best-known generic top-level domain is .com, but .net, .biz, .info and a growing number of others exists.

This arrangement should ensure that the domain name system has enough flexibility to accommodate the needs of businesses using the same identifiers, but trade mark owners prefer to grab domain names in several, or many, top-level domains so as to create a monopoly – something the trade mark system is designed to prevent. Moreover, some cc top-level domains are attractive in their own right – .tv for television broadcasters, .fm for radio, .tm for trade mark owners, .md for (American) doctors, with no need for a real connection to Tuvalu, the Federated States of Micronesia, Turkmenistan or Moldova respectively. Some countries have done rather nicely out of these peculiarities.

Topography Right

A *sui generis* intellectual property right, protecting the layout of a computer chip. Council Directive 87/54/EEC of 16 December 1986 on the legal protection of topographies of semiconductor products required EC Member States to introduce protection, to take advantage of the reciprocal protection offered by the US Semiconductor Chip Protection Act (17 USC 901) of 1984. In the UK, the original *sui generis* right was subsumed into unregistered design right by the Copyright, Designs and Patents Act 1988. **See integrated circuit topography, Washington Treaty.**

Trade Dress (US)

The 'total image and overall appearance' of a business: *Blue Bell Bio-Medical v. Cin-Bad, Inc.*, 864 F.2d 1253, 1256 (5th Cir. 1989). It may include 'features such as size, shape, color or color combinations, texture, graphics, or even particular sales techniques': *John J. Harland Co. v. Clarke Checks, Inc.*, 711 F.2d 966, 980 (11th Cir. 1983).

There may be a number of components to trade dress, some of which may be registrable as trade marks (including, these days, colour and shape). In *Two Pesos, Inc. v. Taco Cabana, Inc.*, 112 S.Ct. 2753 (1992), the US Supreme Court held that inherently distinctive trade dress may be protected without proof of secondary meaning, resolving the split between the Second Circuit, which required proof of secondary meaning for trade dress protection, and the Fifth and other Circuits which did not. See **get-up**.

Trade Libel

See **slander of goods**.

Trade Mark

In the Trade Marks Act 1994, section 1(1) defines a trade mark as:

> Any sign capable of being represented graphically which is capable of distinguishing the goods or services or one undertaking from those of other undertakings.

It may include words (including personal names), designs, letters, numerals or the shape of goods or their packaging. In the United States, in *Qualitex*, the Supreme Court confirmed that the Lanham Act defines the universe of things that can qualify as a **trademark** 'in the broadest of terms' and that human beings might use 'almost anything at all that is capable of carrying meaning' as a 'symbol' or 'device', terms used to define trade marks in the Lanham Act. 15 U.S.C. § 1127. at 2. (I like the phrase about carrying meaning.)

The word 'sign' denotes a larger set of which trade marks are a specialised subset, with the properties mentioned in section 1(1) of the Act. In an infringement action, what the defendant is using is therefore properly called a sign but not a trade mark. The subject-matter of an application for registration, logically, should also be referred to as a sign, although there are signs that fall within the statutory definition of a trade mark but which are excluded from registration for one of many reasons enumerated in the Act; the Act uses no special expression for these purported trade marks, perhaps giving them the benefit of the doubt.

Trade marks are registered, importantly, for specified goods or services, and the applicant must have at least an intention (under the trade mark laws of most countries of the world) of using the mark for those goods or services. Unfortunately, it is possible by using a high level of generality and an extensive list of goods and services to thwart the policy goals of the legislation, and create from a trade mark application something that has more of the qualities usually associated with copyright, or even a patent.

Trade Mark (or Trademark) (vt)

Often misused to mean the act of registering a trade mark, or even the mere act of applying to register a trade mark. If it means anything it must logically be confined to applying a trade mark to goods or their packaging, or perhaps to using a trade mark to indicate the origin of services. But cf. **patent**.

Trade Mark Agent

Section 82 of the Trade Marks Act 1994 allows acts required or authorised by the Act to be done by or to an agent authorised for the purpose. Anyone may hold themselves out as a trade mark agent, but only those entered on the register of trade mark agents kept in accordance with section 83 may call themselves 'registered trade mark agents'. A person who falsely represents himself to be a registered trade mark agent commits an offence. In the Committee proceedings on the bill that became the Copyright, Designs and Patents Act 1988, where the registration of trade mark agents was introduced, the opposition spokesman (one Tony Blair) said:

> This may represent one of the more eccentric beliefs about human behaviour, but it has been put to me that someone may, in order to bring upon himself greater social standing, represent himself as a registered trade mark agent. It was suggested that such a claim could be a useful first chat-up line at a party. I might have had a much better time at University if I had realised that.

Trade Mark Attorney

Section 86 of the Trade Marks Act 1994 provides that no offence is committed by a **trade mark agent** using the description 'trade mark attorney'. Otherwise, until 1873 the word 'attorney' was historically reserved to those practitioners in the courts of common law who corresponded to solicitors in the courts of equity. In 1988, a similar exception was created to enable patent agents to call themselves 'patent attorneys': see **patent attorney**.

Trade Marks Act 1994

The most recent statutory restatement of the law relating to trade marks in the UK. It implements Council Directive no 89/104/EEC, makes provision in connection with the Community trade mark regulation, and gives effect to the Madrid Protocol and certain provisions of the Paris Convention. It also made long-overdue changes to a 56-year-old statute that had passed its 'best before' date decades earlier.

Trade Name

The name used by a person (a legal or natural person) in the course of their trade, and by which their trade is known. It often carries with it the good-will of the business and may be protectable as a **trade mark**.

Trade-Related Aspects of Intellectual Property

See **TRIPS**.

Trade Secret

A type of commercially valuable confidential information, expressly protected under state laws in the USA and a special class of confidential information in the UK which can be protected from use by an employee or former employee (see **Faccenda**). In deciding whether something is a trade secret, consider the nature of the employment, the nature of the information, whether the employer impressed on the employee the secrecy of the information, and its separability from general skill, experience and knowledge. In *Faccenda*, details of customers, routes and prices were not trade secrets.

Trademark

In the US, the two-word expression has become unified, in much the same way as 'copy right' or 'copy-right'. Given that the UK has merged the latter, it is sometimes argued that merging the former is an inevitable and even desirable step. As with the pronunciation of 'patent', the user can to some extent please themself, but it is pretty clear from the title of the **Trade Marks Act 1994** what the official version is. See also **trade mark (noun)**.

Trademark Law Treaty

Designed to approximate and streamline national and regional trade mark registration procedures through simplifying and harmonising certain features of those procedures. Trade mark applications, and the administration of trade mark registrations, in multiple jurisdictions should therefore be less complex and more predictable. Concluded 1994; 45 contracting parties.

Traditional Knowledge (TK)

Knowledge held by particular communities, especially of indigenous peoples. Formerly, it was easy for more 'advanced' societies and organisations to misappropriate this knowledge, for example by isolating the working principle of a traditional medicine, and patent it. TK is becoming recognised as a form of intellectual property in its own right, though this is still at a nascent stage and there is no universal legal framework for protection of TK. China grants patents for traditional medicines, but this is one small instance of TK being protected (and it fits awkwardly into a patent system, where novelty is the essential qualification for protection). WIPO is now working on ensuring that the owners of TK are rewarded, and patent offices understand its significance as prior art. In May 1995 the US Patent Office granted to the University of Mississippi Medical Center patent no. 5 401 504 for 'Use of Turmeric in Wound Healing'. Following an international outcry, a re-examination took place and the patent was revoked

Traditional Speciality Guaranteed

A form of protection for a designation of a foodstuff produced in a traditional manner or to a traditional recipe but without the connection to a geographical location that would merit Protected Designation of Origin (PDO) or Protected Geographical Indication (PGI) status.

Trafficking

In trade mark law, this word bears a specific meaning – and one much less unsavoury than the meaning it has acquired in some other areas. Under the (UK) Trade Mark Act 1938, the registrar was required to refuse to register a trade mark if registering it would facilitate trafficking in trade marks – in other words, treating trade marks as items of commerce in their own right. In the *American Greetings Cards* case [1986] RPC 421 (known as the Hollie Hobbie case) the House of Lords confirmed that this meant that it was not possible for a trade mark to be registered for a wide range of goods in respect of which (or part of which) the applicant proposed to grant licences. This did not accord with the way that trade mark owners expected to be able to use their trade marks in the late twentieth century and the law was changed in the 1994 Act.

Transformative Work

A work that uses other works for purposes including criticism, commentary or parody. An expression used in US copyright legislation, where it defines a form of fair use of copyright works, and in the **Gowers** report. There, it is said to 'enable creators to rework material for a new purpose or with a new meaning. Such new works can create new value, and can even create new markets.' In the US, Gowers explains, it enabled the 'Hip Hop industry' to develop in the late 1970s and early 1980s, which should have been reason enough to reject such an exception in UK law. Gowers's notion of 'value' is purely monetary, although the report goes on to quote Picasso's dictum, 'Good artists borrow; great artists steal', which he might have appropriated from Stravinsky ('a good composer does not imitate: he steals'), or T.S. Eliot ('immature poets imitate; mature poets steal'), though no copyright point appears to have been taken, perhaps because creators of their calibre are above such matters.

Transmedia Intellectual Property

In the entertainment and computer games world, content delivered via a plurality of media, which may include video games, social networks, mobile platforms, print and film.

Transmission

1. The transfer or assignment of a piece of property from one person to another.
2. In copyright, a **restricted act** in the laws of some countries analogous to **communication to the public** or **making available**. Also, the noun used for the service delivered by cable, analogous to a broadcast, in the original version of the Copyright, Designs and Patents Act 1988 (UK).

Triple Identity Test

The first test devised by the US courts to help with the application of the doctrine of equivalents. Under *Graver Tank & Manufacturing Co. v. Linde Air Products Co.,* (1950)), something is deemed equivalent if it performs substantially the same function, in substantially the same way, to yield substantially the same result.

See also **insubstantial change**.

TRIPS

The Agreement on Trade-Related Aspects of Intellectual Property Rights, made under the auspices of the General Agreement on Tariffs and Trade (GATT) Uruguay Round – which also decided to rename GATT the World Trade Organization, in part reflecting its new interest in intellectual property. Formally, TRIPS is Annex 1C of the Marrakesh Agreement Establishing the World Trade Organization, signed in Marrakesh on 15 April 1994. Being an integral part of the WTO agreement, it is automatically binding on members, of which there are 153 (July 2008 figure). There were also 29 observers at that date – including some large countries, Russia being the largest – which are, by virtue of their status, committed to membership within five years.

TRIPS imposes the basic principles (national treatment, most-favoured nation treatment) and minimum standards of IP protection (including most of the requirements of the Berne Convention in the copyright field) across a wider range of countries than had hitherto been the case. It also contains provisions about the enforcement of IP rights and does what it can to prevent procedural difficulties in acquiring or maintaining IP rights from undermining the purpose of the agreement.

TRIPS-Plus

A shorthand term denoting the efforts, generally attributed to WIPO, to impose on developing nations and least-developed countries obligations going beyond the norms set out in the TRIPS agreement. Not popular with Brazil or Argentina, which have launched an initiative for a development agenda within WIPO.

Troll

Trolls in Scandinavian folklore were originally supernatural creatures, sometimes dwarves or giants. One type of troll lived under bridges, and would try to eat users of the bridge – as in the Norwegian fairy tale, *The Three Billy Goats Gruff* (*De tre bukkene Bruse*). By extension, 'troll' has become a term – perhaps a pejorative term – for a patent owner with little or no interest in working the patent. Rather, the owner uses it merely as a source of revenue, threatening and suing businesses who use the patented technology – which might have lain unused for years before being acquired by the troll. Patent trolls often have no technical skills, only an aptitude for patent litigation. There is also a species of trade mark troll, who have fared rather worse than their patent equivalents.

The term was first applied to aggressive patent claimants in 1993, and popularised in 2001 by Peter Detkin, former Assistant General Counsel of Intel, whose company was involved in litigation with one. When Detkin referred to the other side as a 'patent extortionist', a libel suit followed, and the term 'troll' was adopted as a non-defamatory alternative. Surprisingly, it seems to have worked. '**Non-practicing entity**' is a less pejorative alternative, and given that banks in the ordinary course of their business might find themselves looking rather like trolls (Deutsche Bank and Credit Suisse having recently created funds for buying unused patents) it is probably appropriate to have such a neutral term in the lexicon.

The phenomenon remains one that is almost entirely confined to the US, and there attempts are being made to control such activities. In his concurring judgment on *eBay v MercExchange* in May 2006, Justice Kennedy in the US Supreme Court attacked the right of trolls to a mandatory injunction, noting that:

> An industry has developed in which firms use patents not as a basis for producing and selling goods but, instead, primarily for obtaining licensing fees . . . For these firms, an injunction, and the potentially serious sanctions arising from its violation, can be employed as a bargaining tool to charge exorbitant fees to companies that seek to buy licenses to practice the patent . . . When the patented invention is but a small component of the product the companies seek to produce and the threat of an injunction is employed simply for undue leverage in negotiations, legal damages may well be sufficient to compensate for the infringement and an injunction may not serve the public interest.

In the US Senate a bill for a Patent Reform Act was introduced in August 2006, which would have required US courts to consider when awarding damages:

> the economic value that should be attributed to the novel and non-obvious feature or features of the invention, as distinguished from the economic value

attributable to other features, improvements added by the infringer, and the business risks the infringer undertook in commercialization.

Patent trolls flourish in the **Eastern District of Texas**. Trade mark trolls, it seems, do not flourish particularly anywhere. The most talked-about example of that subspecies is one Leo Stoller, who (by 2007, according to Wikipedia) had brought 47 infringement actions, won none of them and been enjoined by the Northern District of Illinois from bringing more actions without the Court's consent. Mr Stoller's efforts are hampered by the requirement in US law that a trade mark be used in commerce. In the UK, the BBC reported in 2008 that a company called Never Give Up Limited claimed to own trade marks identical to established businesses' names and demanded payments for a licence or an assignment. Such an application or registration would probably be vulnerable to attack on grounds of **bad faith**.

A similar scam in earlier times involved setting up ransom companies; and incorporating a company is a great deal cheaper than registering a trade mark. The introduction of the Companies Names Adjudication Service has gone a long way towards resolving that problem. See also **cybersquatting**.

Trundlehumper, Trundlene

A device or substance that, perhaps because of its great novelty, has no common name. Alternatively, a non-specific device or product which might appear in examination questions, examples and the like, along with similar figments of the imagination, viz. 'a *trundlehumper*, comprising a sprunglechump connected to a worfblender'. A patent application for a trundlehumper (GB0612681.7) appears in the *Patents and Designs Journal*, 6116, p. 3891, dated 9 August 2006, published as GB2427603, by which time it had become 'a wheeled hoist for lifting, lowering and transporting material'. A pity: trundlehumper seemed the perfect name for it – perhaps a little bit too descriptive.

Trundlehumpers are obviously closely related to widgets and blodgets, though those devices tend to predominate in the world of competition lawyers.

TSM

See **Teaching–Suggesting–Motivation Test**.

TTAB

1. Trademark Trial and Appeal Board (TTAB) – administrative body that hears *ex parte* appeals, oppositions, cancellations and concurrent use proceedings.
2. John Welch's influential **blawg**.

Typeface

A type of artistic work which may be protected by copyright, provided it has the requisite originality and qualifies by reference to its author or the country of first publication.

Typographical Arrangement

The layout of the page of a 'published edition' may receive copyright protection under this rubric. This means the published edition of the whole or any part of one or more literary, dramatic or musical works. 'Typography' includes logotypes (see **logo**), so the notion of a typographical arrangement should extend to elements of page design and layout other than writing (which in the Copyright, Designs and Patents Act is a key feature that identifies literary, dramatic and musical works, a literary work being defined as any work that is written, spoken or sung other than a dramatic or musical work).

The Newspaper Licensing Agency was originally set up to exploit newspapers' copyright in typographical arrangements. In *NLA v Marks & Spencer plc*, the defendant argued that it had not copied a substantial part of the copyright work (it had copied only individual articles, and – so the argument went – the copyright work was the typographical arrangement of the whole newspaper). In the High Court, Lightman J held that each article constituted a published work, and its typographical arrangement was capable of being a copyright work ([1999] EWHC Patents 266). The defendant's copies were therefore copies of a substantial part of the respective arrangements. On appeal, the majority in the Court of Appeal considered that a published edition had to be viewed as a whole, so there was no infringement unless a substantial part had been taken ([2000] EWCA Civ 179). The articles that had been copied did not in themselves amount to substantial parts of the whole newspaper. The House of Lords agreed ([2001] UKHL 38).

U

UDRP

See **Uniform Domain Name Dispute Resolution Policy**.

Uncopyright

The verb 'to copyright' has no place in UK copyright law, or indeed the copyright laws of almost any country other than the US: and since that country joined the Berne Convention in 1989 copyright has been an automatic right like it is in the rest of the world, or so nearly all of it that it makes no difference. 'Uncopyright' appears to be used mainly as a verb, although a noun form and an adjective form might also exist. It is usually employed to denote the purported dedication of a copyright work to the public domain, which could alternatively be characterised as a voluntary waiver of the usual incidents of copyright protection. It is impossible to renounce a right that arises automatically, though abandoning it might have a similar effect.

Not unrelated to copyleft, it is a less sophisticated approach because it does not subvert the way that copyright law works to enforce licence terms that perpetuate the liberal licensing model.

Undistributed Middle, Logical Fallacy of

A logical fallacy that is committed when the middle term in a categorical syllogism is not distributed. The classic example goes like this: 'All Zs are Bs. Y is a B. Therefore Y is a Z'. Or, in the instance familiar to lawyers, all passing-off actions must display the five elements identified by Lord Diplock in **Advocaat**, but merely because those five elements are present does not necessarily mean that a passing off is taking place.

Unfair Advantage

One of the alternative legs of a trade mark **dilution** claim in European Community trade mark law. Following the *L'Oréal v Bellure* case in the Court for Justice of the European Union, the adjective 'unfair' might be redundant.

Unfair Competition

Commercial conduct that some countries' laws might prohibit. A person injured by an act of unfair competition may be entitled to relief in a civil action against the perpetrator of the act. Trade mark infringement has long been considered to be a form of unfair competition, and the prohibition may extend to false advertising, product disparagement or trade libel, infringement of a trade secret, infringement of the right of publicity, and slavish copying. Protection against unfair competition is mandatory under the Paris Convention: the UK has always argued, not very convincingly, that a combination of the law on passing off and criminal statutes on trade descriptions met this requirement.

Unified Patent Litigation System (UPLS)

One element in a bundle of reforms proposed to create a pan-European patent system, also including a single Community patent. Successor to the politically difficult **European Patent Litigation Agreement**, the Commission proposed the creation of the UPLS. Unlike the EPLA, the UPLS is designed to cover Community patents (as and when implemented) and European patents. The UPLS would establish a unified court structure with jurisdiction over European and future Community Patents for both infringement and revocation actions and a single judiciary following uniform procedures and comprised of highly specialised and trained judges. Its decisions will have effect throughout the territories where the patent is in force.

Uniform Domain-Name Dispute-Resolution Policy (UDRP)

The policy, which has an associated procedure, for resolving disputes about domain names in the generic Top Level Domain (gTLD). In other top-level domains there are more or less similar, or even identical, procedures, although there may be significant differences between them. The UDRP derives its authority from **ICANN**'s requiring all accredited registrars to impose it through their registration agreements. It is mandatory for registrants in gTLD. Registrants must agree to submit to the application of dispute procedures as a condition of registering a domain name.

Unity of Invention

In principle a patent should be granted for a single invention. If there is more than one invention, each should be the subject of a separate patent application: but the simple rule is not uniformly applied. In the US, they take a strict view about unity of invention, and the USPTO often raises objections which can be met by filing divisional applications. In Europe, a patent may claim a compound, a process for making the compound, use of the compound and a product containing the compound, and they will all be considered to form part of the same **inventive concept**.

Universal Copyright Convention (UCC)

An international copyright convention, ratified in 1952, in effect from 1955, and revised (in Paris) in 1971, created under the auspices of the United Nations Educational, Scientific and Cultural Organization (UNESCO) but very much the work of the United States, which was not prepared to meet the requirements of the Berne Convention.

It was based on the principle of national treatment, just like Berne, but the minimum period of protection was 25 years (the US gave 28 years from publication, which was renewable once) and it avoided any mention of the troubling subject of moral rights. The US did have to accept that it had to do away with copyright formalities, but this was made conditional on copyright owners placing a notice on their work with a copyright symbol together with the copyright owner's name and the year of first publication (so, the requirement to give notice was waived only if notice were given).

The US also had to remove any requirement for foreign works to be registered, and to abolish the **manufacturing clause** for UCC works (it was not completely done away with until 1986). This last change provided the incentive needed to convince other countries that there was merit in creating a second international copyright system in parallel with the Berne Convention one. One hundred states are currently parties to the Convention.

Unpatentable Subject-Matter

Scientific theories, discoveries, programs for computers, methods of doing business, methods for the presentation of information, and literary and artistic creations are generally excluded from patentability, often by being excluded from the definition of an invention. Patent laws also commonly contain exclusions on grounds of **ordre publique**, and often provide that methods of medical treatment may not be patented (sometimes deeming them to have no technical effect).

Unregistered Design Right

An intellectual property right directed to the protection of certain designs. It comes in two flavours, one of which is unique to the UK and the other spread throughout the European Union. It also comes in two distinct strengths, though both are watery. Both rights contain a substantial amount of copyright.

1. UK unregistered design right was introduced in the Copyright, Designs and Patents Act 1988 with the specific aim of replacing copyright protection for industrial designs. It is a pathetically weak form of intellectual property, with a maximum duration of 15 years from when the design is made (but more usually ten years from when articles to the design are first marketed), with **must-fit** and **must-match** exceptions to prevent car spares deriving any protection from it, and, in case any should slip through, licensing of right provisions applying during the last five years of protection. It does not protect surface decoration, either. The design must be original and protection requires copying in some form: in these respects it closely resembles copyright. A **commonplace** design will not possess originality. Non-EU designers or manufacturers are unlikely to enjoy any protection at all, unless they contrive to market their products first in an EU Member State. Reciprocal protection is available to any country adopting a similar law: designers and companies from New Zealand and Hong Kong may benefit.
2. Community unregistered design right (CUDR) supplements Community registered designs, giving three years' automatic protection for designs that qualify for registration having novelty and individual character. However, this is a very high threshold, resulting in many highly optimistic claims: CUDR is often the last straw to which someone with no other intellectual property clings. Again, infringement requires some sort of copying – it is not a monopoly right.

UPOV

Union Internationale pour la Protection des Obtentions Végétales. See **plant breeders' rights**.

Use

1. Noun: something without which a trade mark, in the fullness of time, will become liable to revocation. In most trade mark registration systems five years is the key period, with a period of grace provided for, so that a prospective challenger can approach a trade mark owner without the risk that an instant resumption of use will save the trade mark and thwart his purpose. In the UK it is necessary for an applicant for registration to state that it uses or intends to use the trade mark for the goods and services concerned; if this statement is given falsely, the application will be regarded as having been made in bad faith. EC trade mark law does not demand such a statement, but an application may still fail if it is in bad faith.
2. Verb: what an applicant for registration of a trade mark must have an intent to do in the US system (unless the mark is already in use). 'Intent to use' applications in the US are a relatively new departure. This sense of the word is also relevant in the UK and EC trade mark systems.

USPTO

The United States Patent and Trademark Office, the government agency that issues patents (both utility patents and **design** patents) and registers **trademarks**.

Utility

What is required in US patent law, the equivalent of the requirement for industrial applicability elsewhere. The US requirement permits a wider range of subject matter to be patented.

Utility Certificate

The name given to a form of utility model or **petty patent** protection in Trinidad & Tobago and Uganda.

Utility Model

See **petty patent, Gebrauchsmuster**.

Utility Patent

In the US patent system, designs are protected by design patents and to distinguish the two types of patent what are called 'patents' in the UK and elsewhere are often referred to as 'utility patents'.

V

Validation

The stage at the end of the process of obtaining a European Patent, when the patentee must decide in which of the countries originally designated in the application they now wish to have patents. Validation involves submitting an application to the national offices concerned, with a translation in most countries. Three months is allowed for this (except in Ireland, where it is six months).

Validity Opinion

A legal opinion directed to how a court might rule on the validity of an issued patent, trade mark or other registered intellectual property right. Often sought prior to litigation, when the validity of the right sued on is likely to be challenged by the defendant.

Validity Search

A search carried out to establish the validity of a patent. It will be directed to the twin issues of novelty and inventiveness, and will therefore be designed to identify the prior art both in the patent literature and elsewhere.

Valuation

A dark art when applied to intellectual property, sometimes dismissed as a type of shamanism. Several different techniques can be used to place a value on intellectual property: the market approach, the historic or replacement value approach, the capitalisation of historic profits, the gross profit differential method, the excess profits method or the relief from royalty method. One of them should produce the desired answer.

Value Recognition Strategy

A theory put forward by the Music Business Group in response to the **Gowers** review's proposals on format shifting. It is described (with links to sources) much more eloquently than I could ever manage by Bill Patry in his **blog**. In brief, the 'Strategy', dreamt up by Capgemini, the consultants, attributes a value to the transferability of the computer files containing a consumer's music collection – so that the record industry can lay claim to a share of that value. In other words, format shifting should be something for which the consumer pays (see **double dipping**). There is no sign of the UK government swallowing this.

VARA

The Visual Artists' Rights Act of 1990, the first federal legislation in the United States to protect artists' moral rights.

Vienna Agreement

An Agreement, concluded in 1973, amended in 1985, establishing an International Classification of the Figurative Elements of Marks (the Vienna Classification). Only 28 parties, but used by the industrial property offices of at least 30 States, as well as by the International Bureau of **WIPO**, **OAPI**, the **Benelux** Organisation for Intellectual Property and **OHIM**.

W

Wands Factors

In unpredictable areas of technology, in particular biotechnology, it is not easy to tell whether the enablement requirement in patent law is met. The skilled addressee can be expected to carry out a certain amount of experimentation, but how much? In *In Re Wands*, 858 F.2d 731, 742 (Fed. Cir. 1988) the Court set out a series of factors to determine whether the enablement requirement had been met: undue experimentation is determined by a standard of reasonableness, which can be assessed by examining: (1) the quantity of experimentation necessary; (2) the amount of direction or guidance presented; (3) the presence or absence of working examples; (4) the nature of the invention; (5) the state of the prior art; (6) the relative skill of those in the art; (7) the predictability or unpredictability of the art; and (8) the breadth of the claims.

War Loss

An old ground for extension of patent term in British law, now extinct. A similar concept is encountered in French copyright law, which applied a complicated formula designed to add to the post-mortem term of certain copyrights a further period representing the duration of the First or Second World War, or both. The Cour de Cassation abolished the extensions in 2007, except for musical works in respect of which the Loi no 85-660 du 3 juillet 1985 preserved them.

Wares

In Canadian trade mark law, the equivalent of goods in other countries' trade mark laws. Canada does not use the Nice classification.

Washington Treaty on Intellectual Property in Respect of Integrated Circuits

An international treaty that has not yet come into force, having been ratified only by Egypt and acceded to by Bosnia & Herzegovina and St Lucia. Having been around since 26 May 1989, this is an undistinguished record. It is designed to establish principles for the protection of integrated circuits and their topography.

Watch List, Special Watch List (US)

A list of countries, such as Canada, whose intellectual property laws are judged by the United States to be wanting. The Omnibus Trade and Competitiveness Act of 1988 created the so-called Special 301 mechanism under which the United States Trade Representative issues an annual Special 301 Report which 'examines in detail the adequacy and effectiveness of intellectual property rights' in many countries around the world. Countries may be placed on a Watch list or priority watch list, or be given Section 306 Monitoring status. The 2009 Report designates 46 countries in total

Watching Service

A commercial service that informs trade mark owners, or their lawyers, about applications filed by third parties that might be considered to conflict with the trade marks of the person paying for the watch to be kept. Although many trade mark offices inform owners about earlier rights of conflicting later applications, it is conceivable that trade mark owners would perceive conflicts where trade mark offices might not, so maintaining a watching service is an important precaution – especially in systems such as those in the UK and the EC, which depend on oppositions to deal with conflicts.

WCO

World Customs Organization. There is a page on the organisation's website devoted to intellectual property, where of course customs have a major enforcement role to play.

Webcast

A term without precise legal meaning but commonly used to refer to a transmission analogous to a broadcast but delivered over the World Wide Web.

Weblog

A type of **website** characterised by the inclusion of regular items of commentary, descriptions of events and other material, commonly in reverse chronological order. It may also provide a facility to leave comments, which may be moderated at the administrator's choice. The expression is commonly abbreviated to '**blog**'. See also **blawg**.

Website

A collection of what might loosely be called 'digital assets', comprising a number of web pages, which are documents written either in hypertext markup language (HTML) or extensible hypertext markup language (XHTML) and linked together to form a coherent collection.

Welfare Loss

The consequence of monopolists charging super-normal prices and failing to meet potential demand for their products. Because intellectual property rights confer monopolies (theoretically limited monopolies, though IP owners seem to strive to turn them into the closest possible approximations to monopolies) there is a strong chance that they will lead to welfare loss – though they should usually deliver countervailing benefits.

Well-Known Trade Mark

A trade mark that enjoys the exceptional protection of Article 6 bis of the Paris Convention (and Article 16 of TRIPS). The Convention does not specify how well-known trademarks should be protected, or how they can be recognised, leaving it for each signatory country to decide how to address these matters. Most countries do not process applications for recognition of well-known trade marks unless their owners show a need for recognition, and most countries do not have a separate or independent application procedure for recognition of well-known trade marks.

Whelan v Jaslow

Whelan Associates v. Jaslow Dental Laboratory, 609 F.Supp. 1307, 225 USPQ 156 (E.D. Pa. 1985). The American case that is the starting point for all cases on copyright in computer software, sufficiently influential to have been reported in the UK in [1987] FSR 1. The court recognised that literal copying of the code was not the important thing for a software house, and focused on the '**look and feel**' of the software or, putting it a different way, its '**structure, sequence and organisation**'.

Whitford

1. Mr Justice Whitford (Sir John Whitford) (1913–2001) was from 1970 until 1988 a Judge of the High Court and assigned to the Patents Court. In 1974 he was commissioned to chair a departmental committee set up by the Department of Trade and Industry to consider the law on copyright and designs. The report, invariably known as
    . . .
2. . . . the Whitford report (Cmnd 6732), helped shape the reform of copyright law in the Copyright, Designs and Patents Act 1988, though its recommendations (including a minority report) on designs proved less persuasive

WHO

The World Health Organization.

Whole Contents Approach

An approach taken to the state of the art, as in *Asahi Kasei Kogyo KK's Application* [1991] R.P.C. 485, that includes all prior disclosures in earlier applications. In that case, Lord Jauncey approved the Banks Committee's statement:

> that it is against public interest to grant a patent for subject matter which has already been publicly disclosed in an earlier application, notwithstanding that the disclosure was not public until after the priority date of the latter application or that no patent may be finally granted on it. In other words, only the first person to take steps to disclose such subject matter to the public by means of a patent application has the right to a monopoly for it.

Rejected (in line with EPO cases) by Laddie J in *Re Woolard's Patent*, where an earlier patent that had been withdrawn by the same applicant did not form part of the state of the art, on the basis that the law was only concerned with preventing double patenting which could not happen if the earlier application were withdrawn.

Windsurfer, *Windsurfing International v Tabur Marine*

In the *Windsurfing International* case, the Court of Appeal set down a test for determining whether an invention had the necessary qualities of inventiveness to justify the grant of a patent. It was a 1949 Act case, but the test is still applied. The elements of the test are:

- Identify the notional person skilled in the art and then identify the relevant common general knowledge of that person.
- Identify the inventive concept of the claim in question or, if that could not readily be done, construe it.
- Identify what, if any, differences existed between the matter cited as forming part of the state of the art and the inventive concept of the claim or the claim as construed.
- Viewed without any knowledge of the alleged invention as claimed, did those differences constitute steps that would have been obvious to the person skilled in the art, or did they require any degree of invention?

Pozzoli SpA v BDMO SA and Moulage Industriel de Perseigne SA is a recent example of this test being applied.

WIPO

Pronounced variously with a long 'i' sound, a short 'i' and a long 'e'. To avoid confusion and embarrassment, perhaps it should be referred to it as **OMPI**, which has the merit of having only one possible pronunciation. See **World Intellectual Property Organization**.

WIPO Treaties

Although WIPO is responsible for a multiplicity of treaties in the IP field, this expression has a more limited meaning. Collectively, two international treaties dating from 1996 initially proposed as protocols to the Berne Convention, which modernised copyright and neighbouring rights law to meet the challenges of the digital age: the WIPO Copyright Treaty (WCT) and the WIPO Performances and Phonograms Treaty (WPPT). They resulted in national and regional legislation including the **DMCA** in the US and the EC Directive on copyright in the information society (**Information Society Directive**).

Withdrawal

In the EPO, an application may be withdrawn either at the request of the applicant or following a decision of the Office to consider the application to be withdrawn because the applicant fails to:

- pay fees in due time (Article 90(3) EPC);
- file a request for examination within the given time period (Article 94(3) EPC);
- reply in due time to any invitation within the examination procedure (Article 96(3) EPC).

It may be possible for the prosecution of the application to be resumed. See also **abandonment**.

Work

1. Noun: The subject-matter protected by copyright. UK law (Part I of the Copyright, Designs and Patents Act 1988, as amended) protects original literary, dramatic, musical and artistic works; films, sound recordings and broadcasts; and the typographical arrangement of published editions. Each of these categories is the subject of a separate entry.
2. Verb: To use an invention.

Work (made) for hire

See **Hire, work made for**.

Work of Architecture

See **architecture, work of**.

Work of artistic Craftsmanship

See **artistic craftsmanship, work of**.

Workshop Improvement

An old term in British patent law, describing a modification that a skilled worker would automatically make in the normal exercise of their trade to make something work: it is therefore inherently non-inventive.

World Intellectual Property Organization

An agency of the United Nations, based in Geneva, which is responsible for the administration of many important international intellectual property treaties. The International Bureau handles applications under the **Madrid Agreement** concerning the international registration of marks and **Madrid Protocol**, and receives and processes applications under the **Patent Co-operation Treaty** and the **Hague Agreement**. It also promotes the virtues of intellectual property to the international community and offers mediation and arbitration services, including dealing with the majority of **UDRP** cases.

World Patent

Definitely a figment of the imagination, but one that appears to be supported by the use of the letters WO to designate a PCT application.

Writing

Defined in the Copyright, Designs and Patents Act 1988 to include any form of notation or code. This makes the definition of a literary work extremely wide: it rightly does not discriminate between different alphabets, nor does it exclude encrypted material, but the definition is also broad enough to include material written in binary code, such as computer programs.

Written Description Requirement

In the words of 35 USC 112, a patent application must describe an invention 'in such full, clear, concise and exact terms as to enable any person skilled in the art to which it pertains, or with which it is most nearly connected, to make and use the same'. The written description requirement also demands that the best mode of performing the invention be described.

WTO

The World Trade Organization, formed from the old General Agreement on Tariffs and Trade. This change, of name and substance, was effected by the Marrakesh Agreement in 1994 and coincided with the introduction of the Agreement on Trade-Related Aspects of Intellectual Property Rights (TRIPS).

X

X-Patent

A very early US patent, issued by the United States Patent and Trademark Office between July 1790 (when the first US patent was issued) and July 1836, when the first 10 280 patents were destroyed in a fire. Fewer than 3000 were recovered and reissued with X numbers. The X is a suffix in the handwritten numbers on full-page patent images but commonly appears as a prefix, like a patent type – 'D' designates a design patent – in patent collections and for search purposes.

X-Ray

Because of the wide definition of a photograph in UK copyright law – it is carefully technology-neutral – X-rays are capable of being protected as copyright works. They might find it hard to pass the originality test, though.

Y

Yorkshire Relish

The product involved in the passing-off case of *Powell v Birmingham Vinegar Brewery* [1897] AC 710, which established that a geographical name can nevertheless serve as a trade name and receive the protection of the courts. Very useful for anyone trying to compile an alphabetical collection of expressions used in intellectual property law: other suggestions about words or phrases beginning with 'Y' would be gratefully received.

Z

Zeta Jones, Catherine

One of the claimants in the important English privacy and confidential information case, *Douglas v Hello!* [2007] UKHL21 in which Lord Hoffmann effectively reduced the **Coco criteria** to the simple proposition, 'follow the money'. Increasingly, that principle seems to work for all areas of intellectual property.

Zhing-Zhong

See **fong kong**.

Zoetrope

A device that uses a sequence of static images to produce an illusion of movement – which is not very different from how a motion picture works, and appropriately the Copyright, Designs and Patents Act 1988 defines '**film**' widely enough to catch zoetropes.

Z Sections

Sections of a British Act of Parliament which has been much amended with additional sections being infiltrated into the body of the statute. Suffix letters are common enough (sections 50A, 50B and 50C of the Copyright, Designs and Patents Act were inserted by the Software Directive). The term Z section is a convenient shorthand for a (usually obscure) addition to a statute, and is usually employed to refer to some of the provisions (sections 296 ZA to ZG) of the Copyright, Designs and Patents Act 1988 that impose strict liability for devices marketed for circumventing technical measures protecting copyright works.

Zwart Maken

Dutch, literally 'to make black'. A technique for avoiding a court automatically granting a seizure order under the **Enforcement Directive**. The party that anticipates such an order being made against it informs the court by letter that the claimant's rights might be invalid, pre-empting the grant of an order.